MACEDONIA
Its People and History

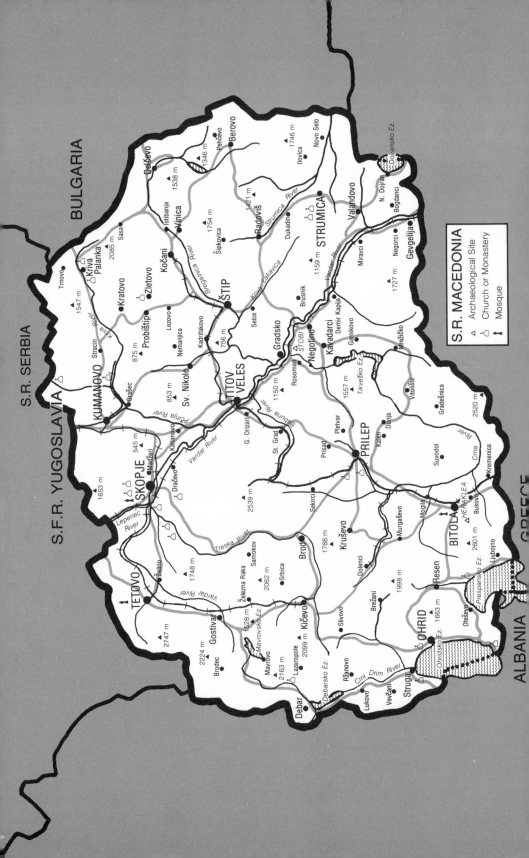

S.R. MACEDONIA

△ Archaeological Site
⌂ Church or Monastery
⊑ Mosque

BULGARIA

S.R. SERBIA

S.F.R. YUGOSLAVIA

ALBANIA

GREECE

Dojransko Ez.

Trnovo
Kriva Palanka
1547 m
2085 m
Sasa
Kratovo
Zletovo
Kočani
De, Deljevo
Istibanja
Vinica
1346 m
1538 m
Pehčevo
Berovo
Novo Selo
Ilovica
1746 m
1754 m
Šipkovica
Radoviš
1421 m
Strumica River
Dukadin
STRUMICA
Valandovo
N. Dojran
Bogdanci
Gevgelija
Negorci
Miravci
1727 m
Vardar River
1159 m
Demir Kapija
Garnikovo
Mrežičko
Kadrifakovo
Nemanjica
Lezovo
Probištip
875 m
ŠTIP
Selce
Gradsko
STOBI
Negotino
Kavadarci
Brusnik
Rosoman
Tikveško Ez.
1557 m
Vitolište
Gradešnica
Crna River
2520 m
Kremenica
Kriva Lakavica River
Bregalnica River
756 m
TITOV VELES
1150 m
Babuna River
St. Grad
G. Orizari
Katlanovo
Pčinja River
Stracin
853 m
Sv. Nikole
KUMANOVO
545 m
Orašec
Madžari
Dračevo
SKOPJE
1653 m
Lepenec River
Pletvar
Prisad
PRILEP
Kalen
Dupija
Suvodol
Mogila
HERAKLEA
BITOLA
2601 m
Bukovo
Ljubojno
Prespansko Ez.
Oteševo
Resen
1998 m
Brežani
Murgaševo
1788 m
Kruševo
Sekirci
Dolenci
Slivovo
Silovo
Brod
Samokov
2062 m
Srbica
Železna Raka
1528 m
Kičevo
2099 m
Lazaropole
Mavrovo
2163 m
Mavrovsko Ez.
2539 m
Treska River
1748 m
Žeino
TETOVO
2747 m
2224 m
Brodec
Gostivar
Vardar River
Debarsko Ez.
Ržanovo
Debar
Crni Drim River
Lukovo
Vevčani
Struga
Ohridsko Ez.
OHRID
1663 m
Vardar River

MACEDONIA
Its People and History

Stoyan Pribichevich

The Pennsylvania State University Press
University Park and London

Library of Congress Cataloging in Publication Data

Pribichevich, Stoyan, 1905-
Macedonia, its people and history.
Includes bibliography and index.
1. Macedonia—History. I. Title.
DR701.M2P74   949.5′6   82-80455
ISBN 0-271-00315-4   AACR2

TABLE OF CONTENTS

INTRODUCTION

A Maze of Frontiers and Nationalities

IN the Balkan peninsula there are no less than six countries: Yugoslavia, Bulgaria, Albania, Rumania, Greece and the European strip of Turkey with Istanbul. The first two are Slav. The first four are Communist ruled, but only Bulgaria and Rumania are in the Soviet bloc. Greece and Turkey belong to NATO.

Yugoslavia alone is more complex than all the rest of the Balkan nations; it is perhaps the most complex country in the world. Of the approximate size of Wyoming (98,740 sq. miles) and with a population of more than 20.5 million (1971 census), Yugoslavia is a federal republic consisting of:

- Six republics: Serbia (including the autonomous provinces of Vojvodina with a large bloc of Hungarians and Kosovo with numerous Albanians), Croatia, Slovenia, Bosnia-Herzegovina, Montenegro and Macedonia;
- Five nations: Serbs (more than 8 million), Croats (more than 4.5 million), Slovenes (almost 1.7 million), Macedonians (1.2 million), Montenegrins (500,000); to whom must be added Moslem Slavs (1.5 million) and 270,000 people who declared themselves Yugoslavs pure and simple;
- Three languages: Serbo-Croatian, Slovenian and Macedonian;
- Three principal religions: Eastern Orthodox (Serbs, Montenegrins and Macedonians), Roman Catholic (Croats and Slovenes) and Moslem (Turks, most Albanians and a large number of Slavs in Bosnia-Herzegovina);
- Two scripts: Cyrillic (used by Serbs, Montenegrins and Macedonians) and Latin (used by Croats and Slovenes).
- Numerous national minorities populate certain frontier areas and inland enclaves: Albanians (1.3 million); Turks (some 130,000); Hungarians (some 480,000). The remainder consists of Slovaks, Gypsies,

1

Rumanians, Bulgars, Ruthenians, Czechs, Ukrainians, Germans, in that order; plus some others, including Vlachs and Tsintsars.

IN the dead center of the peninsula, forming the southernmost part of the Federal Socialist Republic of Yugoslavia, lies a region about the size of Vermont and known as the Socialist Republic of Macedonia. It is flanked by Albania in the west, Greece in the south and Bulgaria in the east, with the Serbian part of Yugoslavia to the north. The area is sometimes called "Vardar Macedonia," after the river Vardar, which empties into the Aegean Sea near the Greek port of Salonika. Skopje, the capital of Macedonia, is now the third largest city in Yugoslavia, although in 1963 a terrible earthquake almost destroyed it.

Not all of Macedonia's 1.65 million people are Macedonians. More than 100,000 are Turks, and some 280,000 speak Albanian. The urban Tsintsars and the Vlach shepherds are now largely Slavicized. But the Yugoslav population statistics still recognize the Vlachs as a separate national entity. (There are Vlachs in Serbia, Greece and Bulgaria, too.)

The Gypsies, also, are a separate ethnic group in Yugoslavia. The Gypsies of Macedonia are sedentary. Skopje has a Gypsy section with people working in factories, as craftsmen or as domestic help. There are whole villages of land-tilling Gypsies in the Struma region of Macedonia.

The Macedonian republic within Yugoslavia does not embrace all of Macedonia nor do all Macedonians live in Yugoslav Macedonia, although by far most of them do. Some 180,000 Macedonians form almost the entire population of Bulgarian Macedonia, often called "Pirin Macedonia" after Mt. Pirin. Greek Macedonia (sometimes called "Aegean Macedonia" by non-Greeks), with its big port of Salonika, contains some 100,000 Slavs, a definite minority in the region. The Macedonians of Bulgaria and Greece do not have self-government, in contrast to those of Yugoslavia.

Terra Incognita

THE Macedonians of today are not, as many in the West think, descendants of the long since vanished Macedonians of Alexander the Great. They are Slavs, who speak a language related to the Serbo-Croatian and the Bulgarian. Together with other Slavs, they came from the Russo-Polish-Ukrainian plains at the end of the Great Migrations, in the sixth and seventh centuries A.D. and settled in the mountainous Balkan land then ruled by the Byzantine emperor.

All the Slav tribes that almost fourteen hundred years ago had established themselves in the Byzantine provinces known of old as Macedonia in the second half of the nineteenth century began to use the name of that province as their own national appellation. And only at the middle of the twentieth century, after the Second World War, did these Slav Macedonians form their own national state, called "Macedonia," within federated Yugoslavia. Today it is proper to call the distinctive Slavs of Macedonia "Macedonians." That is what they call themselves and that is the official name of their nation and their state within Macedonia.

THERE has been a lack of a comprehensive work on Macedonia in any language, not even in that of the natives, describing Macedonia and its peoples from antiquity to the present day, from Alexander the Great to the Slav Workers' Council.

The closest to a well-rounded presentation of Macedonia is a mimeographed series of lectures on the history of Macedonia from antiquity to the twentieth century, authored by Professor A. S. Šofman of the University of Kazan, U.S.S.R., and put out in Russian in two volumes in 1960. This work, though confining itself to political and social history, is so useful that one can forget its ritualistic Marxist language. Its one great fault is that it closes with the Balkan War of 1912–1913 which ended Turkish rule in the Balkans. It ignores both World Wars and makes no mention of the creation, in 1945, of the People's (since 1963, Socialist) Republic of Macedonia within the Federal People's (Socialist) Republic of Yugoslavia. The Soviet Communist Party adjusts its changing views on Macedonia to its shifting policies inside and outside the Communist world, and Communist scholars do not commit themselves in advance.

The student and the interested reader must wade through a disorderly mass of unrelated data and uncoordinated special studies about Macedonia, strewn about in various countries in many languages. Many events from more recent times are deliberately kept from public knowledge and many will never be known because the witnesses are dead. Nationalistic and cultural prejudice permeates much of the Slav and non-Slav writings on Macedonia, accounting for spurious facts, dubious theories and wrong emphases.

Thus it happens that, while Alexander's battles have been written about in great detail, we don't know much about the villages which furnished his phalanxes, about their living conditions, customs, religion, even language; nor do we know much more about the Slav Macedonians for long periods under the Turks; and a great deal of material about Macedonian terrorist organizations and great power intrigues will probably never be available. Briefly, we don't know much about Macedonia, and the little we know is sometimes wrong and often disputed.

MACEDONIA is such a little-known land that some scholars even today question whether the ancient Macedonians were Greeks or belonged to another subgroup of Mediterranean peoples. It would be easier if modern Greeks had not appropriated Alexander the Great as another Greek national hero, despite Demosthenes' patriotic speeches against the "barbarian" Philip.

Ancient Macedonia seems to have been little known even to Greeks of the Classical Period, although men like the philosopher Aristotle, the playwright Euripides and the painter Zeuxis at one time or another lived at the Macedonian court. It is rather extraordinary that in his writings Aristotle never mentioned his pupil Alexander, described court life in the ancient Macedonian capital of Pella, or commented on the great changes that Philip and Alexander were bringing to Greece and the world beyond.

Nor has our knowledge of Macedonian and Balkan geography progressed much since antiquity. Indeed, until well late into the second half of the last century, European cartographers insisted against all evidence that a west-east mountain barrier prevented a north-south Belgrade-Salonika passage. This was so because the Greek Strabo in his *Geography* (first century B.C.) and Ptolemy of Alexandria in his *Guide to Geography* (second century A.D.) had erroneously claimed that an unbroken and insurmountable west-east mountain chain separated Greece, Macedonia and Aegean Thrace from the northern Balkan lands, establishing a formidable barrier between the agreeable and polished South and the savage and inhospitable North with its snows and frosts, a land—said the Hellenes—inhabited by barbarians. The classical misconception found its way into Renaissance cartography. The supposedly solid west-east Balkan mountain chain was grandly named *Catena Mundi* or *Catena del Mondo* (the Chain of the World). Most cartographers of the first half of the nineteenth century designated the same impenetrable Balkan rampart as the *Zentralkette* (Central Chain).

The German explorer August Grisebach insisted in vain in his monumental *Journey Through Rumelia to Brussa in 1839* that one could travel in a coach the entire distance from Belgrade through Macedonia to Salonika. It was only after the travels of the French explorer and historian Ami Boué in the first half of the last century that European geographers and cartographers gradually began to admit that there was not and never had been a non-negotiable Central Chain

4

in the Balkans. The German geographer H. Kiepert's maps of the mid-nineteenth century disposed of the west-east Balkan barrier legend. In 1858, Johann G. von Hahn, the Austrian consul in the then Turkish Salonika and a hardy traveler, made a journey from Belgrade through Macedonia to Salonika by coach and canoe specifically to prove that a Belgrade-Salonika railroad, in which Austria had become interested, was entirely feasible. Even so, according to the illustrious Serbian anthropologist-geographer J. Cvijić, one could as late as 1870 come upon maps showing the "impassable" west-east mountain chain of Strabo and Ptolemy.

In his *Mission Archéologique de Macédoine* (1876) the French scholar Leon Heuzey claimed that he and his party were the first Europeans to penetrate the gorges of the Mariovo region of present-day Yugoslav Macedonia. Actually, Philip of Macedon and his men had marched through the wilderness more than a millennium earlier. As late as 1894 the Pindus Mountains were described in a paper to a Berlin scientific society as being utterly savage and inaccessible. The Serb J. Cvijić, in his capital work *La Péninsule Balkanique* (Paris, 1917), drew the same picture. Yet roughly a century before, the French diplomat and explorer F. C. H. L. Pouqueville crossed the Pindus Mountains on horseback in springtime, and produced a magnificent description of that country and an account of his Balkan travels, published in 1826.

Trains have been running between Belgrade and Salonika through Macedonia for many decades now. The fact is that a north-south passage from the Danube to the Aegean through Serbia, Macedonia and Greece has at all times been available through the northbound river Morava and the southbound river Vardar, both connected by three passes cutting through the "Central Chain." It is astounding that mapmakers should for so long have ignored the evidence that the Morava-Vardar valley was used in prehistoric migrations, in Roman times, in the times of the Great Migrations and of the Byzantine Empire; that the Turks had constantly used that route; and that the Austrian General Silvio Piccolomini, pursuing the Turks after the failure of their second siege of Vienna (1683), in 1689 penetrated the "Central Chain" and captured Skopje in Macedonia.

The story of the impenetrable west-east Balkan mountain chain is a textbook example of how political prejudice can create and maintain geographical ignorance.

Even after the rediscovery in the last century of the north-south passage, Kiepert's revolutionary maps contained a blank area in Macedonia ("south of Serbia"). As late as 1858, European cartographers, conversant with human settlements in Paraguay, were unaware of the venerable, beautiful and prosperous town of Kruševo in what is now Yugoslav Macedonia. On the maps of the same year, the wild Mariovo region of the present Yugoslav Macedonia was marked with dots, as are still certain areas in the Amazon jungles.

Regrettably, the Greek archeologist Fotios Petsas, well known in the United States, felt compelled to call *The Encyclopaedia Britannica* of 1954 publicly to account for having published on Pella, the capital of Philip of Macedon and Alexander the Great, only six lines, "almost all wrong."

In default of writings and "stones" there are myths, traditions and folklore to fall back upon. These are the oral, artistic and behavioral records of the illiterate or prehistoric peoples. If we with the philosopher Socrates, the classicist Belloc, the historian Toynbee and others dismiss all unprovable traditions and myths like so much fancy, the result is much lost history. The written record, the "document," to which our legalistic-minded society attaches so much importance, is no proof in itself. The proof is the reliable man behind the document, the man who truly experienced or witnessed what the document states as a fact. Herodotus's statements have often been questioned, not seldom unjustly, while certain written records about Alexander the Great were forgeries. There had been much truth in the *Iliad* about Troy all the time before Schliemann proved it. Nor would the Flood of the Bible have remained a tale if Sir Leonard Woolley had not shown it to have been a historical event.

IT is always important to see the places where events occurred and people lived that one reads or writes about. In his *Hellenism*, A. J. Toynbee says that "... it is a great help to have seen something, however little, of the theatre in which the drama was performed. One instant's glimpse of a landscape with one's own eyes can tell one more than years spent on studying maps and texts." Yet Toynbee himself wrote about Macedonia without having visited its more important areas. "I have not yet," he says in the quoted book, "seen ... Epirus or Paeonia [the present Yugoslav Macedonia]; Amphipolis or Philippi or Mount Pangaeum. . . . To venture to write about such important regions without having set eyes on them is hazardous; but the alternative would have been to put off writing till the Greek Kalenda. So," Toynbee adds, "the best I can do is to put my cards on the table." Later Toynbee did pay a visit to the indicated areas.

The trouble is that students of Balkan affairs could hardly ever travel freely through Macedonia, choosing at will the places or the duration of their visits. The great Serbian anthropologist-geographer Jovan Cvijić complained that under the Turkish rule large sections of the Balkans were off limits to scholars for political reasons. In 1927 a noted German geographer of the University of Jena made a similar complaint about Yugoslavia and Greece. In 1962 I myself was unable to travel in Bulgaria to do research.

This should not weaken the spirit of the earnest traveler or ruin his disposition, as indeed it did not in those scholars whose accounts are mentioned above. Prejudices seem to be more frequent in non-travelers. Nor should bureaucratic annoyances prevent the enterprising wanderer from lighting up, even if only with a match, the dark places and times still connected with Macedonia and the Balkans. Above all, to understand a country one must love it.

It is gratifying to record that one of the best books on Macedonia and the Macedonians that have come my way was written by a member of an ex-enemy nation, the German naturalist Dr. Franz Doflein, of the University of Breslau (now Wroclaw, Poland). He served with the German army in the First World War in what is now Yugoslav Macedonia. He roved and looked around, made copious notes and published them in the form of a book after the war (*Mazedonien*, Jena, 1921). Not refraining from fair criticism, he closed his observations, written in the midst of the bloodiest carnage the world had known up till then, with the following lines about that beautiful and wounded land, "A book like this... should make an unknown land, a blank spot on the map of Europe, better understood by our people and show how much all branches of our knowledge and our culture still have to learn from that land."

Memorable Places

AT the northern end of the Mt. Athos isthmus, east of Salonika, there is a low hill above the Aegean Sea where once the Hellenic colony of Stagira stood; it was the birthplace of Alexander the Great's teacher, Aristoteles. In the one-time Hellenic colony of Abdeira, in eastern Greek Macedonia, Democritus was born, father of the theory of mobile and colliding atoms. Near the international highway south of Skopje, the capital of Yugoslav Macedonia, is the site of the village where the codifier of the Roman Law, Emperor Justinian, was born. Just a little further south are the ruins of the classical city of Stobi, where in 388 A.D. Emperor Theodosius proclaimed his edict forbidding religious disputes about the Mother of God.

In parts of Yugoslav and Greek Macedonia you drive past Roman milestones along the old Roman Via Egnatia between Durazzo on the Albanian coast and Salonika; the road was eventually extended to the Hellespont (the Dardanelles) for transport of Roman troops to and from Asia. The oldest Eurasian highway was the one Xerxes built from the Hellespont through Thrace and Macedonia to Greece, including the still visible canal across the Mt. Athos isthmus to be used by his fleet.

In the Battle of Pydna, near Mt. Olympus, in 168 B.C., the Romans defeated the last Macedonian successor of Alexander the Great. The ancient nation and realm of Macedon disappeared forever.

In 48 B.C. Caesar defeated his rival, Pompey, at Pharsalus, south of Olympus, this battle being one of the birth pangs of the Roman Empire. Six years later, in the battle on the plains of Philippi, east of Salonika, Octavian and Antony defeated Cassius and Brutus, Caesar's assassin, who committed suicide on the very spot and with whom the Roman republic itself died.

In 31 B.C., on his march to Roman imperial power, Octavian (the later Augustus) routed Antony's and Cleopatra's combined fleets off the promontory of Actium in Epirus, Macedon's western neighbor. The local legend has it that the ghosts of the drowned ancient warriors, pirates and shipwrecked people still wander on stormy seas there during autumn nights.

In the early tenth century A.D., Tsar Simeon of Bulgaria established himself at the Macedonian town and lake by the name of Ohrid, having conquered a major part of the Balkans. In the early eleventh century, near Lake Doiran in Macedonia, Byzantium overwhelmingly defeated the Macedonian (western Bulgarian) Emperor Samuel. In the fourteenth century, in Skopje, Dušan of Serbia founded a Serbian empire. Upon his death, the newly arrived Turks shattered the Serbian army on Kosovo Field, just across the Macedonian border. Having secured the strategic Balkan center, the Turks captured Constantinople (1453) and extended the Ottoman empire to the gates of Vienna (1529).

From the fields of the Yugoslav-Macedonian town of Kumanovo are seen the summits and the gullies where the Serbian army, in 1912, broke through the Turkish positions, in the Balkan War in which the Serbs, the Montenegrins, the Bulgars and the Greeks for the first and only time acted together and put an end to the long overdue Turkish rule in Europe.

There is a French military cemetery on the heights of Kaimakčalan and a British military cemetery above Lake Doiran, in Yugoslav Macedonia, dating from the First World War. What sometimes on many another Yugoslav-Macedonian slope looks from a distance like a well-ordered vineyard is nothing but a grimly impeccable forest of crosses—Serbian, French, British, German. These cemeteries mark the advance toward Belgrade of the Allied armies of the Salonika front in September-October 1918. The breakthrough precipitated the dissolution of the 400-year-old Habsburg empire and helped create the new states of Yugoslavia and Czechoslovakia following the Armistice of November 11, 1918.

In many places in Macedonia there are graves, memorials, burned down houses and despoiled gold ornaments in churches, which indicate the trail of fratricide among Serbs, Bulgars, Greeks and Albanians. However, high above the Yugoslav-Macedonian plain of Pelagonia the summit of Bear's Rock represents a call to act in common. Trenches are still discernible where the last few picked Macedonian rebels of the "St. Elijah Uprising," in 1903, succumbed to an overwhelming Turkish force. Militarily, the uprising was of no consequence. But the "St. Elijah Proclamation" called for the self-government of Macedonia under Turkish suzerainty and appealed to all the other Balkan nationalities to fight to obtain autonomy. This was the first stand for a Balkan federation. The message still reads that it was not enough for the great powers to leave the Balkans alone. It is equally necessary for the Balkan peoples to make peace among themselves.

WHAT THE LAND
LOOKS LIKE

MACEDONIA is a country of picturesque mountains and crags and deep silences; of dark forests and glittering mountain lakes; of bizarre rocks and sun-scorched high plateaus; of lush lowlands, grassy highlands and arid badlands; of unexpected waterfalls, primeval swamps and underground rivers; of Asian buffaloes, extraordinary costumes and miles of fields of tomato, green pepper, tobacco, poppy and grain, vineyards and orchards; of picturesque towns, medieval ruins, lost ancient cities and remains of prehistoric settlements; of villages hidden in gullies, sheltered by vegetation or hanging over precipices; of churches and monasteries pinned to cliffs or looking at themselves in tranquil waters. It is an altogether enchanting country.

Macedonia is more than a landscape. It is an artistic composition. Its natural and esthetic unity makes the Yugoslav, Greek and Bulgarian frontiers wholly artificial. Its distinct personality is balance and imagination. In this, the Macedonian landscape reflects the traits of the Macedonian people: "Its face reveals its soul."

There is hardly anything immoderate in this land. Almost all that is inordinate lies on its fringes or just outside. The imagination displayed by this landscape is beyond human capacities. What architect, for example, has ever thought of combining Venice and Niagara Falls as an idea for a town? There is such a town, Edessa (Voden, in Slav), in Greek Macedonia.

Macedonia is an optimistic and intensely human countryside that can instill deep homesickness into its men. Stories of natives returning from abroad and embracing and kissing the trees are literally true.

Mountains

THE word *balkan* means "mountain" in Turkish. Specifically, the Turks gave that name to the eastern section of the so-called "Central Chain," running west-east through the middle of Bulgaria and called Haemus in ancient times. In 1808, the German geographer A. Zeune applied the name to the entire peninsula, which has ever since been known as the Balkan Peninsula.

Some sections of the Pyrenées are said to be the only European mountains resembling to some extent the Balkan mountains. The Alps, royal and monumental, have not quite the dramatic effect of the raw Balkans. Nor does the colossal Alpine skyline compare with the impetuous profiles of the smaller but unruly Balkan mountains. These mountains seem to be in constant movement—closing in on you, surging like successive waves, marching as though in battalions, writhing as if in agony or passion, rearing against each other, reaching for the heavens. They sometimes seem to grow taller as one comes closer, and they often look brooding, scowling, lurking, as if about to do something to the spectator. After all, there has for so long been so much to avenge. The Germans and the Italians sincerely feared the Balkan wilderness. Yet to the natives it seemed friendly and protective, as indeed it has always been. "Get thee to the hills, the forest is thy mother," advises an old folk poem, an advice that was widely taken during the last war.

It is said that there are still recesses in the Balkans unknown to man, such as the forests in the rugged hills southwest of Skopje where human foot has supposedly never trodden. However that may be, it is true that many Balkan places are not at all or are sparsely inhabited and hardly if ever visited. For instance, the Mariovo region in the south of Yugoslav Macedonia, inhabited by picturesquely costumed and rustic people, is still very much off the beaten track, and local papers still report that persons have disappeared because of bad weather, or have been killed by wild beasts, especially in winter.

MACEDONIA is rimmed by the biggest Balkan mountains: Pirin (9,564 feet) to the northeast, in Bulgaria; Šar (9,010 feet) to the northwest, in Yugoslavia; Korab (9,066 feet) to the south, in Greece.

The Macedonian mountain landscape is all broken up. The mountains stray in all directions and are fitfully cut off, pushed apart or crowded together by valleys, plains or high plateaus interpolated at random. Because of this chaotic structure, much of the Macedonian interior has long been quite unapproachable. Even today these mountains lack roads and trails, and the best way of visiting the most interesting parts of Macedonia is on horseback or on foot.

Mountains in the shape of a cone or a pyramid are frequent in Macedonia and in Epirus. Thus an impressive mountain rises like a perfect cone in the very center of Yugoslav Macedonia; its name is

"Salonika Head." From its height of more than 8,300 feet a magnificent view embraces almost the entire country, including some gleaming white marble slopes amidst the velvet of the forests. Far to the south, on a clear day one can discern Salonika. Hence its name.

All the mountains along the Yugoslav-Greek frontier have a resolute look. Mount Kaimakčalan of First World War fame, viewed from Greek Macedonia, is nothing but bare, dark, vertical walls with projecting towers, pointed peaks, crenelated ramparts and a sawtoothed skyline. It is not the biggest Macedonian mountain, but it is the haughtiest and the most forbidding—standing guard against the south.

Just north of Kaimakčalan extends the Mariovo region, a tormented landscape of hills literally slashed by ravines. Some bristling pointed rocks appear from afar like a forest of giant poplars. Nearby rise the grotesque Konjsko crags, where the folk-poem hero Marko Kraljevic is said to have competed with his piebald steed in jumps from summit to summit.

At the northwestern end of Yugoslav Macedonia rises the massive Šar, the second-highest mountain of Yugoslavia and one of the highest in the Balkans. From its top pyramid, now available for skiing, one can glimpse, farther northwest along the Albanian frontier, the weird Cursed Mountains and the beginnings of the unassailable Montenegrin crags. This whole northwest is a turbulent panorama of seemingly storm-tossed land masses, a veritable cauldron of seething land. Some of these rocky heights, especially the Cursed Mountains, are surmounted by pointed peaks with concave sides and look like enormous fangs bared toward the heavens. Toward the south, along the Macedonian-Albanian border, there are mountains whose sheer drops and smooth sides glitter with an elusive diamond blue under the resplendent snowcaps. Among them is the formidable Korab with its glistening pinnacles and battlements and its cleanly sliced-off stone flanks, hovering like an ice palace over the lesser crests. Only Kaimakčalan ranks in stature with Korab and the northwestern mountains, which awed and humbled the few European explorers who during the last century ventured into this desolate country.

In this tumultuous mountain mass are also found the Macedonian river canyons of Radika and Drim, with their bridges with names like "Devil's Bridge" or "Stag's Leap," their snows, high pastures, woods, cascades, goat paths and solitudes.

THERE are five "religious" mountains in or just outside Macedonia.

Just south of Salonika Head, in Yugoslav Macedonia, stretch the deep and mysterious forests of the Babuna Mountain. Leaders and members of the powerful medieval religious-social sect of Bogumils or Babuni, which opposed the church, the state and the nobility, used to have their hideouts and hold their gatherings there for centuries.

From Salonika, on a clear afternoon, one can see across the bay to the southwest the bluish silhouette of something like the hump of a whale—Mt. Olympus, where Zeus and his gods and goddesses once ruled, feasted and feuded. It lies just outside Greek Macedonia and is the highest mountain in the Balkans. Its snowy heights are surrounded by peaks, forests and precipices.

East of Salonika, on the other side of the three-pronged Chalcidice Peninsula and fronting the Aegean Sea, stands the Pangaeum Mountain. Flat-topped, it rises brusquely from the ground, as does more than one Macedonian mountain. Its back is turned to a big and almost level plain, the scene in 42 B.C. of the battle between Octavian and Antony and Brutus and Cassius. The plain contains the ruins of the ancient Macedonian town of Philippi, constructed by Alexander's father, Philip of Macedon, who exploited the gold mines in the surrounding hills. The ruins include the remnants of the cell where the Apostle Paul is supposed to have been imprisoned after he first set foot in Europe, near the present-day Greek port of Kavalla. The Pangaeum Mountain supposedly sheltered in its interior the seat and altar of the great ancient Thracian and later also Greek and Roman god of life, Dionysus-Bacchus.

From the Pangaeum Mountain, when it is clear, one can see to the south the outline of a big mountain rising straight up from the sea. Its top, at the extreme southern end, has the form of a cone. The mounain runs the length of the easternmost prong of the trident peninsula and is called Mount Athos, or the Holy Mountain. In long-forgotten times, some pagan temples used to stand there. Now twenty Eastern Orthodox monasteries, mostly Greek, perch like eagles' nests on cliffs high above the sea or balance hazardously on overhanging rocks. This mountain is also the only place in Europe where hermits live and pray out in the open.

In southwestern Bulgaria, which constitutes the Bulgarian part of Macedonia, the so-called Pirin Macedonia, soars the biggest Macedonian mountain, Pirin. The mountain is named after the ancient pagan Slav thunder god, Perun. He is supposed to have taken up his residence at the top of this mountain upon the arrival of the first Slavs in the Balkans. In the 1930s the people of this region, it is said, still believed that he lived up there and made thunder, lightning and storms. The highest of Pirin's summits, named Vihren (Storm), is usually shrouded in haze, and then the villagers in the plain say that Perun is breathing. When heavy dark clouds envelop the Storm Peak, they claim that

Perun is smoking his pipe. Pirin is a "growing" mountain. On the National Geographic Society's map of 1958 it yields only seven feet to Mt. Olympus, but it has not yet become the highest Balkan mountain. According to some sources, the natives are piling up rocks on the Storm Peak so that every new map adds to the height of Mount Pirin.

Forests

YUGOSLAVIA is right behind Finland and Sweden in European forest wealth; nearly one-third of its territory, or almost 20 million acres, is covered with forests. Within Yugoslavia, Bosnia still has some untouched areas and is the number one forest country in the Balkans. Macedonia does not rank last, and there are primeval forests in the Chalcidice Peninsula.

It is estimated that in ancient times two-thirds of Yugoslavia was wooded. Macedonia, too, was heavily forested, and its rivers were bigger. Since then, forests have been disappearing from large tracts all over the Mediterranean, and the bared soil was not always fit for agriculture. Those responsible for the destruction of the original Macedonian—and Mediterranean—woodlands have been man, goats and nature, in that order.

THE ancient Macedonians and Thracians felled lumber for the Athenian navy and merchant fleet. The Romans cut down the Macedonian oak and pine for construction work, mining installations and ship building. Waves of the Great Migrations ravaged the Balkan forests, whereupon the natives made the invaders pay for fuel and reconstruction. And thus the invader-destruction-reconstruction cycle continued. The Slavs came and needed wood for fuel and the building of villages. Medieval Serbian kings needed Macedonian lumber for mining. Then the Turks came and a general "robber economy" began—despoliation without plan or replenishment. Daut Pasha of Skopje was not the only one to denude the hills around the city for his monumental *aman* (bath). Peasants are notorious everywhere and at all times for indiscriminate use of the ax and ignorance about conservation of forests. The Balkan Wars and the two World Wars further reduced the Yugoslav, and Macedonian, forest wealth, not only for fuel and building material but for defense, for the woods were the fortresses of the Partisans. In short, throughout history, foe and friend, alien and native, applied the ax and the torch to the Balkan forests.

The number two destroyer of the Macedonian forests has been the goat. In fact, throughout the Mediterranean one can observe the pernicious effect of the undisturbed browsing of the goat. In 1949

Macedonia passed the so-called Goat Law, often described as the Law on Liquidation of Goats. The goats were confiscated against compensation and slaughtered for meat, tanning and so on. The peasants were reoriented toward sheep breeding. Only a white goat variety which could be kept and fed at home was exempted from the massacre. Other Yugoslav republics followed suit, Serbia being the last, in 1953. The result was that the number of goats in Yugoslavia dropped from 2.8 million in 1931 to 200,000 in 1955, most of them of the white variety. As for Greek Macedonia, it remained a free country for all goats.

As soon as large areas were deforested by man and goat, forces of erosion set to work by cutting barren gorges into the mountains. Thus it happens that the great and beautiful Šar itself is disfigured by ugly gashes. Ice, torrents, landslides and winds have done even more damage to the Black Hills north of Skopje, once dotted with shrubbery and evergreens.

THERE is nevertheless more forest than arable land in Yugoslav Macedonia. Bald mountains and arid lands take up 13 percent of the republic. Western Macedonia next to the Albanian frontier is the real forest country, with the beech replacing the pine and pushing back the oak.

Forestry is a "developing" science in Yugoslavia. It is partly also a state secret, for economy and defense reasons. After Tito's breach with Stalin in 1948, considerable woodcutting by mobilized peasant forces, unreported in the press, went on for several years in Yugoslavia, surpassing the prewar activities.

One must not forget that wood is used for most heating and cooking in Yugoslavia, and much construction, especially in the villages. Thin fumes on Macedonian heights tell that forest murder is being committed in charcoal kilns by people who know only *mangale* (braziers). The Yugoslav *Encyclopaedia of Forestry* states that a considerable amount of power for Yugoslav industry is still generated by the burning of wood. And one will regularly hear comments that too much wood and its products are exported for hard currency.

For reforestation, the Macedonians import poplars from Canada, because of their fast growth rate. Tourists at Lake Ohrid can watch whole areas planted with pine and cypress saplings. In accord with a new Yugoslav policy, the Macedonian government has placed some forest complexes under state protection and established vast national parks.

ELKS can only rarely be heard calling in certain mountains of Macedonia. Deer are also not too frequent; neither are chamois. But wild boars, foxes, martens, ermines, weasels are plentiful, and hares are exported. Every winter local newspapers report wolf packs appearing in the streets of villages in broad daylight. In the summer, the press will carry a story about big brown bears attacking grazing cattle. Western Macedonia is one of the very few remaining European regions where the lynx still lives and makes sorties against sheep. Packs of jackals and dogs gone wild roam both Yugoslav and Greek Macedonia.

Eagles, vultures, hawks and falcons patrol the Macedonian skies, while storks like to nest in the fields near Skopje and pelicans inhabit the Prespa Lake. The *poskok* (jumper), the horned viper common on the Yugoslav littoral and in the southern regions, lies in ambush on much of Macedonian soil; and an area in western Greek Macedonia literally crawls with them. In the summertime, in hot rocky gulleys, scorpions scamper about.

A plant behaving like a lizard also belongs in this company. In swampy spots on the heights of Pelister, on the Yugoslav-Greek border, a butterwort variety with fleshy leaves and big violet flowers (*Pinguicula grandiflora Lam.*) devours insects.

MAN, especially Slav man, has always been influenced by the forest, the unity formed by its countless trees, the ceaseless growth and the struggle and the peace, the mystery of its ongoing life.

European man's first idols were forest deities. Humans of the forest believed they had come from forest trees and continued to live in them after death. The trees became seats of higher beings who decided on man's good and ill fortunes. The oracle was the oak of the thunderbolt-thrower Zeus. It was also under the protection of the Slav thunder god, Perun. Many classical temples have been stylized architectural replicas of the forest, the trees reduced to pillars supporting the stream-lined roof of tree crowns.

Forests have often influenced the fate of nations. The Germanic tribes drew the northern frontier of the Roman Empire at the rim of their endless, deep forests. The Irish fought the English in their forests for centuries. The Tartars got bogged down in the Russian woods during the long war between the steppe and the forest. The southern Slavs have through centuries battled the invader with *hayduk* guerilla bands in the forests. They waged two big successful national liberation wars with the aid of the forest, one against the Turks and the other against the Germans. To the Balkan Slav, the forest is freedom.

The wildernesses of the world are in peril everywhere today. This is particularly true in the "developing" countries, where the drive for electrification has often become a "progressive" political craze among peoples now searching for respectability. There have already been outcries in the Yugoslav press against the spoliation of magnificent sceneries for the purpose of over-industrialization of doubtful benefit.

The wildernesses of the world, including the Balkans, represent the Free Territories of Nature. They ought to be preserved for the rejuvenation, inspiration and balance of industrial society. We must, as Justice William O. Douglas has said, keep in contact with "the startling beauties of creation" in places of "quiet and solitude where life exists without molestation by man." Roads are necessary for a free society. But do roads have to go everywhere? Roadless nature is also necessary for a society to be free.

In Macedonia and the rest of the Balkans, the roads only yesterday paved the way for the enemy. It is by no means certain that the hills and the woods will never again be needed. Man must find his place in the energy-creating world, of which he is only an infinitesimal part. Contrary to *Genesis* and *Das Kapital*, nature was not made for man alone. Nature's forces have not yet really challenged the forces of man. With all his science, man still has no idea where he fits on earth or in the universe. But if he is only a link in the chain of life, he should protect rather than destroy other life.

Lakes and Plains

THERE are six big and glorious mountain lakes in Yugoslav and Greek Macedonia—Prespa, Doiran, Mavrovo, Ohrid, Ostrovo, Kastoria (Kostur in Slav). All are surrounded by different and picturesque landscapes. All, except one, Lake Ohrid, lie in regions not often visited by foreigners. On the low ground east of Salonika, two more big lakes, Koronia and Volvi, separate the Chalcidice Peninsula from the Greek-Macedonian mainland. Smaller lakes will appear before the traveler. Great heights hold tiny immobile glacial lakes glimmering greenishly out of gray rocks. The natives call them "eyes."

Lake Prespa, shared by Yugoslavia, Greece and Albania, is the largest of all. It is also the wildest and the most solitary, with dense forests literally plunging into the placid waters, which in the evening often turn milk-blue. This lake, which harbors pelicans and small islands topped by medieval ruins, was one of the residences of a tragic and controversial medieval Macedonian Slav monarch, Tsar Samuel. The same lake afforded rest to many Hungarian "freedom fighters" of 1956.

From the beautiful artifical lake of Mavrovo, which feeds a postwar power plant high up in the woods of western Yugoslav Macedonia,

17

opens a stunning panorama of the Korab and other mountains along the Albanian frontier. The lake of Doiran, astride the Yugoslav-Greek frontier near Bulgaria, was the scene of a year-long artillery duel between the Allied and the German-Bulgarian forces in the First World War, leaving not a wall standing. It is also the only place in Europe where fishing is done with the aid of migratory birds, as in pre-historic times.

Most bewitching is the view of Lake Kastoria, in the far west of Greek Macedonia, near the wilds of Greek Epirus and southern Albania. Ringed by mountains, it is nearly halved by a thin tongue of land with an abruptly rising point, from which a town seems to descend like a charmed city below the invisible waterline to the very bottom of the translucent lake.

The universally glamorized Macedonian lake, however, is Lake Ohrid. The lake looks like a piece of the Dalmatian Adriatic transplanted into high wooded hills. The waters are an indigo blue, which turns a clear green along the immaculately white beaches and match the mellow violet of the mountains reflected in the lake. All of this harmonizes with the red, gray and brown roofs of the white town, which with its church steeples climbs a hillock toward the ruins of Tsar Samuel's old fortress. Of this lake, just behind the German lines on the Salonika front in the First World War, a visiting German naturalist wrote at the time that its view "can compare with the most beautiful in the world." Regardless of the battle line, he said, young lovers went out in the evenings and sat on the rocks and sang their melancholy songs. He added that "when dusk fell, and the mirror of the lake darkened, and only the mountain peaks and the wandering clouds radiated the red flame of the sun," this was the only place in the war where he could think of peace.

SOME twenty low plains and high plateaus hollow and intersect the Macedonian mountainland. All, except the vast Salonika coastal plain, are walled in by high mountains. The Yannitsa plain, west of Salonika, was a bay of the Aegean Sea in the times of the ancient Macedonian kings.

Macedonian plains, high and low, sometimes have a touch of the African lion country with their scattered bushes and lonely trees amidst green oceans of young grain swaying in the wind. Unfortunately, those beautiful and characteristically Macedonian trees, the great solitary oaks of the plains, were in large numbers cut down for fuel and construction by the occupation armies in the two World Wars. But the other common Yugoslav tree types, the poplar and the weeping willow, still dot the Macedonian plains. Everywhere poplars stand in long lines along a road, or in clumps, indicating a village, or man the fields all by themselves, tall and slender between the earth and the sky. Sometimes, however, poplars keep mute and solemn company to sinuous rows of willows bent weeping over a stream in the field.

The high plateaus, like Ovče Pole (Sheep's Field) in Yugoslav Macedonia, are known for the rush of the winds and a blazing summer heat which often cracks the earth. In the big plains below—like the Polog, Pelagonia, Gevgelia plains in Yugoslav Macedonia or the Florina, Seres, Yannitsa plains in Greek Macedonia—the soil is uncommonly fertile, excellent for the growing of grain and fruit, and is in many places suitable for double harvests and subtropical plants. However, these plains are also subject to droughts and floods. From the Kumanovo plain on the Macedonian-Serbian border to the Yannitsa plain in Greek Macedonia there are numerous irrigation and drainage works, some still under construction. Many more are needed.

The town of Bitola, on the Greek border at the southern end of Yugoslav Macedonia, was stormed in 1912 after a long siege by the Serbian troops wading chest-deep through swamps and the water which the Turkish defenders released by opening the dikes. For ages this region was one of Macedonia's main breeding places of malaria. Although malaria has been stamped out—in Yugoslav Macedonia partly even before the Second World War, thanks to the Rockefeller Foundation—many of the great spaces of Pelagonia have not yet been cleared of marshes. Large tracts of the Salonika coastal plain, also, are still only endless black mire. There are stagnant waters elsewhere, too. Nevertheless, drainage dikes and irrigation pipes and sprays have restored much human health and food by eradicating malaria and opening new fields to cultivation. Even the Katlanovo lake and swamp in the Skopje plain, long a malaria distribution center, is now a spa with a controlled Georgia-type swamp, underwood and reeds, and with all the noisy world of the water birds.

The Story of a River

FIVE main rivers traverse Macedonia: the Vardar (the ancient Axios) in Yugoslav and Greek Macedonia, the Halyakmon and the Ludias in Greek Macedonia, the Struma (the ancient Strymon) in Bulgarian and Greek Macedonia, and the Black Drim in Yugoslav Macedonia. The first four enter the Aegean Sea on a southward or eastward course, the Black Drim heads northward and through Albania empties into the Adriatic.

The Vardar forms a part of the Balkan north-south passage. Through two short overland links with the northbound Serbian river Morava, it connects the port of Salonika on the Aegean Sea with the Danube and Central Europe. This route has been traditionally named "the Morava-Vardar Valley."

The Vardar, Macedonia's main river, has been navigated since the Bronze Age. In classical times, when almost all of Macedonia was overgrown with thick forests, the Vardar carried three times more water than it does today. The ancient Greek triremes—big seagoing vessels with three ranks of oars, one above another—used to ply that river all the way up to where the city of Skopje is located.

Contrary to Homer's eulogies of the Axios beauties (*The Iliad* II, 850), the Vardar is only sometimes a green river and mostly a muddy yellow or a coffee-brown or black stream carrying slime and silt. Except at its terminus in the Salonika plain, the Vardar is rather swift, with an average speed of six miles an hour. It is not of great depth, and although in places it reaches a width of 800 feet, in a time of drought it may only be knee-deep and not even twenty feet wide. But in the winter and spring months, the Vardar brings broken ice and melted snow from the mountains and causes floods both in Yugoslavia and in Greece. In the Skopje plain, the Vardar also overflows from underground inundations coming from a subterranean network of water ducts whose sources are not known. South of Skopje the mountain stream Topolka gushes in deep-green waterfalls through a defile of red-yellow cliffs into the Vardar. There was a time when monks, from a monastery on a green turf and ringed by trees, contemplated the turbulent entry of the rivulet into the unruly Vardar. A little farther down, at the junction of the Babuna River, the vertical rock walls rise to 1,300 feet out of the water. Nearby, a boulder in the midst of the greenish Vardar carries the reddish ruins of a chapel.

The capital river of Macedonia swirls on and sculpts away at the upright colored cliffs, relaxing every now and then past cheerful groves which relieve the nudity of northern and central-eastern Macedonia. Before the narrows of Demir Kapu (the Iron Gate), the landscape turns, first, into bare desolate banks with nothing but miserable scrubs hanging onto crumbling stone, then into stark naked hills with ravines eaten into them. In the afternoon sun, these hills appear in bizarre shapes of glaring colors—brick red, orange and violet above brown and white. A painter has said that this part of the Vardar land reminded him of some landscapes along the Red Sea and in Mexico. Demir Kapu was known even to the ancient Macedonian kings before Alexander as Macedon's gate to and from the forbidding north. Here the winding, compressed and somber river passage cuts through gray basalt of reddish-brown tinge. The Vardar snakes back and forth between several hundred yards of towering cliff walls so steep that tunnels had to be bored for the road and the railroad. There are no houses, no fields, only stones and bears.

Wresting itself free of the twisted Demir Kapu hold and leaving behind the jagged rocks, the Vardar sets out for the Gevgelia plain. To the east looms a mountain chain. To the west, one purple mountain rises above another. Behind them soar the snowy pyramids of Kaimak-čalan and others with radiantly blue gullies on their white slopes.

The Vardar now emerges into the apparently endless Aegean coastal plain, exuding damp mist. Here the energetic river, depositing several feet of silt, settles down to a lazy pace and to slowly spreading its waters as far as they will trickle. The Vardar ends its lively journey rather undramatically, just southwest of Salonika, by coming to a standstill in an immense delta, where its many very slowly moving water arteries can hardly be traced in what looks like an enormous black quicksand.

Sky, Wind and Soil

THERE is a marked difference in climate between the Balkan north and Greece. The former is influenced by Russia, the latter by Africa. Both are influenced by the Near East. Being on the crossroads like the Balkans themselves—only more so—Macedonia has an even more varied climate.

In the winter, icy northern winds from the Eurasian steppes break through the Rumanian plains and the Hungarian Carpathian passes into the Balkans and reach parts of Macedonia. On the other hand, the subtropical high-pressure zone extends from Africa across the Mediterranean into the Balkans. In addition, climatic influences from the hot Near East are responsible for much of the drought in the Balkans. In the Gevgelia low plain and on Sheep's Field high plateau, summer temperatures may rise to more than 107 degrees Fahrenheit. In the winter, temperatures below zero have been noted.

GREEK mythology knew two principal Balkan winds, endowing one with creative and the other with destructive powers. One was the ice-cold north wind Boreas, protector, fertilizer and world creator. The other was the hot south wind from Africa, unhealthy, evil-smelling, blighting and causing "nightmares" (headaches and hallucinations).

21

Boreas inhabited a cave on Mount Haemus (the present-day Mount Balkan, in Bulgaria). He also had a home beside the river Struma, in today's Bulgaria. From there he blew down all the way to Attica. He was worshiped by all within his domain—the Thracians, the Macedonians, the Hellenes.

Agamemnon, the leader of the Greek amphibious expedition against Troy, sacrificed his daughter Iphigenia on the altar to Boreas before sailing, imploring him to be a good wind to his fleet. Later the Athenians invoked Boreas to destroy Xerxes's fleet, as he had sunk the ships of Xerxes's father Darius off Mount Athos. And after their crushing naval victory over Xerxes at Salamis (480 B.C.) they built him a temple. Blowing in wintertime, Boreas was also believed to impregnate Attica each year with spring flowers. Considering what we know about dissemination of pollens by the wind, this may be called a scientific guess.

Before people knew how pregnancy came about, they widely and for a long time assumed that females were impregnated by rivers or winds. Pliny himself, following Homer, thought that Spanish mares conceived by exposing their hindquarters to the wind. Church father Lactantius, in the late third century A.D. explained impregnation of women by the wind as an analogy of the Virgin's conception by the Holy Ghost. The "breath of life" that God blew into Adam's nostrils also belonged to the category of beliefs in the life-giving force of the wind.

The ancients may have derived their Boreas cult from the Pelasgians. These rather misty Neolithic precursors of the Hellenes, of some 5,000 and more years ago, also revered the North Wind. In their myth of Creation, the North Wind, in the form of the great serpent Ophion, fathered with Eurynome, the Goddess of All Things, the great Universal Egg, out of which tumbled sun, moon, stars, the earth and the rest.

OF the four north winds of Yugoslavia, two are Macedonian, blowing onto the Aegean Sea via the rivers Struma and Vardar.

The Struma north wind, coming from Bulgarian Macedonia, can make the Aegean Sea literally boil along the eastern shores of Mt. Athos—enough to have sent Darius's ships to the bottom, and to have forced Xerxes to dig a canal across the Mt. Athos isthmus for his fleet that met with disaster at Salamis. The Struma wind is the wind of ancient Boreas. It is also the wind of the old Slav thunder god Perun, who took over from Boreas and installed himself on top of Mt. Pirin, only a few miles south of Boreas's cave. As in the case of the Yugoslav folktale about the three-headed god Trajan's Ass's ears, repeating a prehistoric King Midas myth, we have here another transmission of an important Hellenic myth. The question immediately arises: were the

Macedonian Slavs of the Pirin region the first Slavs to settle permanently in the Balkans?

The other Macedonian northern wind is called Vardarac. It is an almost equally aggressive northerly, which storms from Yugoslav Macedonia toward Salonika through the narrow Vardar river passes and dies in Thessaly. This cold wind rises without warning within an hour and always, like the Adriatic *bura*, under a clear sky. It blasts anywhere from one to five days in one uninterrupted gale, not in buffeting gusts, like the other two Yugoslav northerlies. It ceases as abruptly as it starts. Because of the Vardarac and the generally prevalent strong winds blowing from the north, towns and villages in Greek Macedonia are preferably built on the southern slopes of the hills.

Sometimes, in parts of Yugoslav Macedonia, Dalmatia and Bosnia, yellow rain falls or the countryside is covered with yellowish or reddish snow. Very strong and hot southern winds from the Sahara, called *jugo* (south) in Yugoslavia and generally known as *sirocco*, cause more than oppressive, humid, warm weather and dirty-green heaving seas in the eastern Mediterranean and the Adriatic. Blowing at great heights and at a speed of sixty miles an hour, they drive before them enormous quantities of the hot Sahara air saturated with microscopically fine sand particles. This dust regularly descends upon western Yugoslav Macedonia and certain other Yugoslav regions. Discharges of clouds at such times create colored rain or snow, another of the many startling wonders of Macedonia.

CROSS-CLIMATE influences show in the produce of Yugoslav and Greek Macedonia. They account for grain, especially wheat, and also for white-speckled fields of cotton and opium poppies (for medicinal purposes only). They make it possible to grow the Indian sesame medicinal plant and are also responsible for some water-glistening rice fields. The climate combinations have also made Macedonia a country of sweet chestnut, walnut and hazelnut forests, and the only Yugoslav area producing peanuts. Macedonia's vegetable gardens are in particularly high repute. The Yugoslav-Macedonian valley of Polog produces the renowned "Tetovo beans." Top-quality tomatoes and green peppers for export to the West carpet great expanses in Greek Macedonia. Green peppers are not mere seasoning in Macedonia, they are food.

Thracian and Macedonian wines have been appreciated since the times of the cult of Dionysus, and vineyards still spread through all three Macedonias. The late King Alexander had some of his choice vineyards in Macedonia, and today vast new collectively owned vineyards cover its plains and rolling hills. Beautiful and extensive orchards, on the plains and in the valleys between Mt. Šar in the north and Mt. Olympus in the south, produce the finest apples, pears, peaches, apricots, cherries. Much of this fruit is exported to Western countries. From the Yugoslav Macedonian plains of Polog and Lake Prespa come internationally known apples as well as a certain type originally imported from California. Miles of the Gevgelia, Pelagonia and other plains in Yugoslav and Greek Macedonia carry mulberry trees for the growing of silk worms. Figs and pomegranates grow in Greek and southern Yugoslav Macedonia. Even olives do—in Greek Macedonia. Oranges and lemons do not.

Much fruit grows wild in Macedonia. Parts of the northern and southern slopes of the Yugoslav-Greek border mountains abound in whole forests of wild cherry, apple and pear trees; so much so that on the Greek side villages are sometimes named after the wild fruit surrounding them. Macedonia must have possessed much more wild fruit in ancient times. For instance, one of the Illyrian provinces in those times, embracing parts of present-day Albania and Yugoslav Macedonia, was called "Dardania." Significantly, *dardhe* means "pear tree" in the language of the Albanians, believed to be descendants of the Illyrians.

Tobacco, ranking among the best in the world, is grown in Greek Macedonia, particularly in the plain of the town of Drama, and in Yugoslav Macedonia, particularly in the plain of the town of Prilep. Few people know that it is this Macedonian tobacco which, under the commercial name of "Turkish" (for the Turks first introduced and exported it), is used for "blending" with the Virginia tobacco in U.S. cigarettes.

Camels are no longer bred in the Strumica region, in the southeastern corner of Yugoslav Macedonia, as transport animals. One will hardly see a goat in Yugoslav Macedonia, the domestic animal being prohibited in the interest of reforestation. Nor will one find a mule, except with army units. Horses are not numerous, neither are pigs. Chickens by far exceed turkeys, geese and ducks. Black Asian buffaloes, a familiar sight, are a reminder that the real East is not very distant. Cattle, rather on the bony side, are not the main livestock. As in many another place in the Balkans and the Mediterranean lands, not to mention Latin America, one will most often meet two domestic animals in Macedonia: the poor peasant's greatest friend and transport, his universal standby as old as history, the donkey; and his chief provider of food and clothing since the time of Abraham, the sheep. In the spring and in the autumn, flocks thousands strong may halt all traffic on back country roads, heading to and from their summer pastures high up among the blue asters in the green hills. Ferocious shaggy

"Šar Mountaineers" (big sheep dogs which will attack wolf, bear and man alike) keep them together under the watchful eye of the hooded shepherd with the crooked staff and the eagle cruising above. In Turkish times, at the beginning of this century, when there were no frontiers, Macedonian shepherds used to take their flocks annually to Thessaly, even to Asia Minor.

The Underground

PRESIDENT Josip Broz Tito's celebrated wartime headquarters in a Bosnian cave were really nothing exceptional in the porous limestone territory which harbors an underground wonderland between Trieste and Sparta. Yugoslavia alone has some 6,000 known caves.

Yugoslavia, Albania and Greece are underground countries in more than a political sense. The bald toothy limestone heights between the Italian frontier and the Peloponnesus hide a whole world of little explored subterranean caverns, rivers, waterfalls, lakes, terraces and pillared halls. The inhabitants of these folklore-laden regions add their own stories of fabulous underground castles and palaces and beings living in them.

In the mountains of Bistra, Stogovo and others in Yugoslav Macedonia, many streams get lost underground. The name of one such on the Bistra mountain is Tonivoda, meaning "Sinking Water." Many Yugoslav rivers disappear among the rocks, and mostly no one knows what happens to them down below except that they reappear elsewhere, often with nobody the wiser whether it is the same river. Some have been certified as making repeated entries and exits in a sort of dolphin-like terrestrial diving and surfacing. Such rivers are called *ponornice* ("abyss rivers"). As far as now known, the biggest is the Dubrovnik River which, on its 60-mile course, plunges underground and breaks surface four times, with a different name each time, before entering the Adriatic near the famed medieval city and modern sea resort of Dubrovnik.

The ancient Roman and Greek writers recorded various stories of mysterious underground rivers in what is now Yugoslavia and northern Greece. The Roman poet Virgil, in the first century B.C., noted the river Timavos, between Trieste and Aquilea, as the most famous of these underground streams (*The Aeneid*, I, 24). The Greek historian Theopompus, of the fourth century B.C., reported the popular belief that an underground river running under the soil of Macedonia linked the Aegean and the Adriatic. Perhaps this tale is the distant origin of the occasional modern suggestion that Lake Ohrid is connected by an underground waterway with the Adriatic Sea. Still more widely held and less disputed is the belief that Lake Prespa feeds the lower-placed Lake Ohrid through a subterranean outflow under the high mountain of Galičica, which separates them. However that may be, the fact is that in the Balkan limestone many rivers negotiate heights by submerging rather than by circumnavigating.

There may be no underground castles in Macedonia or elsewhere in the Balkans, but there are underwater villages and towns. There is a submerged village in Lake Ostrovo, in Greek Macedonia; the streets of a village at the bottom of the sea may be seen off one of the Dalmatian Kornati islands; and nearby the town of Aigion in the Bay of Corinth a city may be discerned below a calm sea, drowned in the earthquake of 373 B.C. According to the geographer L. Schultze-Jena, of the University of Jena, it has been observed since 1896 that Lake Ostrovo has periodically risen, flooding the neighboring fields and villages, then subsiding. Nothing more was known about this, but Schultze-Jena called attention to the possibility of an underground filling and draining of the lake in this land of cavernous limestone.

The town of Edessa, or Voden, in Greek Macedonia, the early seat of ancient Macedonian kings near Lake Ostrovo, reposes on a waterfall cliff, which is all hollow underneath, with caves behind the waterfalls. No one dares to break them open for fear the town may cave in. In 1964 the Yugoslav press revealed that the new housing construction erected in the village of Madžari in the Skopje plain for some of the 1963 Skopje earthquake victims, had to be abandoned because underground waters had begun to lap at the foundations.

All this is the reason why the nine-headed Hydra, the ancient Greek Loch Ness monster, should be realistically regarded as the unknown source of underground waters which, bursting into the open, flood the land and devour people and animals.

The ancient Greek conception of Hades, the "lower world" of the dead, with its five underground rivers, Styx, Lethe, Acheron, Cocytus and Phlegeton, to which various entrances led from the earth through caverns or beside deep lakes, had indeed a basis in fact in this part of the world.

NOW for the earthquakes.

The Balkan underground is permanently restless, having had minor and major shakes and seizures since time immemorial. Almost every Yugoslav has at one time or another felt the earth tremble under his feet, if ever so imperceptibly. Every coast inhabitant has heard the distant rumble and seen the glassy sea turn dark with minuscule wave-

1. Church of St. John the Divine, Ohrid

2. Church of St. George, Nagoričani

3. St. Mark's Monastery, Skopje

4. Lesnovski Monastery, Lesnovo

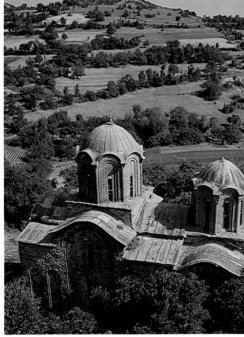

5. *The Annunciation*, Church of St. Clement, Ohrid   6. *The Virgin Savior of Souls*, Church of St. Clement, Ohrid

7. Church of St. Clement, Ohrid

8. Church of St. Panteleimon, Nerezi

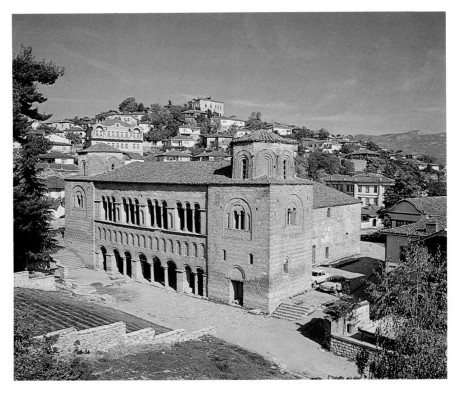

9. Church of St. Sophia, Ohrid

10. Street in the old section of Ohrid

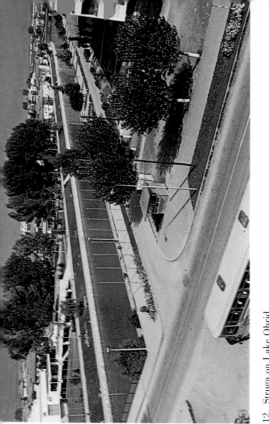

11. Skopje on Vardar River

13. Tetovo

12. Struga on Lake Ohrid

14. Titov Veles

15. Bitola
16. Kumanovo
17. Prilep
18. Strumica

19. Marble quarry, Prilep

20. Steel works, Skopje

21. Lead smelter. Titov Veles

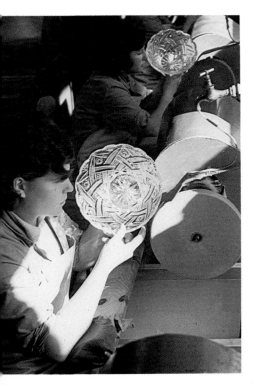

22. Crystal grinding, Kratovo

23. Textile factory, Kumanovo

24. Harvesting wheat

25. Gathering grapes

26. Tomatoes, covered irrigation system

27. Sheepfold

28. Silkworm cocoons

29. Rice fields

30. View of Old Ohrid

31. St. Stefan's Beach, Ohrid

32. Tsar Samuel's Fortress, Ohrid

33. View of Lake Ohrid

34. Stag Jump Bridge

35. Pelister National Park

36. Šar Mountain

37. Houses in Kruševo

38. Stilt house and fishing on Lake Dojran

39. "Teškoto," folk dance

40. Bride's gown, Mariovo Village

41. The village well

lets. Eighteen months before the devastating Skopje earthquake of July 26, 1963, a serious tremor rocked a section of Dalmatia. Skopje itself had several concussions in the past. In 518 A.D., with the first Slav waves from the north just beginning to cross the lower Danube, a tremendous earthquake shattered all of Macedonia, destroying all its cities.

The cavernous substructure from the Alps to the Peloponnesus, the jumbled mountains and the thousands of islands in parallel strings along the Yugoslav Adriatic coast and across the Aegean Sea are only a small sector of the global belt of faults in the earth's surface. The belt stretches from the tip of South America across the Caribbean and the Atlantic to the eastern Mediterranean, Iran, Indonesia, Japan, Kamchatka, Alaska and all the way down the American Pacific coast. The global belt has long been subject to volcanic explosions and tectonic convulsions. So has the eastern Mediterranean, along with southern Italy and Sicily. Very powerful eruptions of the magma, the melted matter beneath the earth's crust, in far-off prehistoric times raised the mountains, split them asunder, formed the hollows, set and reset the face of the land.

The ancient Greek myth which tells of the time when there were no humans yet and when the big and terrible Giants, born of Mother Earth, revolted against Zeus and hurled rocks and firebrands from their mountains at the heavens, indirectly describes volcanic explosions and fires of long ago. It also points in epic images to the massive attacks of the prehistoric Macedonians against the early Hellenic fortresses in the north.

The myth goes on to say that the gods, with the aid of Hercules, destroyed the Giants and that, to avenge them, Mother Earth's youngest monster-son made a rush for Olympus. His name was Typhon ("stupe-fying smoke"), his legs were a mass of coiled snakes (the whirlwind), his arms reached to both horizons, his wings darkened the sun, his eyes flashed fire, his breath carried an evil smell, and rocks hurtled from his mouth. In a colossal combat over vast territories, in which most of the gods fled to Egypt, Typhon took his final stand on Mount Haemus (Mount Balkan in present-day Bulgaria) and threw whole mountains at Zeus's position on Mount Olympus. Zeus retaliated by firing his thunderbolts at the flying mountains and making them rebound upon Typhon. And the blood streaming from Typhon gave Mount Haemus its classical name (ancient Greek *haima* means "blood"). Typhon fled to Sicily, where Zeus crushed him underneath Mount Aetna, from which fire and smoke belch to this day ("it is Typhon's anger boiling up," says the classical poet).

Geologically, this myth describes another of the great volcanic and tectonic upheavals in the eastern and central Mediterranean in the remote past. Historically, it may indicate the turbulent overthrow of the matriarchal society by the patriarchal society. Also historically, according to Robert Graves, the flight of the gods to Egypt may refer to a frightened exodus of priests and priestesses from the Aegean archipelago shortly before 2000 B.C., when a volcanic eruption engulfed half of the large island of Thera, north of Crete.

There are great quantities of hydrogen-sulphur gases in several places in Yugoslav Macedonia (Kratovo, Prespa, Ohrid, Debar). They were created by volcanic eruptions in the distant past. Although after the 1963 Skopje earthquake these gases were joined by those in the Katlanovo swamps, so far it has been held that present-day Balkan earthquakes are caused by the fragile subterranean structure rather than by volcanic action.

No geological work to speak of has been done in any part of Macedonia. The reason is that no army, government or private enterprise has had the desire, money or opportunity to explore Macedonia. Macedonia's underground structure remains almost as little known as ever. In this field, as in much else about Macedonia, people still guess rather than know and tell stories rather than facts.

MATTERS do not stand much better with the Macedonian mineral subsoil. Some ores have been despoiled by foreign occupants and domestic rulers, but most sites are unexplored.

The gold riches of the Mt. Pangaeum region, western Macedonia and Illyria vanished before the Romans did. A little gold sand here and there is all that is left in Macedonia. Sulphur is abundant. It was observed in antiquity that in the river Pontos (Strumica, in Yugoslav and Bulgarian Macedonia) there were rocks called *marithán*, which occasionally flickered with a light flame. These rocks were simply brown coal or lignite impregnated with pyrite (a sulphurous mineral known as "brimstone" or "firestone"), which in contact with water catch fire in the sun. Yugoslavia is rich in coal, brown (lignite) rather than black or bituminous (anthracite), but not much of it is extracted in Macedonia. Some Macedonian mines have even been closed (Raduša, in the north). Yet the foremost prewar Yugoslav geologist, G. Tućan, insisted in 1937 that "mighty coal deposits" lay below the big Macedonian plains. He also claimed, on the ground of the big magma eruptions in the past, that there must be oil deposits in the Lake Ohrid region.

In olden times, as the Romans very well knew, copper was plentiful throughout the Balkans. Yugoslavia is still the number one copper

28

producer in Europe. There is still some copper in Macedonia, too, for instance near the town of Kratovo; but there is not as much as there was under the medieval Serbian kings who mined it with the aid of German miners. In the production of lead, which the Romans also dug zealously, Yugoslavia is still the leader in Europe. In Yugoslav Macedonia, big deposits of lead-and-zinc-bearing ores are also to be found near Kratovo. The main iron ore regions of Yugoslavia are outside Macedonia. The once rich iron ore deposits of Greek-Macedonian Chalcidice have long been exhausted. But there are still some areas with iron ore in Yugoslav Macedonia. Quite recently, new and substantial iron ore sites have been discovered near the town of Kičevo in western Yugoslav Macedonia. Again, Yugoslavia takes first place in Europe in the production of antimony, which also owes its presence to the long-past eruptions from the earth's insides. Serbia, particularly, abounds in it, and there is much of it in Yugoslav Macedonia, specifically in the Skopje Black Hills in the north and the Tikveš region in the central south.

If there is no more gold in Macedonia, there is gold-bearing chromium, again a product of Typhon's explosive activities. Yugoslavia, Albania and Greece are the only chromium-producing areas in Europe. The chromium vein extends from Albania all the way to Turkey, the largest chromium producer in the world. In Yugoslavia, the biggest chromium mines are in northwestern Macedonia and the adjoining Serbian autonomous province of Kosovo, on the Albanian frontier. Next to tobacco, chromium is Yugoslavia's and Macedonia's best dollar-earning export article.

In lieu of the exhausted gold, there is also marble in Macedonia, an equally noble raw material. A big vein extends from the Babuna Mountain in central Yugoslav Macedonia to Lake Ostrovo in Greek Macedonia, where it glimmers, light gray, on a hill above the waters. Marble goes together with walnut forests and the poetic landscape of the people who, aside from being singers, dancers, fresco painters and wood-carvers, are expert stone masons known in every capital of the world. For instance, Macedonians were hired for various kinds of work during the construction of the Empire State Building.

On the Road

ONLY those who have seen the mud, rocks and holes of the Serbian and some other Yugoslav country roads during the last war will know what an adversary they can be to the invader in wartime and to the natives in peacetime. The roads of Macedonia were few and among the most discouraging in prewar Yugoslavia. After the Second World War an impressive road construction effort literally opened Macedonia to the world and to all-around improvement. Macedonian roads can now be classified as good, fair or passable for automobiles. Often asphalted or otherwise paved, even in outlying regions, they now penetrate into most sections of the country. Naturally, there are still roadless areas. One will hit upon some fearsome dirt or rock roads in the back country. The roads in Greek Macedonia west of Salonika, equally ravaged in both World Wars and the subsequent civil war, are generally in an even better condition than those in Yugoslav Macedonia. A NATO frontier needs good communications.

A modern international highway with service stations now crosses Macedonia from north to south. It is part of the postwar Belgrade-Salonika-Athens highway, itself connected with western Europe via Trieste and Vienna. Nevertheless, the most beautiful and intriguing spots in Macedonia can be reached only on horseback or on foot.

ONE bright autumn afternoon, while driving for less than fifteen minutes on the road between Skopje and Kumanovo, I passed a rattling tractor, a woman with a baby in her arms on a horse led by a boy, four peasant boys lying on their stomachs on a hillock and watching a motorcycle whizz by, a group of white-bearded hook-nosed Turks in white-banded red fezzes riding their ponies, people kneeling and praying among wooden crosses in a copse, hooded shepherds with big furry dogs rounding up black and white sheep, a vast "plantation" (socialist farm) of peach trees, and a factory smoke stack.

Many scenes on the Macedonian road are typical of any largely peasant country going through the great urban-industrial transformation or halfway arrested in it. It does not matter whether this Second Industrial Revolution is occurring under communist, democratic or other form of government: these countries will for a long time remain peasant. In India, too, one meets oxcarts moving at an indifferent pace in hectic modern traffic. In Nigeria, also, chickens, children and women run in panic before an automobile and in the last minute decide to cross onto the other side. People ride in two-wheeled carts with American army surplus tires in Casablanca as well as in Skopje.

It is very Macedonian, however, when in autumn one passes streets of red peppers hanging everywhere, dangling in every town and village in countless bunches, clusters and garlands from windows, walls, eaves, porches and fences; while tobacco leaves dry in the sun in rows of frames set up like easels in every courtyard. Stately flocks of geese

30

sometimes stroll near the curiously turbaned and tilted tomb posts in Moslem cemeteries, which always look neglected. Often peasant women, chins wrapped in white kerchiefs, sit on a slope by the roadside spinning and minding the sheep, a scene thousands of years old. Customarily, the woman walks behind her man on the donkey, and he will say that the donkey does not like the woman. But occasionally one will be startled by the unusual and beautiful sight of a peasant woman on horseback galloping past like a Valkyrie, her great white cape fluttering in the wind.

The whole landscape encompasses several ages: the arched Turkish bridges, *amams* (baths), mosques, caravanserais, *kales* (fortresses); medieval Byzantine or Slav churches; remnants of Roman roads, milestones and forts; disinterred remains of Illyrian tombs with gold death masks; relics of classical theaters, tumulus graves of the warriors of ancient Macedon; bones of prehistoric animals, or sites of Neolithic Pelasgian settlements of 6,000 or more years ago. Here and there a catastrophe has left imposing palaces of kings and princes to time and snakes. Somewhere else the asphalt road cuts through stony silences to reach ultramodern skyscrapers.

MORE than any other part of the Balkans, Macedonia provides a feast of national costumes. It would be truly difficult to find anywhere else such an inexhaustible wealth of color, embroidery and design, such an imagination straight out of the Arabian Nights, as appear on the Macedonian, Albanian, Turkish, Tsintsar and Gypsy female costumes on the roads, streets and markets of Yugoslav Macedonia. One meets black-and-white costumes with black kerchiefs; preponderantly crimson or black-white-red costumes; black with diagonally red-striped heavy black aprons; white-brown-violet with white kerchiefs shrouding the chin; costumes like leopard skins. And sometimes women look like Persian rugs incarnate. Often women wear heavy aprons, mostly like solid oriental mats, in front or in the back or both. The Tsintsar women of eastern Macedonia are noted for tall, heavy, dark caps pushed back on their heads and a tattooed pre-Christian cross symbol between the eyebrows indicating man. Moslem women along the Albanian frontier walk in wonderfully ornamented wide, baggy Turkish trousers (*dimlije, šalvare*), sometimes mottled or dark blue with white rosette points; while their heads, with no veils to hide their features, are often enveloped in white or yellow kerchiefs, their aprons sometimes a light red. In Skopje streets, Moslem women—Albanian, Turkish and Gypsy— look particularly graceful in high-heeled shoes, their "balloon" trousers tightened above slim ankles.

Men use the folk wardrobe less than do women, except for headgear, often worn with urban clothing: brown Macedonian sheepskin caps; Albanian skullcaps, usually white; red Turkish fezzes with an occasional white band around (*čalma*). Macedonian peasant men mostly wear a knee-length white shirt above the trousers with sometimes a broad red sash and usually a dark jacket, the trousers strapped below the knee and tucked into many-colored heavy socks in mocassin-type sandals. In a few regions, Macedonian men even wear aprons. The Albanian men adhere more strictly to their national attire: tight white woolen trousers with vertical black stripes. The mountaineers, instead of the skullcaps, wear a loose white cloth around the head with flaps down over the ears, making them look like Bedouins.

In Macedonia people go about in folk dress more often than in other parts of the Balkans. It is especially on market days, at country fairs and church festivals that one can see the display of costumes, hear the folk music and songs, and watch the folk dancers.

In Macedonia one does not encounter peasant women in all-black garb, a sight common in Serbia, Montenegro, Greece, Italy, Sicily, Spain.

MACEDONIAN towns often present an uncommonly attractive view because, unwittingly following an idea of Corbusier's, they fit into the landscape as if they had been deliberately designed for the effect. For instance, the red and brown roofs of Veles literally cascade down the two slopes of a Vardar gorge to meet at the waters below. The setting of the town of Ohrid against the lake and the wooded mountains is doubly impressive because the houses, climbing the hill, have their upper storeys jutting out like so many steps. The town of Edessa rides a waterfall delta, while in the town of Bitola a tree-shaded rivulet forms the middle lane of the main boulevard. The town of Kavalla, a promontory studded with shimmering houses, rises from the sea. The great city of Salonika, on the other hand, lowers itself down a mountainside into the sea.

Even Hitler's soldiers called Kratovo, in Yugoslav Macedonia, "the end of the world," for it has medieval towers, high bridges and flower-heavy balconies over narrow winding streets in the midst of cozy copses below wooded mountains. At the northern end of the green Pelagonian plain, the prettily modernized and flowery tobacco town of Prilep lies beneath a double peak of a granite crag carrying the ruins of the fortress of the medieval folk-poem hero Marko Kraljevic. This is set against the backdrop of a lofty mountain with an Apollo temple inside an old monastery just below the sharp-pointed summit, named "Golden Peak." To the west of this panorama, at a height of

4,000 feet, is located the dignified old Tsintsar town of Kruševo, where at dusk cows clang their bells in the streets on their unhurried way from mountain pastures.

The majority of towns are still largely "old towns," where one's car bumps along narrow, tortuous, cobblestone or unpaved hole-pocked streets between rows of small shops or houses which often have balconies on overlapping upper storeys. In some towns one may drive along the main street past high walls concealing from view the houses of the Moslems, traditionally more bent on privacy than the Slavs. Flowerpots stand in many a window along the road, but this is nothing particular to Macedonia. It is the exquisite flower gardens and parks in or outside some modernized Macedonian towns that will surprise and move the visitor. The fascinating parks in and outside Skopje, the beautiful flower-adorned public squares and streets of Ohrid, Prilep, Tetovo, more than faintly remind one of the magnificent flower gardens within some Moorish castles in Spain. The Macedonian flower cult is said to go back to the not so mythical rose gardens of prehistoric gold-rich King Midas, reputedly blooming once in present-day Greek Macedonia. The Turks, too, were known for their love of flowers. So were the Arabs, whose manifold influence on the Balkans, through the Turks and otherwise, has not yet been properly studied.

Villages often have an air of wishing to keep out of sight and reach. For the most part they stay away from the main roads, where for so long various armies, raiders and marauders used to pass. In the plains, villages cannot hide and a congregation of poplars and orchard trees will give away a cluster of village roofs. In the hill country, a settlement is not seldom tucked away in some gully not immediately visible. Occasionally one may perceive a hamlet cautiously peering from behind a mountain bend. Or the village is openly perched high above a streamlet. Some villages in Yugoslav and Greek Macedonia, Epirus and Peloponnesus hang so high up on the mountainsides that they seem literally suspended from the cliffs. Narrow dirt roads or paths climb to them in never-ending, hair-raising turns around gorges, twisting up and up above the precipices.

Galičnik, famous for its site, its war history, its costumes, its wedding ceremonies, its fresco artists, its nomadic shepherds, its migratory craftsmen and skilled laborers—described by Louis Adamic as the village of grass widows—is one such cliff-hanging village in Yugoslav Macedonia. It is flung, so to speak, down the wall of a yawning abyss.

ABOUT two hundred monasteries, of the Eastern Orthodox Church, still crowd Yugoslav Macedonia. There was a time, in the seventeenth century, when the town of Ohrid alone was supposed to have had more than three hundred churches, "one for each day in the calendar." Some of the Slav monasteries date back to the tenth century. All have, or have had, frescoes in their churches, many of them extremely valuable. Several of the churches, like the Holy Saviour in Skopje and the St. Jovan Bigorski in western Yugoslav Macedonia, boast internationally admired wood-carved iconostases.

Like most other Balkan monasteries, the Macedonian, too, are mostly concealed in the mountain recesses or only visible from a distance on inaccessible heights. Some are hewn into almost perpendicular cliffs, like the St. Jovan Bigorski or some of the Mt. Athos monasteries. Some, weather beaten, stand on platforms teetering above canyons, as in the Treska River's stony wilderness near Skopje. Some churches in towns, like the Holy Saviour in Skopje, have no steeples and are half buried and hidden behind a high wall, for the sight of a bell tower would have offended the eyes of the true believer. The rattles do not hurt his sensitive ear to the same extent. Massive, built like fortresses, the old monasteries were places of Slav refuge and resistance, keepers of the national identity through centuries.

In the construction of monasteries, Slav monks have shown a love of freedom as well as an almost acrobatic art of architecture, a taste for beautifully wild places, and an appreciation of great spaces. Again, this is not uniquely Balkan Slav—there were majestic architects in Peru, too. Yet just below the southernmost Greek Macedonian boundary, in Thessaly, between Olympus and Pindus, giant granite rocks by the name of Meteora rise out of the plain like so many Chrysler Buildings, slender tall rock towers with monasteries "suspended" on their tops between heaven and earth, and until recently reachable only by pulleys.

An old legend says that one night, as the Turks came, all the monasteries and churches in the valleys fled into the mountains.

PART I

THE PAST

ANCIENT MACEDONS

AROUND 3500 B.C. a little known people invaded the Balkan peninsula, until then inhabited by cavemen. Some say they came from southern Russia; others say they came from Palestine. At any rate, although both the Germanic and the Slavic language schools claim them, they were not Indo-European, or Aryan. They used stone tools, made colored pottery and lived in underground habitations. Hellenic tradition refers to them mostly as "Pelasgians," a name meaning "Plain Dwellers" to some and "People of the Sea" to others. Traces of this dim race can be found in many places, including the Greek Macedonian plain just south of Lake Ohrid on the Yugoslav border.

About 2800 B.C. Helladic emigrants from Asia Minor arrived in the Peloponnesus via the Aegean Islands. Around 2300 B.C., it seems, the Thracians appeared in the Balkans from Asia Minor, followed about 2000 B.C. by the Greeks from the south (some say, from the north) and the Illyrians from the north. The Macedonians, some claim, came from the north with the Dorians after 1200 B.C. The Greeks brought agriculture with them. The Illyrians introduced bronze craftsmanship into the Balkans. The Macedonians were the first to develop iron civilization there and to introduce cavalry. The Greeks, though mixed, have stayed where they settled until the present day. Descendants of the Illyrians live in present-day Albania; the Tsintsars and the Vlachs are the descendants of the Thracians. The Macedonians have left no descendants.

The Early Makedones (Tall Men)

THE words Makedón, Makedónes are supposed to stem from Makednós, meaning "high" or "tall" in Homeric Greek. The only inhabitants of the mountains of present-day western Greek Macedonia, just below the Yugoslav frontier, seem to have been people of more than average height, and their main conquering tribe, according to Herodotus and Strabo, apparently called itself "Tall Men" (Makednói).

37

It is difficult to discuss the origin of the ancient Macedonians—no less than the nationality of Slav Macedonians—because there will be hurt sensibilities whatever one says. The Greeks, especially Demosthenes, called the Macedonians "barbarians"—people with a way of life different from or contrary to the Greek way—the definition embracing the Persian Empire. Herodotus and Thucydides did not call the Macedonians "barbarians," but they did not call them "Hellenes," either. Modern Greeks mostly regard the ancient Macedonians as Hellenic. True, the Macedonian dynasty claimed Greek descent, but could the people claim it? The ancient Macedonians have been described as Hellenic (Dorian), half-Hellenic, being close to the Illyrians and being close to the Thracians. As for the language, we have only a few glosses and a few words mostly describing places, people, plants and animals, indicating Greek and non-Greek elements. Thus the question of whether the Macedonians were more akin to the Greeks, to the Illyrians or to the Thracians is as unresolved today as it was in antiquity.

Whatever else they were, the ancient Macedonians, on a low cultural level and with no artistic or scholarly talent, were a sturdy rustic race at the time of the civilized Greek city states, their language being hardly known to the ancient Greeks. Their cattle-breeding and farming peasants lived in unwalled villages under a warlike nobility who filled even the Thracians with fear. In peacetime these rugged nobles often arranged feasts and drinking bouts which sometimes ended tragically. But the Macedonian kings were able rulers and had a gift of state and empire building in the midst of the fragmented Balkans. They subjugated the Macedonian hill tribes to the north and the adjacent Hellenic and Thracian provinces to the south and the east, though their court became Hellenized. They constructed roads and fortresses and created the most modern army of the time. It was King Philip II who organized his peasants into those terrible infantry phalanxes with which his son Alexander crushed his enemies.

The plains and the hills of Macedon abounded in wild animals, such as lions, panthers, wild boars, aurochs, wolves, chamois, lynxes. Lions did great damage to Xerxes's army supplies, but in the end were only to be found in Roman circuses. There were large forests of pine, spruce, walnut, chestnut, oak, beech, poplar, cherry, alder and so on. Wood was the main export, a monopoly of the Macedonian kings, later of the Romans.

The Macedonians had their own religion, similar to the Greek, but with a mysterious air-water goddess Bedu and the Thracian life-and-wine god Sabazius-Dionysus. Along the coast west of Salonika and approaching Pella one comes upon a series of high mounds like pyramids, some of them marking prehistoric settlements, but most of them tombs, called *tumuli*, of high-ranking Macedonians. Generally, the walls inside are covered with paintings. The Macedonian nobles had a habit, often observed among the Etruscans, of depositing their dead in sumptuous vaulted chambers, with funeral beds. A grave near Pella is an underground vaulted cave topped by a cradlelike arcade, and with marble double doors underneath, leading to marble beds. In some such graves sometimes a sculpted lion or family serpent watches under the bed.

The Macedonians wore wide-brimmed felt hats with upturned brims, called the *kausia*. The king's was purple red, resembling a cardinal's, with a gold-embroidered white cloth wound around and fringes falling down the back. Distinguished warriors wore a *chlamys*, a short mantle, purple red for the king, with one corner rounded. The helmet of the phalangists was made of rawhide with an upturned round rim. The walls and the ceiling of the Macedonian commoner's house were blackened with soot from the hearth. Inside the wall beside the gate and facing the front of the house there was a roofed colonnade for storing tools and harboring livestock. Separate from the house stood the steam bath, the use of which seems to have come from the Slav or Scythian east.

Until the time of Alexander's father Philip II, the Macedonians were not an urban people, but afterward some seventy towns could be counted in the Macedonian plains, many of them with Macedonian names. Most of them have not been excavated. Besides grain, the Macedonians produced fruit and wine and felled great quantities of timber, important for Athenian ship building. Like the Thracians and the Thessalians, the Macedonians excelled in horse breeding, which in Greece was considered a luxury sport. Copper was generally plentiful in the Balkans, as it is today. There were long since exhausted silver mines along the present-day Greek-Yugoslav border. And there was the no longer existing mined and river gold in the coastal mountains around the Pangaeum east of Salonika. All was depleted in Roman times. Incidentally, all mining under the Macedonians and afterward was done by slave or convict labor.

There is supposed to have been a Macedonian tribe that took over and started a period of conquest about 850–750 B.C. From this ruling tribe the dynasty and the nobility are presumed to have come. Perdikkas I, in the first half of the seventh century, is assumed to have been the founder of Macedon. Between him and Alexander the Great's father Philip II in the fourth century some eight kings are somewhat inexactly counted, many of short or dubious tenure and some, including Philip II, coming to a violent end. It was a court where, as King Archelaos explained in Plato's *Gorgias*, it could happen that a pretender to the throne, such as his brother, drowned in a pit chasing a goose. Archelaos himself, illegitimate son of a slave woman, was also murdered.

The kings spent a long time subduing the Upper Macedonian mountain tribes of Lyncestes, Orestes and others, after which they leaned on the upper aristocracy of the lowlands. We are not told which Macedonians were free landowners, but it is reasonable to assume that the estates of the nobles were worked by serfs or slaves. The king had as much power as he had personality. However, he was bound by the ancient custom of consulting tribal chieftains and the council of nobles. The most prominent nobles had all the best land in the country and composed the so-called "Companions" of the king. They ate at his table and at the time of Philip II, according to the Greek historian Theopompus, counted some 800 families, having as much land as 10,000 Greek families. The king was not only supreme commander in war but high priest and supreme judge in peacetime, except in the case of murder. A sentence of death could be passed only by the assembly of men capable of bearing arms who then stoned or speared the convicted man to death. In case of a disputed succession, which was not infrequent, the army—"the people in arms"—decided.

It was King Archelaos who in 403 B.C. moved from the remote beautiful Aigai (Edessa) and built himself a palace in low-lying Pella almost on the sea, near the estuary of the river Axios (Vardar). At the court of this murdering and murdered king, at whom Socrates used to shake his head, Euripides wrote *Bacchae* and produced several plays for the Pella theater. Archelaos built roads, improved his cavalry with Hellenic equipment and laid the basis for the great military organization perfected by Philip II. Nevertheless, Socrates mocked him saying that people went to see his palace, not him, unless offered money, which no serious-minded man would accept.

Alexander's Underground City

IN Skopje, the capital of Yugoslav Macedonia, many a tourist inquires eagerly, "Did Alexander the Great pass here?" He did not, nor did his father Philip II, although ancient Macedonian coins have been found in the vicinity. Some thirty miles west of Salonika one can see the excavations of Pella, the ancient capital of Alexander the Great (356–323 B.C.) and of the Macedonian kings between Archelaos (end of the fifth century B.C.) and the conquest by Rome (168 B.C.). On the way through the lowlands, which in classical times were largely swamps along the Aegean Sea and now feature grain, cotton, fruit, pasture and drainage works, one may discern a big mound here and there. As indicated earlier, most are ancient Macedonian tombs, some are prehistoric settlements.

The humble Pella excavation site lies lonely beside the highway in the vast plain—a simple workshop-workhouse affair of one storey in what looks like an abandoned construction lot. Across the road, in a wired enclosure, stand heaps of ancient broken pottery and earthenware. In the distance a village or two can be spotted. Men labor in the fields, a dog barks at sheep, and a rooster crows in the solitude above the buried city of Alexander the Great.

In the scanty excavated grounds, crisscrossed with ditches, parallel streets are clearly recognizable. One can follow the water mains, walk along the remnants of walls almost three feet thick and trace large rectangular houses with columns and capitals. Practically nothing has been preserved from the superstructure of the buildings so far uncovered. Only the floors can give us a glimpse into their interior and the style of life of their inhabitants. Several large buildings seem to have been exceptionally luxurious. They have several floors covered with mosaics, a central courtyard, and a multitude of rooms. One room alone, apparently an antechamber, has a blue-and-white diamond-pattern mosaic floor of some 1500 feet square. Some of the scattered roof tiles of the mighty house bear in Greek letters the inscription PELLHS ("of Pella"), while others are decorated with flower designs. It is obviously a public building, but experts say that this is not the royal palace King Archelaos is supposed to have built toward the end of the fifth century B.C. We know that Demosthenes brought an Athenian delegation there to negotiate with the foe of Athens, King Philip II, and that the father of Alexander's tutor Aristoteles was a physician at the Macedonian court in Pella.

The four pebble mosaics, uncovered on the Pella house floors in 1957, show a young handsome Dionysus in the nude, his thirsus staff in hand, riding a panther that looks like a cheetah; a griffin fastened on a buck in full flight and snapping his spinal cord; a male and a female centaur—a rare combination; and two men fighting a lion. One of them holds a lifted spear and the other is about to strike the lion with his sword. Both are practically nude, but the one with the spear wears the ancient broad hat of distinction. The lion, charging the man with the spear and the hat, is turning around to ward off the sudden attack by the swordsman. It has been suggested that this pebble mosaic depicts the well-known incident during a lion hunt near Sousa in Persia in which Alexander was saved from a charging lion by the swift intervention of his friend Grateros, whom he later killed.

Pella's prehistoric name is said to have been "Bounomos," a Greek word meaning "meadow." As for "Pella," some say the name derives from the town's alleged founder "Pellas," and others claim it refers to a "dark cow." Most modern scholars think the meaning is "rock." The contradiction between "meadow" and "rock" is explained as meaning a transfer of the original settlement from flat land to rocks. As a matter of fact, the walls excavated in Pella in 1957 were found to be resting on solid rock.

Information about the town itself is equally scanty. The classical Greek historian Thucydides twice barely mentions the town. Herodotus says no more than is quoted above. The historian Xenophon describes Pella as "the greatest" Macedonian city. The Athenian opponent of Macedon, Demosthenes, calls the town "an obscure little place."

It is almost unbelievable that so far the one and only factual report, however brief, on Alexander the Great's capital comes from the Roman historian Titus Livy, who lived at the time of Jesus Christ. He described the town as it had looked to the Roman consul and commander Aemilius Paulus after the final conquest of Macedonia in 168 B.C., and for this he apparently drew on a Greek historian of the time, Polybius. Paulus thought, Livy writes, that Pella had not been chosen as the Macedonian capital without good reason. It stood on a hill and was surrounded by an impenetrable swamp, formed by the rivers entering the sea. From the swamp rose the walled island of Phacos, connected by a bridge with the fortified town on the hill. In the island fort Macedonian kings kept their treasury.

These lines of Livy's, nearly two thousand years old, served as chief guidance to scholars who between the eighteenth and the twentieth centuries tried to fix the exact location of Alexander the Great's capital. They never succeeded and constantly disagreed. For the earth had flattened out and practically nothing visible remained of Pella on the surface. A few sherds here and there, a broken tile, the fragment of a column, these were no leads.

Such was the state of affairs until the First World War.

IN 1914, Professor G. Oikonomos began the first excavation work in Pella, with the aid of the Greek Archeological Society. However, he brought few finds to light and made no general survey. The First World War came to Greece's northern frontier, and in 1915 Pella was forgotten again.

After that, according to Photios M. Petsas, to whom goes the credit for most present-day information about Pella—contributions to the meager literature on that ancient town were scanty and misleading. A few pages in the 1938 edition of the imposing and authoritative *Real-Encyclopädie* in Germany erroneously assumed that the ruins of Pella were covered by the waters of a nearby lake. The few lines in the *Guide Bleu* and in *The Encyclopaedia Britannica* are not correct. The few words in a new Swedish lexicon repeat *Britannica*'s error to the effect that Philip II was the first to make Pella the capital of Macedon. The catalogue of the Library of Congress, in Washington, contains several entries under "Pella." They refer to places and persons in North and South America, not in Greece. This about sums up the present-day Western printed information about Alexander the Great's capital.

By sheer accident a spade was sunk in the right spot in 1957. One day in that year Vassilios Stergioulas, a peasant in the Pella region, was digging in his cellar and struck the base from an Ionian column. The local schoolmaster notified the Salonika archeological service, and soon Ph. M. Petsas undertook the new excavation effort. When this proved to be a success, the Athens government granted an annual subsidy. The excavator's workshop-storehouse was built near Vassilios Stergioulas's farmhouse, and he became a guardian of Alexander the Great's underground city.

There are no more marshes in the area where trial trenches have located the former island of Phacos. Archeological evidence has not yet confirmed the existence of the royal palace. Where that palace is—and everything else that must be learned about Pella—will be determined by archeology, not by speculation.

Nevertheless, it is incomprehensible and reprehensible that the civilized West, with all its scientific, technical and financial resources, should not yet have opened to the world the city which was the birthplace and the capital of Alexander the Great, the man who through Hellenization of the Near East contributed to the preservation of the classical Graeco-Roman culture during the Western Dark Ages.

Macedon's Sturdy Neighbors

THE Illyrians, to the north and northwest of ancient Macedon, and the Thracians, to the east and northeast, were vigorous, stock-breeding and soil-tilling warriors, living in the fields and mountains, with a few primitive towns, under tribal kings who were a coarse barbaric imitation of oriental monarchs. The Illyrians lived in all of today's Yugoslavia and overflowed into Hungary and Italy. The Thracians occupied all of Bulgaria, western Greece and Rumania. Both nations were made up of two main social classes, the land-owning and the land-working.

The Illyrians

MANY Illyrian kings and nobles owned gold mines. Their excavated graves still show solid gold masks on the faces of the dead. But that does not mean that the Illyrian people were rich. Some of their tribes were so poor that the Greeks had a saying, used by the playwright Aristophanes, "Hungry like an Illyrian."

The Illyrians produced good wine, olive oil, cheese and pickled fish, but their specialty was Roman-coveted gold. The country seems to have been gorged with it. "Alluvial" or "placer" gold in the riverbeds or on the surfaces of valleys, plains or high plateaus was the most common. In Paeonia, present-day Yugoslav Macedonia, gold was, according to Strabo, quite often ploughed up; while in nearby Dalmatia, according to Pliny, in the time of Nero as much as 50 pounds of gold could be scraped up from the surface in one day.

In the 1960s, gold death masks were still being dug up near the Yugoslav-Macedonian lake of Ohrid and elsewhere, dating back to the sixth century B.C. Actually they go back to the Mycenaean times of the second millennium B.C. in the Peloponnesus, when dead kings wore gold-mask replicas of faces and gold breastplates for protection against malign influences after death. No one has as yet explained whether there was any connection between the Mycenaean and the Illyrian gold masks on dead potentates. They were the products of the Bronze Age, which came at different times to different peoples; but gold was the first metal discovered and worked, before bronze, silver or iron.

THE famous Illyrian tribe of Dardans were described as unclean people. They lived in huts roofed with dung, and they bathed only three times in their lives: at birth, marriage and death. But they loved music and expertly played the flute and the stringed instruments. They, like the other Illyrians, were also excellent soldiers, whose fierce yelling and brandishing of arms frightened even the Spartans, and the phrase was soon coined in Greece, "To shout like an Illyrian." The Illyrians who lived along the present Yugoslav and Albanian coasts were fine sailors and devoted themselves to piracy, preying especially on Greeks. They became the terror of the Adriatic Sea until they took on the Romans.

Unlike the Thracians, the Illyrians treated their women with respect. These women were strong and emancipated. They moved about without chaperones, and often went alone to the men's councils and banquets.

44

Some had several husbands, and even ruled as tribal chiefs or queens. The Illyrian men, rather big, were given to drinking and loved orgies as much as the Thracians and the Macedonians. Ancient writers frequently describe Illyrian women taking their drunken husbands home from parties. However, these people were most hospitable and cherished liberty above all. Being pirates themselves, they knew what slavery was. Roman historians recorded cases of battles where Illyrian women with shrill voices urged their men to throw torches before them and charge; in other cases they threw their children into the fire and jumped into the flames after them to escape becoming Roman slaves. It was in particular an Illyrian queen, Teuta, at one time ruling the territory from the middle Adriatic to the frontiers of Greece, who put up a stubborn resistance to the Romans, so much so that she was glamorized in a famous Croatian play. The Yugoslavs proudly point out that they have Illyrian blood, but it is actually the Albanians who can make that boast.

The Romans spent about two hundred years subduing the Balkans—the Macedonians, the Greeks, the Illyrians and the Thracians. The conquest was completed at about the time of Christ.

It is the prevalent view that the Albanians are direct descendants of the Illyrians, though they may partly come from the ancient Thracians or even the prehistoric Pelasgians. Their language, mixed with Greek and Latin roots, is a puzzle, too.

In west-central Albania there lives a tribe called Lapiths. In this ancient mountain people there prevailed before the First World War the custom of "Amazon" girls joining a war band in men's clothes; this custom, one may add, was widely practiced during the Second World War by thousands of girls among communist partisans in Albania, Greece and Yugoslavia. "Amazon" is usually derived from *a* and *mazon*, Greek for "without breast," for the women were believed to sear away their right breast in order to shoot the arrow better—a fantastic notion. More probably it is an Armenian word meaning "moon woman." For the priestesses of the moon goddess in certain prehistoric areas around the Black Sea and the Mediterranean bore arms. The mythological victories over the Amazons by Heracles, Theseus, Dionysus and others record, in fact, the overthrow of the matriarchal system in Greece, Asia Minor, Syria and Thrace.

There is another custom that survives in some Albanian regions from the Illyrian times, couvade: the husband goes groaning to bed while his wife is in labor—a custom known in many parts of the world, an example being the Jivaro headhunters of Peru.

THE Illyrians never lost their military qualities. Conquered, they offered their services to Rome. As from century to century the supply of native Roman soldiers became more and more exhausted, the Illyrians supplied more and more recruits, especially as the headquarters of the Roman army were set up in Illyria so as to be able to send troops either west, north or to the Near East. In the third century A.D., the Illyrians had virtually obtained command of the Roman army. Since the legions were the source of imperial power, this meant command of the Roman Empire. A number of powerful emperors came from the ranks of sturdy Illyrians with close-clipped military beards and indomitable features: Claudius, Aurelian, Diocletian, Trajan, Justinian, Constantine the Great.

The son of an Illyrian shepherd, Aurelius Valerius Diocletianus rose to be a legionnaire, provincial military governor, commander of the emperor's guards (Praetorians), and in 284 the army proclaimed him emperor. He was the last representative of the old militant Rome and made the last big effort to consolidate the empire by disciplining the army and reorganizing the civil service. The Dalmatian city of Split was built around the enormous palace he constructed near his peasant birthplace, there to spend the remaining eight years of his life, tending his vegetable garden. The palace covers more than 30,000 square yards. Its ruins are inhabitable and harbor some 3,000 tenants. It was enclosed by a wall 17 to 23 yards high and 2 yards thick and it was strengthened by 16 towers. A sphinx can still be seen at the entrance to the mausoleum, but Diocletian's body has never been found. One version has it that as a fervent sun worshiper he was cremated. Diocletian is not held in fond memory by the Christian Church, but then the Christians, whom he persecuted severely, were considered the Reds of the Roman Empire. It must have been a great blow to him when, in 313 Emperor Constantine issued the edict on religious tolerance. His busts were destroyed by rioting Christians in Rome, his daughter had to flee the capital, and he himself died in the same year.

The Thracians

THRACIANS were big men with blond or reddish hair.

The skins of the Thracian nobles were distinguished from those of the common people by picturesque tattoo designs which still can be seen on certain Attic vases. A tattooed Thracian sometimes looked like a walking picture gallery. They used blue dye derived from the herb woad. Characteristically, the Vlach and Tsintsar women of present-day Bulgaria and Yugoslavia, supposed descendants of Romanized ancient

Thracians, still occasionally tattoo the cross symbol of man on their foreheads with a blue dye.

The noblemen wore caps, usually of fox skin, gaily colored sheepskin coats and high leather boots. The commoners went bareheaded, often went half-naked and sometimes lived in underground habitations. The country had the same wild game as Macedon, and the hunt was a favorite occupation of the nobles. This ruling class also enjoyed polygamy, and favorite wives were sometimes sacrificed at their husband's funerals in the company of slaves. The women, socially inferior, were known for their housekeeping qualities. The Athenians used to employ them as wetnurses for their babies. The Thracians sometimes sold their daughters or let them live freely before marriage.

The Thracians, like the Macedonians, were remarkably incapable of arts and were scorned for having no cultural achievements but the glitter of gold and silver ornaments. Yet, as in Illyria, music seemed to have flourished in Thrace. They also liked to dance with high leaps. Xenophon describes in his *Anabasis* how Thracians in full army dress danced to the flute, leaping and striking each other with their swords.

The Thracian noblemen were also immoderate eaters and drinkers. Xenophon tells how King Seuthes I used to toss the meat around to his guests. Athenian playwrights and the public ridiculed the "butter-eating, tousle-haired ruffians," who helped themselves to soup out of "bronze cauldrons larger than wine vats," got drunk, sang and caroused. Yet behind this contempt lay a wholesome fear of the potential ferocity of the Thracians.

The Thracians had fixed rules and coastal posts for wrecking and looting Greek ships. They would break up roads that invaders built in their country and for protection would not build their own. They often went abroad as mercenaries and in Athens served as mounted and unmounted bowmen. Alexander the Great used them as javelin men, archers, slingers, light cavalry, mounted scouts.

Thrace was full of gold and silver, including the rich Pangaeum area gold mines, all subsequently despoiled by the Romans. Its orchards, like those of Macedon, produced rich harvests of apples, pears, peaches, cherries, mulberries, figs, plums, melons, pumpkins—as they do today. Also like Macedon, Thracian forests produced much timber, used by the Greeks for ship building. The land also had green pastures for livestock and fertile plains and valleys producing cereals. The Thracians knew how to make beer either from barley or from hemp. Then there were the vineyards. Homer spoke of the "dark sweet wine" of Thrace, so potent, according to Pliny, that it admitted twenty parts of water to one of wine. Unlike the Greeks, who always mixed their wine with water, the Thracians never drank it but neat, which the Greeks considered barbarous. Today tobacco growing has ousted the Thracian vine.

Herodotus considered the Thracians the tallest people after the Indians. Thracian tribes were smaller but more numerous than the Macedonian. There were supposed to be forty-three of them, ruled by local kings, princes and chieftains. On the other hand, Thrace had fewer native towns than Macedon, and its people lived mostly in open villages.

Unlike the Macedonian, the Thracian tribes never got together to form a Thracian state. Terea, prince of the Odrysian tribe, was the first who, after Xerxes's defeat in Greece (480–479 B.C.), tried to carve out an empire of the vast Thracian territory, but the mountain tribes insisted on independence. His son, King Sitalkes, continued to enlarge the big Odrysian-Thracian kingdom, with some mountain tribes submitting. It became larger than continental Greece and more powerful than Macedon. Sitalkes was credited with an army of 150,000, of which one third consisted of cavalry. This would imply a population of at least 600,000. In 429, Sitalkes had in mind a grand Thracian-Macedonian-Athenian confederation, but nothing came of it. The Athenians were halfhearted, and the Macedonians were shifty. Had his plan succeeded, Athens inevitably would have become supreme in the Balkan north. After Sitalkes came Seuthes I, under whom the Odrysian-Thracian kingdom reached its high point in wealth and military power. In the fourth century B.C., the kingdom fell to pieces. Philip and Alexander of Macedon did not have to contend with it.

IF the Macedonians gave the Balkans the first nation state, and Europe the first intercontinental empire, the Thracians gave the Greek and Roman world religion: two gods, Dionysus-Bacchus and Orpheus.

In his *Birth of Tragedy*, young Nietzsche discussed the two ancient ways of looking at life and its values, and the two gods who represented these views: Apollo was the god of the intellect; Dionysus, the god of the senses. Hellas meant Apollonian moderation but needed Dionysian compensation. Dionysus was imagined as a deity of agriculture, supposed to have been the first to yoke oxen to the plough, which is why he took the shape of a bull in the eyes of his worshipers. He was also sometimes represented as a goat and was then inseparable from the minor goat-shaped woodland divinities like Pans, Satyrs, Silenuses, Silvanuses and Fauns. Dionysius was also pictured as a young man of great beauty and virility. Finally, he was a wine god, supposed to have invented wine, and was connected with the beginnings of vineyard growing. Grapes grew wild on the Asia Minor shores of the Black

Sea, from where their cultivation spread through the Near East, North Africa and, via Crete, to Europe. Everywhere the new drink was celebrated with orgies. In Thrace, the wine cult superseded the beer cult in the late seventh and early sixth centuries B.C.; and with the spread of the wine cult expanded the cult of Dionysus.

This strange god reveler was also a sufferer. Dionysus died each year with the coming of winter. His death was terrible: he was torn to pieces. But each spring he was brought back to life. He died and rose again, like vegetation. He was the lord of life triumphing over death. He granted immortality to his believers.

Every spring Dionysus returned to the Thracian people in the form of a bull, which epiphany gave occasion for a frenzied revelry. Worshipers, for the most part women, gathered at night on mountainsides and dressed like bulls, horns and all, were thrown into ecstasy by intoxication, whirling flutes, and shouted that they recognized the god in the bull and called themselves by the god's name. They finally threw themselves upon the bull, tore him apart and devoured him raw. Through this sacrament they united with the god and received his powers. (Through Holy Communion we ourselves unite with Christ by eating his body in the form of the host, or bread, and, in many churches, drinking his blood in the form of wine.)

Only gradually and against much opposition did the Dionysus cult penetrate Greece. It was particularly the women and the common people who carried its banner in Greece and in other countries. Homer knew only of the "raging" stage of the Dionysus cult. But the tyrants of Corinth and the tyrant Peisistrates of Athens (first half of the sixth century B.C.) spread the wine cult among the peasants and founded the Dionysiac feasts. Dionysus was finally accepted by the divine pantheon and became the most popular Twelfth at the Olympian Round Table, ousting Hestia, the goddess of the hearth. In 186 B.C. the Dionysus cult invaded Rome.

With acceptance elsewhere, the Dionysus cult was slowly Hellenized and humanized. Cities and countries celebrated him in yearly festivals as the dispenser of the stimulating wine, protector and promoter of the growth of plants and entire nature, divine embodiment of all the fullness of life, the ideal of the heightened joy of life.

In the Dionysian mysteries, the essential was the will to life, eternal life, the incessant return of life. And the Dionysian ecstasy was the drowning of the individual in the unity with the godhead, where the soul freed itself not from the body but from its own ego. The Dionysian wanted the removal of the ordinary bounds of existence. He sought to escape from the limits of his five senses, to break through into another order of experience. The Apollonian distrusted this and generally had little idea of what such experience meant. He knew but one law, measure, and he stayed within the known map. Even in the exaltation of the dance, he remained what he was.

Arts received an unlimited inspiration from the Dionysus cult. No other festival in Greece could compare with the yearly Dionysus festival in Athens. The place where the people gathered was not the wilderness, not even a temple. It was the theater. The ceremony was the performance of a tragic dream in an act of worship, a drama never equaled except by Shakespeare—the life and death and resurrection of Dionysus. The god himself was supposed to be present, his priest had the seat of honor. Originally the celebration was a song by a chorus telling of the god. Then a leader would come forward and recite alone, and the chorus would respond. Aeschylus (born 525 B.C.) introduced a second actor who answered the first. Finally, with Sophocles (born 495 B.C.) came a third actor. The dialogue and acting were developed, and the chorus became subordinate to the dramatic action. Up till then the drama had been performed on wooden platforms. In the sixth century theaters began to be built in Athens.

It was particularly the joyful resurrection that was celebrated in the Dionysian theater. The Dionysus cult must have laid the first germ of the belief in the immortality of the soul as taught by many Greek philosophers and preached by certain Greek sects (Socrates, Plato, Eleusian mysteries, and so on). Around the year 80 A.D., a great Greek writer and also a priest at Delphi, Plutarch, received the news far from home that an infant daughter of his had died. In his letter to his wife he wrote, "... we hold it firmly for an undoubted truth that our soul is ... immortal. We are to think / of the dead / that they pass into a better place and a happier condition. Let us behave ourselves accordingly...."

An essential trait of the Dionysian cult was the exaltation into which the god plunged the participants during the orgies. Among his many functions, Dionysus was also the god of all those strange psychic phenomena which the Greek language once designated by the word, *mania*, and which it later called *ecstasis*. Both meant the state of the soul which feels full of a god. Insanity which comes through divine stepping out of accustomed conditions, says Plato in *Phaedra*, must be strictly distinguished from the actual malady. This *ecstasis*, this "stepping out" of the soul, is a "temporary insanity," just as insanity is a lasting *ecstasis*. The passing *alienatio mentis* in the Dionysus cult was taken for a *hieromania*, a holy insanity where the soul united with the deity. It was by Dionysiac enthusiasm, said Plato in *Ion*, that man removed himself from his miserable condition, received the god inside him, became possessed by the god, literally felt him circulating within.

In any population, a certain number of individuals will be capable of a trance experience, especially women—mediums are feminine. Where such experiences are socially accepted, many will have this capacity. But in our Western civilization, such individuals will be scarce and classified as abnormal. In the ecstatic Dionysian state, the borders between here and beyond were transgressed in a breakthrough of the mind barrier analogous to the breakthrough of the sound barrier. Among primitive peoples on all continents except Europe it is simple and natural to commune with the world beyond through shamans, medicine men, priests and sorcerers. Yet even our own civilization, given to hard-boiled materialism since the nineteenth century, knew otherwise. In the Middle Ages the ability to go into a trance was valued, and Catholicism sometimes equaled ecstatic experiences with sainthood. What we read about the spread of the irresistible Bacchic festivals makes us think of the religious epidemics and the dance craze that swept many lands when the Black Death visited Europe in the fourteenth century.

AFTER Dionysus came Orpheus, a mysterious figure, variously explained as a god, a singer, a missionary, a Thracian fox totem, or a personified ideal of the believers. He is supposed to have been the son of the Muse Kalliope and a Thracian king. His mother gave him a super-natural gift of music, and his instrument was the lyre. When he played and sang, everything animate and inanimate followed him. He moved the rocks and turned the course of rivers, and the wild beasts would go with him. If a quarrel threatened, he would play so that the angriest man would forget his ire. If warriors or rowers became weary, he would with his song and lyre restore their strength.

Orpheus was also a teacher. His followers, the Orphics, are known to us as members of closed cult communities, teaching purity, release from the earthly and the transitory, and future life after death. We do not know how the movement spread from Thrace, but in the sixth century B.C. Orphism was already established in Athens and in the Greek colonies in southern Italy. Pythagoras, to whose mystic philosophy Orphism was akin, learned about it in the fifth century B.C., probably in Egypt. It was a religion not localized at any particular sanctuary. It was also an open religion, independent from the social structure, yet a religion particularly of the women, the slaves and the lowly. It was a revivalist religion, one of those reformations that well up from the

51

deep sources of religious feeling when official religion has ceased to satisfy.

The Orphic doctrine teaches that all men are brothers. This solidarity includes all mankind and stretches beyond to embrace all living things. Thus the unity of all life and the unity of the deity are among the cardinal tenets of the mystic faith. Another is the individual responsibility for one's misdeeds, imposing punishment on a man in this world or in the next; or perhaps in a series of lives in this world. Only when purified by suffering did the soul escape this world forever. Transmigration, reincarnation, is still another fundamental tenet of the Orphic religion. The cycle of births and deaths is, in Orphic language, a "sorrowful weary wheel" of the soul on its way toward final liberation from earthly existence. By asceticism and moral purity during life, and by expiatory suffering in reincarnations or in the underworld, the soul may hope for a final release and for reunion with the deity. The alternative is eternal damnation. Other new religious movements arose in the early Roman Empire, and the Orphic religion mingled with them. Christianity also was a doctrine of immortality and salvation, and it too spread at first chiefly among the poor and the unhappy.

More than for his music and his teachings, Orpheus is remembered for his ill-fated marriage with Euridice. When Euridice, upon their wedding, died from snake bite, Orpheus decided to go to the underworld of the dead and try to bring her back. There he struck his lyre, and all that bustling place was charmed to stillness. "See, I ask a little thing," he sang. Even the Furies wept, and Sisyphus rested on his stone. They gave him back his bride, but on the condition that he would not look back at her until they were out. He looked back when he, but not she, was out in the daylight, and in an instant she was gone. Then he forsook the company of men and wandered through the wild solitudes of Thrace, always singing and playing, and the rocks and the rivers and the trees and the beasts listened and followed him. At last a band of Maenads, Dionysus's female worshipers, fell upon him in their frenzy, tore him to pieces and threw his severed head into the river. The head floated to the sea still singing and was buried at the foot of Mount Olympus, where, it is said, the nightingales to this day sing more sweetly than anywhere else.

Philip and Alexander

H. G. WELLS was not alone in suggesting that the true hero of the story of Alexander the Great was his father, Philip II, or Philip of Macedon (359–336 B.C.). It was he who laid it all out for Alexander.

He created an invincible army, subjugated Greece, secured the gold of the Pangaeum area, trained Alexander by assignments in battle, hired Aristotle as Alexander's tutor, and even sent a preliminary expeditionary force into Asia Minor before he was stabbed to death by one of his guards. Nevertheless, ever since Demosthenes's anti-Philip speeches, Philip II has enjoyed bad publicity as a cynic, a drunkard, a lecher; and Alexander had almost all the good press. Yet it was in vain that Demosthenes railed against Philip II and his Macedonians, "This man Philip is not only not a Greek, but not even a barbarian from a country where one could not even buy a decent slave before."

In 367 B.C., as a boy, Philip was taken to Thebes for three years as a hostage for the good behavior of the Macedonians. There he made the acquaintance of the famous Greek military leader Epaminondas and got fresh ideas about military organization and tactics, especially about how to adopt and improve the Theban phalanx. Immediately upon his return, not yet king, he set about reorganizing the Macedonian army.

Homer did not know cavalry. In classical times, the armies of the Greek cities consisted of heavy, densely packed infantry, a small corps of light cavalry, and mercenaries for greater mobility. The bow and arrow the Greeks considered a cowardly weapon. Before Philip II, the strength of the Macedonian army was the cavalry, composed of the hereditary asistocracy of landowners and called "Companions" (*Soters*) of the king. Infantry was an ill-organized mass. There was now to be a well-organized infantry, and the phalanx became the chief striking force of the Macedonian army. This was a body of foot soldiers not too tightly packed, with shields joining and long pikes (*sarissas*) overlapping. The pikes were five to seven feet long and could stab or cut even strong shields. Philip strengthened the phalanx by giving the rear men longer pikes, thus deepening the mass. The phalanx advanced in the center and held the enemy's main body, while on one wing or another the cavalry and lighter units would swoop upon the enemy's flank and rear. The Roman commander L. Aemilius Paulus said that he had never seen anything so terrifying as a Macedonian phalanx as it came on. The Macedonian phalanx was composed of free peasants who communally worked their land. It consisted of 16,000 to 18,000 men. To the phalanx soldiers Philip II gave the name of "Foot Companions," thus raising their status and making them equal to the aristocratic "Companions" of the heavy cavalry. At the same time he retained the traditional tribal organization within the infantry. The heavy cavalry ("Companions") Philip covered with scaly armor. To all this Philip added archers and other light-armed troops. He introduced battering rams, movable catapults to be for the first time used in a field battle, and siege towers 120 feet high. Finally, unlike the Greek armies, Philip's army was constantly drilled. Recruitment was by conscription; altogether Philip commanded 30,000 infantry and 20,000 cavalry.

The balance was in Philip's favor on every count; he even had weak opponents. Athens enjoyed the height of creation in politics, art, literature and thought only for some fifty years after the Second Persian War (480–479 B.C.). Then came the Peloponnesian War (431–404 B.C.), after which, with the predominance of Prussianlike Sparta, the creative period was over. Athens fell from surfeit of corruption and moral degeneration, beginning with the death of Socrates (399 B.C.). It was useless for Demosthenes to preach the grand style and the virtues of an earlier age; democracy had become selfish freedom of living one's own life only. Although the Greeks had one language and script, common heroic epics and the Olympic games, they were fragmented into too many feuding city-states in a land too small. They were not able to make of themselves a nation-state at a time when, besides Macedon, Rome had also become a nation-state.

It was Philip II who imposed unity on the Greeks. In 338, at Chaeronea, Philip crushed the Athenians and their allies in a battle in which eighteen-year-old Alexander commanded the heavy cavalry and defeated the famed "Sacred Band" of Thebes. In the same year Philip formed a League or Confederacy of the Greek city-states (except Sparta) under a common Council and let himself be elected Leader (Hegemon) of the Macedonian-Greek armies. In 337 Philip invited the League's Council in Corinth to vote war on the Persian empire. In 336, his best general and later one of Alexander's commanders, Parmenion, with a scouting party of 10,000 men crossed the Dardanelles. Then violent death came to Philip, and twenty-year-old Alexander took over.

Despite his vices, Philip was always master of himself and could switch in a minute from extreme passion to cool judgment. He was ready to use any means—bribery, pretense of friendship, brutal destruction and magnanimous forgiveness—if it suited his larger scheme. For instance, he razed famous Thebes and cultured Olynth, but he showed generosity toward defeated Athens. He had an uncanny ability to divine the way in which the minds of others would work. If occasionally he failed, he would forget it and return to other tasks. Whether he decided to strike suddenly or wait patiently, all his plans were laid on a large scale and based on a careful evaluation of facts.

The story of Philip and Alexander is incomplete without Olympias, the princely daughter of wild Epirus to the west of Macedon, one of

Philip's six or seven wives, and mother of Alexander. To Olympias, any kind of moderation was unknown. She was a proud and demoniac woman, with strange psychic powers. She was jealous of Philip as he was of her sleeping with snakes. For, with many women, peasants and slaves of her country, Olympias was addicted to the orgiasfic Thracian rites, the wild worship of Dionysus and the snake cult. In the ceremonial dance she would have great tame serpents about her, and her apartments were infested with them. But she kept her son's love all his life. She would write to him abroad about religion and politics, and he would regularly report to her from his campaigns and send her a large share of the war booty. This correspondence has never been recovered, though there have been forgeries. After Alexander's death, Olympias was killed at the instigation of one of Alexander's generals.

Alexander did not seem to have the same respect for his competent father. Plutarch tells of a scene when Philip wedded one of his later wives: after much wine drinking Attalus, the bride's father, exclaimed he hoped there would be a legitimate Macedonian heir. Whereupon Alexander cried out, "What am I then, a bastard?" and hurled his cup at Attalus, upon which Philip drew his sword only to stumble and fall. Blind with rage, Alexander shouted, "Macedonians, see there the general who would go from Europe to Asia! Why, he cannot even get from one table to another!"

Alexander (356–323 B.C.) swept over Egypt and Persia and penetrated Central Asia and India between 334 and 324 B.C. A year later he died, at the age of thirty-three. Alexander is by many thought to be the most glamorous of all world figures. He had youth, looks, courage, brains, was a sportsman, a hand-to-hand fighter, a scholar-explorer, a military leader of stunning performance, and a visionary empire builder. But he, too, was given to excessive drinking and feasting. He not only destroyed whole towns like his father but suffered homicidal spells (his mother's streak), personally committing murders, including the killing of his best friend Cleitus, never forgiven by Shakespeare. In sex matters, though polygamous, he offended less than his father, but his tigerish mother Olympias was probably the only woman he really ever cared for. Legends about Alexander spread all over the world and well beyond the Middle Ages. Greeks, Albanians, Slavs of Macedonia, Hunza natives of the Himalayas, all have claimed Alexander and his Macedonians as their ancestors.

COMMANDER-IN-CHIEF of the forces of Macedon and the Hellenic League, Alexander recalled Parmenion from Asia Minor with the Dardanelles bridgeheads secured. In the spring of 334 B.C., Alexander the Great crossed the Dardanelles at the head of an army of 30,000 infantry and 5,000 cavalry—some say 30,000 infantry and 20,000 cavalry, which was Philip's standing force. Of the infantry, 9,000 were in phalanxes. Alexander usually struck with his heavy cavalry "Companions" from the right. He defeated the Persians at the Granicus and at Issus; he thereupon systematically occupied the whole Mediterranean coast of the Persian empire so that the Persian navy could not join forces with the Athenian navy and attack him from the rear.

Alexander reached Egypt in November 332 B.C. There were no battles, just a plain takeover. The conqueror went to Memphis to sacrifice to Apis, was accepted as Pharaoh, returned to the coast and selected the location of the new city of Alexandria. With a few men he then made his spectacular journey of 350 miles into the Libyan desert to visit the temple of the sun god Amon-Ra in the oasis of Siwah. Alexander entered the shrine alone, was recognized by the priest of the oracle as the god's son but refused to divulge what the oracle had told him except that he was pleased.

In 331 Alexander headed for the interior of the Persian empire and routed at Gaugamela, east of the Tigris, the last Persian army, which in vain used the scythe-hubbed chariots. Alexander then marched to the shores of the Caspian Sea, east into Afghanistan, and north by what is now Samarkand into the mountains of central Turkestan. Following old caravan roads, Alexander in 326 B.C. finally reached the Khyber Pass, descended into India, and on the river Hydaspes (Jhelum, an eastern tributary of the Indus) fought the last and the bloodiest battle of his career against the army of King Porus, which contained two hundred war elephants. After his victory, Alexander wanted to push toward the Ganges, but his army had had enough and refused to budge. It was then and there that Alexander, to no avail, made his famous scornful speech to his mutinous soldiers, telling them that before the time of his father Philip they had been miserable wandering shepherds, dressed in goatskins, driving skinny herds across the hills, and that his father was the first who made them descend into the plains, settle in towns and put on decent clothes.

Alexander built a fleet which took his entire army and supplies down the Indus to the Indian Ocean for a grueling return west. With the main body of his army he started on a grim march through the salt deserts of Baluchistan, while the fleet followed him under Admiral Nearchus along the Persian coast. He arrived at Babylon in 324 B.C., where he spent a year in revelry, murdering his friends and trying to reorganize his chaotic empire. On June 13, 323, at the age of thirty-three, while planning to sail around and conquer the Arabian peninsula, he died of malaria contracted on the Babylon mud flats.

A year before his death, at the age of 32, Alexander the Great had conquered the entire Persian empire up to the river Jaxartes (Sir Darya) and the river Indus; besides, he was the master of Egypt, Macedon, Greece and the eastern Balkans up to the Danube (the present-day Bulgarian-Rumanian frontier). According to some estimates, he had in eleven years covered 22,000 miles, leading his men hundreds of miles farther than anyone had gone before, or the Romans ever did later, marching them "clean out of all maps" to distant regions beyond which, his geographers told him, the world-girdling ocean rolled.

There was no acrobatic feat or engineering device that Alexander would not think of in an emergency, nor icy or tropical climate he and his men would not brave. In Thessaly he cut steps into the flank of a mountain to bypass a fortress—"Alexander's ladders." On the fringes of India his soldiers stormed cliff-top redoubts using ropes on pegs driven into crevices. The fortified port of Tyre, on an isle half-a-mile off the Phoenician shore, fell after a siege of seven months, during which the mole Alexander built was repeatedly destroyed but rebuilt every time, possibly his greatest military achievement. His was the most effective military force the world had ever seen.

Aside from the phalanx, Alexander's army had heavy and light cavalry, archers, javelin throwers, slingers, all in an exceptionally flexible organization. Alexander also had engineers for constructing pontoons and siege machines, the chief engineer being Diades, who is supposed to have invented portable siege towers and rams on wheels. There were sappers, well-sinkers, and surveyors for information about routes and camping sites, who also recorded the distances covered. These records long formed the basis of the geography of Asia.

Poets, artists and philosophers accompanied Alexander on his superbly conceived Persian campaign; among them was Aristotle's nephew, the historian Calisthenes. "Secretary" Eumones of Cardia kept the "Journal," the daily official record of the expedition. There were geographers, botanists, naturalists, who among other things collected specimens for Aristotle. Homer had never heard of India and Aristotle had a poor knowledge of that land. Alexander and his men were the first Europeans to enter India, the first to see and fight against elephants. They also learned about Chinese silken garments and about a reed that yielded honey without bees—the sugar cane. Sailing back from India, Admiral Nearchus also had researchers with him and marked in his log an encounter with a shoal of whales, "monsters" until then unknown to the Europeans. After Alexander, only Napoleon—in Egypt, had a retinue of scientists accompany an army.

ALEXANDER created the first intercontinental empire based in Europe; it extended from Europe to Asia and Africa, from the Adriatic Sea to modern Pakistan, from the Caucasus to Ethiopia. But Alexander did not cross the Dardanelles with a plan to conquer all of Egypt and all of Persia. The idea came to him with his victories. It was Rome which, after arduously defeating Carthage, carried out the idea of a durable universal state, but this necessitated the work of many men and generations.

The young man encountered the Egyptian and Persian civilizations and realized that Aristotle had been wrong teaching him that non-Hellene barbarians must be treated as slaves. When the Macedonians on one occasion shouted, "You have made the Persians your kinsmen!" he shouted back, "I consider you all my kinsmen!" Alexander undeniably had a sense of the brotherhood of man. Where he learned this has remained unexplained. But he dreamed a dream in a world where it could not come true. All he knew was that he must not be a Macedonian king ruling Persians, but a king of Macedonians and Persians alike. Still, to coordinate his empire politically, racially and culturally was a task more complicated than that of the British or the Habsburg empire.

In his administration Alexander employed Persians, Greeks and Macedonians. He kept the old satraps or appointed new ones. In India, defeated King Porus also became a satrap. This did not make Alexander popular among his Macedonians and Greeks, but there was no other way—he was short of Macedonians and Greeks who could do the job.

Putting into practice his idea of racial integration, Alexander married Roxane, the daughter of King Oxyartes of Bactria. Polygamous, as was the Macedonian custom, he also married the elder daughter of Darius, the late Persian Great King, and, in addition, the daughter of a son of Darius. His friend Hephastion married a younger daughter of Darius; Crateros, a niece of Darius; Seleucus, the daughter of a great Persian general; and so on. On the same day, the majority of Macedonian generals married high-born Persian women. Eighty "Companions" of the king and 10,000 soldiers followed the example. A feast was held under an immense tent, and every married couple received a wedding gift from Alexander. In Plutarch's words, Europe and Asia were to be joined "in lawful wedlock and by community of offspring." But after Alexander's death, Seleucus was the only Macedonian general who did not give up his Persian wife.

DURING his brief time Alexander also pursued integration through the building of Greek-Persian cities. He constructed altogether about seventy cities at important military and commercial sites, some seventeen of which were named "Alexandria." Only one of them has remained, in Egypt, in addition to Antioch in Turkey. All these cities had temples, marketplaces, fountains, gymnasia. But the great mass of the people were natives, who lived a poverty-stricken life, above whom a minority of foreign Greeks ran the somewhat autonomous city governments.

The masterpiece of Alexander's city building was, of course, Alexandria in Egypt. It was a magnificently planned city; originally intended as a great commercial port, it developed into a center of Hellenistic civilization. Alexandria's streets were laid out on a rectangular plan, two were ninety feet wide, one was four miles long and lit at night. At the two ends of the long *dromos* stood gates. The city was encircled by a wall and had five boroughs. Alexandria was "the greatest emporium of the inhabited world," said Strabo around the time of Christ. He added that Cleopatra's father derived 12,500 talents or 7.5 million dollars a year from its trade. The lighthouse was one of the Seven Wonders of the World and gave its name, Pharos, to all lighthouses. Built around 280 B.C., Pharos was 530 feet high, with a light visible at a distance of thirty miles. It stood on its isle, connected with the city by a 1300-yard-long dam, until it collapsed in an earthquake in the fourteenth century A.D.

Superseding Athens, Alexandria developed scholarship in addition to commerce. The Library and the Museum fronted the sea and may have covered a quarter of the city. The Library was a depository of books, papyrus rolls, some 700,000 of them. All visitors to Alexandria were required to turn in their "books" at the customs for copying. The Museum was a research institution, with scholars from all over the Greek world coming to live a communal existence there. Here the first steam engine was devised, but there was no use for it at that stage of industrial development. Eratosthenes was only 200 miles off when he calculated the circumference of the earth. Some daring scholars, around 300 B.C., practiced dissection of human corpses. In mathematics, the *Elements* of Euclid (around 300 B.C.) was probably the most influential textbook ever written. Archimedes (around 287–212 B.C.) became a legend. And it was Aristarchus of Samos (around 310–230 B.C.) who, long before Copernicus, taught that the earth revolved around the sun. But Hipparchus (around 150 B.C.) designed a system which had the sun circling around the earth. When completed by Ptolemy around 140 A.D., it became the orthodox view of scholars and churchmen until the scientific revolution of the sixteenth and seventeenth centuries.

One drawback during this expansion of learning in Alexandria was the fact that there was no way of communicating to the masses of the people what had been discovered.

ALEXANDER has been one of the most widely sung heroes in history. Many of the stories, if not true, were invented with a great deal of ingenuity. One such story was the one of Alexander, observing that the stallion Boucephalus facing the west was afraid of his dancing shadow, made him face the blinding sun and tamed him. The story of the Gordian knot was also a good one but is not true. And so on. A good deal of the stories about Alexander were put together in a novel composed about 300 A.D. in Alexandria and falsely attributed to Alexander's historiographer Calisthenes. This "novel" was later translated into Latin and Hebrew. Later, numerous knight-errant epics of Alexander mushroomed in France, Germany, Holland, Spain, England, Ireland, Greece and the Slav lands. In the Orient, from Albania to Pakistan, the deeds of "Iskander" are still parts of the national folklore.

All through his campaigns Alexander slept with a copy of the *Iliad* and a dagger under his pillow. He was a model hero to Napoleon, who remarked that his outstanding trait was his appeal to the imagination of the people. He shaved his face and set a fashion in Greece and Italy for many centuries. Yet the truth is that Alexander, with white wings on his helmet, had inherited a homicidal bent from his mother. Philotas, the son of Parmenion, one of Philip's and his own most faithful generals, was caught in gossip, accused of conspiracy and executed; thereupon Alexander sent men to kill Parmenion before he could learn of his son's death. There was the execution of Aristotle's nephew Calisthenes for opposing divine honors for Alexander. That Alexander's mind was not balanced is shown by the cruel display of grief when his devoted friend Hephaistion died of illness. He had the physician crucified, every mule and horse in Persia shorn, and he ordered all the adults of certain villages to be massacred as a human sacrifice to Hephaistion. This was not his only crime against whole populations. As a warning against revolt, Alexander burned down the ancient Greek city of Thebes, sparing only the house of the poet Pindar, and sold 30,000 people into slavery. Three other cities became the victims of similar fits of cruelty and insanity—Gaza, Tyre and Cyropolis. In Tyre, in reprisal for the killing of Macedonian prisoners, Alexander had the city destroyed, 8,000 fighting men massacred, and many men, women and children sold into slavery. In Cyropolis not a soul, not a child was spared, in revenge for his having been knocked down and wounded in battle—he must have been badly scared, says a commentator. This is not all. Darius's troops contained some 20,000 "Quisling" Greeks. Alexander captured them in the first battle, at Granicus, and had them all executed except for 2,000 whom he sent in chains to forced labor in Macedon. The crime unforgiven by the West, however, was the drunken quarrel with his best friend Cleitus, who reproached him for wearing Persian clothes and quoted from Euripides, "Shall one man claim the trophies won by thousands?" whereupon Alexander snatched a spear from one of his guards and killed Cleitus on the spot. In *King Henry the Fifth*, Shakespeare makes Fluellen say, "What call you the town's name where Alexander the Pig was born? Gover: Alexander the Great. Fluellen: Why, I pray you, is not pig great? ... Alexander—God knows, and you know—in his rages, and his furies, and his wraths, and his cholers, and his moods, and his displeasures, and his indignations, and also being a little intoxicated in his prains, did, in his ales and his angers, look you, kill his pest friend, Cleitus."

As a statesman, Alexander the Great drew more, and rather unjust, criticism than as a personality. Alexander drew together all the known world except the western Mediterranean. It is not altogether idle to speculate what would have happened if he had first turned against the still not strong Rome and Carthage, for even in 281 B.C. King Pyrrhys of Epirus almost succeeded against Rome. The sensible conclusion is that Alexander's empire eventually would have fallen apart. Alexander was accused of *hubris*, the sin of overweening pride, which the gods will not let go unpunished. But ever since his time human thought has been haunted by the idea of possibly uniting the whole world. The Romans in time took over the idea of world dominion.

Macedon's Death and Alexander's Legacy

DURING some fifty years after Alexander died childless, his successor generals struggled for power with all the methods of the Borgias. Finally three were left. Lysimachus controlled the European provinces, Seleucus ruled most of the Asian regions, and Ptolemy held Egypt and Libya. By about 270 B.C. the tripartition had been completed. Most of Greece disintegrated into rival federations. In their quarrels they called in Macedon and Rome. This is chiefly how the Romans established their protectorate over Greece about 200 B.C. Then came Macedon's turn. Toward the end of the third century B.C. Rome was engaged in a mortal combat with Carthage and Philip V of Macedon negotiated with Hannibal for joint action against Rome. With Hannibal driven out of Italy and Carthage beaten, Rome turned her attention to Macedon. In 197 B.C.

the Roman general Flaminius defeated Philip V at Cynoscephalae, but, with his wings clipped, left him king in his own country to remind the Greeks there were others in this world.

Rome continued to worry about Macedon, which was bent on revenge. In the new war the Macedonians put up a much fiercer resistance, but in the Battle of Pydna, near Olympus, Consul L. Aemilius Paulus defeated the last Macedonian king, Perseus. Some 20,000 Macedonians are reported to have fallen and 11,000 were captured. Legend has it that in a valley of the battlefield white asphodels, a sort of lily and a symbol of immortality, sprang up from the blood of the fallen Mace- · donian warriors. Plutarch describes the war booty paraded during the three days of L. Aemilius Paulus's triumphal celebrations in Rome: on the first day, 250 wagons carried paintings and other art treasures; on the second day, carriages loaded with arms passed in procession and behind them 3,000 men carried vessels filled with silver coins; on the third day, 120 fat oxen, adorned with flowers, pulled eighty-seven kettles of gold coins and the gold table service of Perseus; and not far behind, Perseus himself walked in black robes. The loot was so big that the Roman treasury did not have to collect direct taxes in Italy for 125 years. Macedon itself was split into four parts.

This was not yet the end. During the third and last Punic war (149–146 B.C.), the Macedonians rose in arms, followed by the Achaean and Boeotian Leagues. The uprisings were crushed. In the same year that Carthage was burned to the ground (146 B.C.), Corinth was destroyed, the two Greek leagues were disbanded, and Greek freedom was lost—until 1833. Macedon became a Roman province under a Roman governor, never to rise again.

As T. R. Glover puts it, who could have foretold this? Only two generations before, Rome was fighting for her very life against Hannibal at her gates, and now Carthage was gone, Macedon was gone, Greece was gone, and Rome had begun to bring the kings of Asia and Egypt to heel. The Seleucid empire in Asia, with the exception of Persia, came to an end when Pompey appeared on the scene in 65 B.C. Then, after the defeat at Actium in 31 B.C., Cleopatra, queen of Egypt and descendant of the Ptolemys, committed suicide. That was the end of Alexander's empire.

IN the course of centuries the people of Macedon became Hellenized and mingled with numerous other Balkan ethnic groups, including the arriving Slavs. As a group they totally vanished from history. They left no trace of their identity in language, customs or way of life, as did the Illyrians and the Thracians. One could say that Macedon exploded briefly into history, leaving nothing except some imposing tombs in northern Greece and the partially excavated ruins of their two capitals, Aigai (Edessa) and Pella.

Yet something bigger and more lasting remained: the spread of Hellenism, that is, of classical Greek civilization. Alexander laid some of the foundations of the Byzantine Empire, which carried the European torch until the barbarian-ravaged West was ready to accept classical Greek culture as transmitted through the Eastern Empire. In ways known to history rather than to men, Alexander the Great was the necessary transmission belt.

Was Alexander the Great really great? He died too soon to be judged so simply; we do not know how he would have developed. His attempt at racial integration—later strongly emphasized in the Christian creed of the brotherhood of man but never since practiced by an empire builder—did not succeed. Nevertheless, the idea makes him daringly modern. There are historians like A. A. Trever who say, "In his brief career he probably did more to shape the future course of Western civilization, up to the nineteenth century, than any other man except Jesus of Nazareth, and, indeed, it was he who made the legacy of Jesus possible. The 'Legacy of Alexander'. . . passed on to the Western world, still persists as one of the most vital elements in our historical heritage. His expansion of Hellenism is the necessary key to the understanding of succeeding . . . history. It stands with the Roman Empire and Christianity as one of the three great germinal facts. . . ." The greatest germinal fact of Alexander's career was the interracial marriage, proclaimed and practiced by him as the supreme test of the brotherhood of man.

It was the westward thrusts of the Huns that set in motion the waves of barbarian migrations which eventually toppled the Western Roman Empire in the fifth century A.D. Yet long before the Roman Empire was divided into two parts (395 A.D.), Constantine the Great (312–337 A.D.), who accepted Christianity, decided to transfer the seat of the Empire to Constantinople, the second Rome, built by him at Byzantium, an old Greek colony on the Bosporus. The year 330 A.D., when the reformed empire was proclaimed, is looked upon as the beginning of Byzantine history. The Byzantine Empire lasted until 1453 A.D., when the Turks took Constantinople. It existed for one thousand, one hundred and twenty years, outlasting the Western Roman Empire by nearly one thousand years.

Byzantium was more than an empire or a commonwealth of nations, it was a civilization, something we think of when we talk about "the West." The Eastern or Byzantine Empire has generally been spoken of as a continuation of the Western Roman Empire, but actually it was rather like a follow-up of Alexander's Hellenistic empire, built as it was around the stump of what Alexander had created. Although Latin was spoken during the first two centuries, Greek took over in Byzantium as the official and the social language.

SLAV MACEDONIA

The Ancient Slavs

THE original homelands of the Slavs were the plains between Lithuania and the Carpathians, around the rivers Vistula, Pripet, Dnieper and Dniester; those are the plains now belonging to the western Ukraine, southwestern Byelorussia and southeastern Poland. Some of this territory was a swamp expanse around the river Pripet. The root of the word "Slav" itself is supposed to mean "under water."

There are no fixed data about the Slavs until some centuries after the birth of Christ. But it is assumed that these people were peaceful land cultivators. However, the Soviet historian A. S. Šofman maintains that the ancient Slavs, who loved liberty and practiced a kind of democracy, kept many slaves captured in war and engaged in the slave trade. One thing is certain: the original Slavs as they appear in history were not horse-riding and cattle-breeding nomads but settled peasants. They mostly sowed millet and wheat, knew stock-breeding, did much fishing and hunting, and excelled in beekeeping and basket weaving (still one of Yugoslavia's major export industries). To the Black Sea ports they mostly brought furs, bread and slaves.

In the old accounts dealing with the Russian prince Vladimir I of Kiev (980–1019 A.D.), who became a Christian in 989, one may glimpse some features of the primitive Slavs preceding him. Vladimir had a large number of wives. There was no caste of priests, no regular public worship, and no traces of temples have been found. Like the Teutons, the Slavs apparently held their haphazard religious rituals in the open air. Vladimir celebrated the beginning of his reign by putting in front of his palace the wooden figures of the old Slav agricultural gods: three-headed Svarog (Serbian Trojan), the father of gods; Dazhd, the god of rain and bounty; Veles, the god of cattle; Striborg, the wind god; German, the god of fertility; Vesna, goddess of spring; Morana, goddess of misfortune and death; and, chief of all, Perun, the god of thunder, with a huge silver head and mustaches of gold. Vladimir celebrated his accession by offering close to a thousand human sacrifices to his gods. Some of their pagan divinities the Slavs took over into the Christian faith. Thus the thunder god Perun became St. Elijah, whose chariot rolling over cloudy skies causes celestial rumblings.

As to the ancient Slav character and social organization, violent disputes have taken place among scholars. Agreeing with the Soviet historians, the great German social philosopher of the French revolutionary era, J. G. Herder, believed that the early Slavs lived in a truly democratic community. Transport difficulties over the morasses, others said, kept them from having a strong central power. Some Germans pictured the early Slavs as cowards and born slaves, citing as proof their very name. The Slavs could not accept battle on open level ground and, having no armor, preferred to fight with spears and shields in deep forests. Stories have been told about the original Slavs submerging themselves in marshes and breathing through hollowed-out reeds for hours to ambush their enemies. Not inappropriately, a 1943 war report told of Soviet amphibious sappers building at night a subsurface bridge across a river for the Soviet tanks one day to "swim" against the stunned Germans.

Of course, not all Slav lands were swampy, so the "morass civilization" theory is farfetched. On the other hand, the Slavs did suffer from tribal anarchy, with countless clans and petty chieftains seldom agreeing, this in turn leading to serious military weakness. Even today, discord seems to be a curse of the Slavs; a Serbian proverb admonishes, "Only concord can save the Serb." It is also misleading to call the ancient Slavs democratic if we by that mean democratic in the Western fashion. In the absence of an autocratic central power there was a loose federation of tribal autocracies with councils of chiefs and sub-chiefs who, of course, were not elected by secret ballot. The famous Slav "house community" was also neither specifically Slav nor exactly democratic. For the family members who owned, produced and consumed in common had to obey the head of the house—usually the oldest man. But the Slavs still possess the three qualities which have helped them survive all invasions: endurance, high fecundity and a gift of assimilating others.

DARKNESS and anarchy began to fall upon the Balkans toward the end of the fourth century A.D. The great Roman Empire—undermined by concentration of wealth, proletarianization of the masses and rivalries among the military cliques—embarked upon a process of hopeless disintegration. It was unable to put up an effective resistance to the invasion of the barbarian "have-nots."

By the middle of the fourth century something had begun to stir in the immense unknown plains between China, the Caspian Sea and the Baltic, and the great landslide of nations started rolling. This is a rough map of the time: Hunnish nomads, a Mongolian people, lived between the Caspian Sea and the Urals; west of them were the Alans, a Sarmatian tribe; still farther west, in what is now the Ukraine, were two Teutonic nations, the Eastern Goths (Ostrogoths) and the Western Goths (Visigoths). Their cousins, the Vandals, were settled in what is now Hungary. The climate all over the great plains apparently passed through a vast change during the fourth and fifth centuries A.D. A seemingly interminable season of drought set in, grass became scarce, and deserts appeared where formerly there had been steppes. For this reason, it is believed, the huge masses of nomadic tribes began to move west, pushing and trampling each other like a stampeding herd.

The Huns started it all. They were the first to go westward, subjugating the Alans, and making the Ostrogoths pay tribute. The Visigoths moved out of the way by invading the Balkans. After the death of Theodosius the Great (395 A.D.), the Empire had definitely split into the Western part under Honorius and the Eastern under Arcadius. In 410 the Visigoth chief Alaric left the Balkans, marched his men into Italy and captured Rome. Before this migratory tide the Vandals retreated from the Danubian valley into Germany, crossed Gaul and settled in southern Spain. Then their king, Genseric, conquered North Africa, invaded Italy and in 455 A.D. was the next to enter Rome and pillage it. By then the Huns had already reached the Danubian plain, with Attila, one of the greatest military leaders in history, at their head. Rome's central power had collapsed, and the Western Empire, corrupt and boiling with conflict between the poor and the rich, had no force to put forth. Attila invaded Gaul, raided northern Italy and marched to the walls of Constantinople. He conquered a domain of fantastic dimensions, extending from the Rhine to China.

With Attila's death (453), his realm broke up and the Hunnish hordes vanished from the pages of history. The Ostrogoths, then in present-day Hungary, turned west and founded a well organized kingdom in Italy. Then the Longobards, another Germanic tribe, appeared in the north, invaded the Danubian lands, and also crowded into Italy. As these Germanic tribes gradually marched off, the Slavs emerged from what is now roughly southern Poland and western Russia, and took part of the territories abandoned by them.

THE Slavs, like everyone else, were set in motion by the impact of the Huns, but they did not move wholesale. Unlike their transitory nomad conquerors, they had to a large extent become stationary peasants, moving slowly or hardly at all. They did not conquer lands; they occupied them.

It is after the Hunnish empire broke up in the fifth century A.D. that we first encounter the Slavs as a whole. They still held the basins of the rivers in east-central Europe, but they had spread in a westward direction up to and beyond the Elbe and the present city of Berlin. This was their western frontier at the time of Charlemagne, around 800 A.D. The remnants of this westward push still stand firm in Slovakia, Moravia and Bohemia. The second Slav wave rolled south and reached Dacia, present-day Rumania, by the end of the fifth century A.D. These Slavs spread themselves over the swamps and forests of the lower Danube and for nearly two centuries sallied forth to raid the Byzantine possessions in the Balkans. They would cross the broad river in their canoes, push as far as the Adriatic or the Peloponnesus, where traces of their place names can still be found. Together with the Avars, a Mongolian tribe then inhabiting present-day Hungary and to whom they paid tribute, the Slavs once (626), in the absence of Emperor Heraclius who was warring on the Persians, laid siege to Constantinople on land and with hundreds of dugouts from the sea. But the attack was unsuccessful. In the sixth and seventh centuries, alone or with the Avars, the Slavs five times besieged Salonika, but the city, according to the chronicler, was saved by its patron St. Demetrius whose image appeared on the walls and on the sea to inspire the defenders and frighten the enemy.

Not until 527, the year of Justinian's accession to the throne, did Byzantine sources refer to the Slavs under the name of "Sclavini." Contemporary chroniclers described these pillaging hordes as unspeakable barbarians, big bearded men with red hair and blue eyes, very unclean, living in timber huts or mud houses, endlessly quarreling and fighting one another. Byzantine emperors, engaged in a long and deadly struggle with Persia, could do nothing effective against this plague in the Balkans. They had to content themselves with establishing small garrisons in the cities and giving up protecting the countryside. Against systematic Slav invasions, Justinian erected a series of fortresses, about eighty of them, but all in vain. In 548 the Slavs devastated the western part of the Byzantine Balkan possessions up to Durazzo on the present Albanian coast. In the second half of the sixth century the Avars formed a transitory strong state in present-day Hungary and, for a consideration, entered into an alliance with Byzantium against the Slavs. Soon they made common cause with the tributary Slavs. In 559 the Slavs took part in an Avar invasion and ransacked Macedonia and Greece. Some of them reached the environs of Constantinople, and Justinian had to pay ransom. In 568, the third year after the death of Justinian, the Slavs were again in Macedonia. In 578 a hundred thousand Slavs crossed the Danube from their base in present-day Rumania and spread destruction through Thrace, Epirus and Greece. Once in a fit of energy, Emperor Mauricius organized a campaign under Priscus to invade Dacia and subdue the marauders. But the imperial army, after crossing the Danube and defeating the Slavs in battle, refused to advance into forests and swamps full of traps, and the Slavs resumed their depredations. At the beginning of the seventh century the Slavs continued their invasions of Thrace, Macedonia and Greece. At the end of the sixth and at the beginning of the seventh century, with Byzantium's power of resistance becoming ever weaker, the Slavs began to settle in the Balkans in great numbers, gradually assimilating the native population.

Finally, in 629 Emperor Heraclius accomplished a fine stroke of diplomacy. He concluded a treaty permitting the southern Slavs to settle in the Balkans, next door to various now nameless Slav tribes left over from previous invasions. Thus the raiders were transformed into the defenders of that section of Byzantium which now became their own home. At that time Byzantine chroniclers reported some twenty-five Slav peoples living in the Balkans, leading a semi-independent life. Nominally under Byzantine sovereignty, they were generally bound to pay a certain tribute to Constantinople and furnish certain contingents to its army, but they otherwise lived under the direct rule of their chieftains, who occasionally met and wrangled at clan councils.

Byzantium could not stop the tide of Slav colonization. One of the regions first occupied was Macedonia. At the beginning of the seventh century A.D., it had come completely under Slav rule, the neighborhood of Salonika being a special Slav stronghold. It was mainly this region that Byzantine chroniclers called Sclavinia. The following Slav tribes occupied Macedonia: Berziti, Strimoni, Sagudati, Runhini, Smoljani, Dragoviti, Vojniti, Velegeziti, Bersjaks. Of these, the last ones still exist as subgroups of the Slav people in Yugoslav Macedonia.

Very little archeological work has been done on the past of the Macedonian Slavs, and most of this work is based on accidental discoveries. It appears that some of these Slavs built fortifications. Others lived in circular half-underground huts with a hearth at the rim and a roof of straw or grass. Graves have been unearthed with bones and arms and ornaments. But this does not provide us with much information about these Slavs; fortunately, we have additional Byzantine sources.

The High Tide of the Middle Ages

The Slav Apostles and the Cyrillic Script

FEW people know that two centuries before the Battle of Hastings (1066) the Macedonian and other Balkan Slavs had their own script. It came about as the success of a failure.

In the first half of the ninth century, in what is now Czechoslovakia, the German Emperor Louis the Pious had already forced the Catholic faith upon many Bohemian nobles, but the Moravians were still pagans. In 862 the Moravian Prince Rostislav, to avoid German domination, sent to the Byzantine Emperor Michael III for men who could teach the "true faith" to his people in their own language. The following year, the very year of the official Bulgarian conversion, two brothers, Constantine and Methodius, were dispatched to Moravia. They were not Slavs but Greeks, sons of the military deputy commander of the Salonika region, themselves learned men and linguists. Constantine, named Cyril on becoming a monk, was the librarian of the Patriarch of Constantinople and a professor of philosophy at the University of Constantinople. Both monks, later known as the "Salonika Brothers" or the "Slav Apostles," spoke fluent Slav as spoken by the Macedonian Slavs around Salonika.

Cyril invented a Slav alphabet for the Moravians, adapted the local Macedonian Slav language into a common Slav church language, and translated the Holy Books into it. Slav languages were not much differentiated at the time and Macedonian Slav was fully understandable to the Moravians. The German bishops and missionaries promptly declared the two brothers to be heretics and called their language barbarian. Cyril died heartbroken in Rome in 869. Rostislav's nephew Svatopluk, who had sided with the pro-Germans, in 870 overthrew his uncle and had him blinded. Methodius spent two-and-a-half years imprisoned by the German bishops; he was finally released through the personal intervention of Pope John VIII. Moravia definitely turned Roman Catholic.

In 885 Methodius died in Moravia and his numerous disciples, among them the Macedonian Slavs Kliment and Naum, were expelled. Kliment, according to his biographer, was brought to the frontier river Danube naked, with spears to his chest and swords to his throat. Both Kliment and Naum decided to go to the by now independent Bulgaria, where King Boris received them well. Then Tsar Simeon (893–927) mounted the Bulgarian throne and conquered about one-half of present-day Serbia, most of Macedonia and northern Greece, and part of Albania as far as the Adriatic. He received Kliment and appointed him the first bishop of the Bulgarian church. In his diocese of Velice, where the people were still pagan, Kliment trained priests and composed simple sermons for the common people.

Upon their return to the Balkans, the many disciples of the Slav apostles spread the new Slav alphabet, Christianity and the old Slav church language among the Bulgars, the Macedonians, the Serbs. A century later, when the Russians adopted Christianity, they also took over the old Slav church language and the Cyrillic script.

Actually, two Slav alphabets were invented, causing much confusion then and later: the Glagolitic and the Cyrillic. In the virtually unanimous belief of scholars, the alphabet invented by Cyril was the Glagolitic, while the so-called Cyrillic script was invented later by Methodius's disciples in Bulgaria. The Glagolitic was the more complicated of the two, the Cyrillic being a streamlining of the Greek letters with some symbols added for the specific Slav sounds.

It is interesting that the Cyrillic should have been adopted under Tsar Simeon in Bulgaria while the Glagolitic was cultivated in Ohrid by Cyril's pupils Kliment and Naum. The two finally established themselves in this farthest southwestern corner of the then Bulgarian empire, now a Yugoslav Macedonian town near the Albanian-Greek frontier. Kliment built a monastery and lived there, first as a teacher, then as a bishop. He used to order fruit tree seedlings from Greece for the peasants and teach them how to tend livestock. He and Naum founded the so-called Ohrid Literary School, through whose Glagolitic classes 3,500 pupils passed to become teachers and priests. The Glagolitic survived for three centuries, but although the Cyrillic was in general use by the twelfth century, the sect of the Bogumils in Bosnia continued to use the Glagolitic as late as the fifteenth century. The reason that the Cyrillic ultimately won out was its greater simplicity.

THE language of the texts of Cyril and Methodius was the first common literary language of the Slavs; the differentiation into separate literary languages began in the twelfth century. The southern and eastern Slavs are, indeed, indebted to Cyril and Methodius for their alphabet and the beginnings of their national literature and culture. But the Balkan Slavs owe more to Byzantium than entrance into the civilized world. Constantinople had two great ideas. One was that the Gospel must be understood by the converts and therefore must be taught in the native languages, contrary to the Roman Catholic conception of the mystical power of incantations in an unintelligible idiom. The other was that the Eastern Orthodox Church should be a decentralized organization, a loose confederation of national churches, each with its own Patriarch or Primate, bound only by the dogma and the allegiance to the titular Patriarch in Constantinople-Istanbul. This made the new faith part of the feeling of national identity in each people. Thus under the subsequent long Turkish domination, it was the national churches which preserved national consciousness in all the Balkan peoples.

The two Greek monks, the Salonika Brothers who earned the title of Slav Apostles, were not very successful. But through a strange logic of history they won after their death sweeping victories in vast regions of which they had never dreamed. Their disciples, thrown out of Moravia, fled to the Balkans and spread the new Slav alphabet and church tongue among the Bulgars, the Macedonian Slavs and the Serbs. From there the two innovations extended to the newly converted Russians. The Rumanians used the Slav church language until the seventeenth century at which time they replaced it with their own. Even among the Roman Catholic Croats, under the influence of this democratic ecclesiastical movement, the peasants and the low clergy fought a long time to have the Mass celebrated in Slav. Today most Slavs (Russians, Ukrainians, Bulgars, Serbs, Montenegrins, Macedonians), as well as the Greeks, Rumanians, Syrians, Egyptian Copts, Ethiopians—some 250 million people—chant the liturgy in their own languages. And the Cyrillic alphabet is used by the Russians, the Ukrainians, the Bulgars, the Serbs, the Montenegrins and the Macedonians.

To themselves, Cyril and Methodius must have looked like miserable failures. Yet no other two holy men have achieved such epic results. They would rest easier in their graves if they could know that the alphabet, rejected eleven hundred years ago by a few Moravians, is now used by more than 200 million Slavs.

Radical Believers

IN the second quarter of the tenth century, when Macedonia was part of independent Bulgaria under Tsar Peter (927–968), a priest by the name of Bogumil ("Dear to God") began to preach a doctrine which soon gave birth to a powerful radical religious-social movement. It spread like wildfire not only in the Balkans but also into northern Italy and southern France, reaching as far as northern France, Flanders, central Germany, Bohemia. In 1210, an adherent of the sect was burned in London. The members of the sect were called "Bogumils" in the Balkans, while in Western Europe they went under the name of Cathars ("Pure Ones"). They were also called Patarenes and Albigensians, the Waldensians being a related sect.

Of the enigmatic founder of the sect we know nothing except that he existed and when. Even this information comes from only one source, the tract that the Bulgarian Presbyter Cosmas wrote against Bogumil and his teachings around 1072, immediately after the Byzantines occupied Bulgaria. Considering his success, Bogumil must have been a great theoretician, preacher and organizer. There is a legend in Yugoslav Macedonia saying that the priest Bogumil was born in the village of Bogumila, still existing in the Babuna Mountain of that region, the name of the mountain being derived from "Babuns," as the Bogumils were also called. In fact, modern Yugoslav-Macedonian and some Bulgarian historians claim that, contrary to the general assumption that Bogumilism started in Bulgaria, its place of origin was Macedonia, then under Bulgarian domination (hence the misunderstanding). Bogumil communities supposedly were particularly populous on both sides of the steep, dark, heavily wooded Babuna Mountain. The Macedonian Bogumil Dragoviti and the Bulgarian Bogumil churches are considered to be the oldest.

The reason for the scarcity of sources is that none of the Bogumil religious writings, songs and apologies has survived. They were destroyed during the long and severe persecutions, and whatever might have remained must have perished in the subsequent Osmanli inundation. Thus all we know about Bogumil teachings is what their enemy, Presbyter Cosmas, has told us. Similarly, of all the once abundant Cathar religious literature we have nothing but a Book of Rites. Here, too, for their teachings and organization we must rely on the testimony of their enemies and especially on the preserved minutes of Inquisitorial investigations. As the Cathar teachings and organization were the same as those of the Bogumils, the said minutes also throw light on the Bogumils.

AFTER the Second World War the Bogumils and the Cathars aroused new interest among Western and Eastern European scholars. Orthodox historians still maintain that Bogumilism was primarily a religious movement. Marxist and a good many non-Marxist students emphasize the social-political protest in Bogumilism and call it an antifeudal movement. The truth is that the Middle Ages were an Age of Faith; there was no system of values outside the Christian religion, and thus religion was the chief mode of expression, in art as well as in politics, and especially in the matter of justice and injustice.

As a religious formula, Bogumilism and Catharism were a mixture of primitive Christianity and ancient oriental teachings about the eternal struggle between Good and Evil, Ormuzd and Ahriman, with borrowings from the Manichaeans and Paulicians. God created the soul, the invisible, perfect order, where there is no evil, while Satan made the body and the visible, physical world full of suffering and injustice. God ruled the Other World, Satan ruled the earth. In Christian doctrine, man is created as a free being, capable of choosing between Good and Evil. In Bogumilism-Catharism, man is not free to choose and is not responsible for Evil. Bogumils and Cathars believed only in the New Testament. And they believed in the so-called "Inner Light," that is, man's conscience is the supreme judge of Truth. This principle, based on the first seventeen verses of the First Chapter of the Gospel of St. John, means that everyone can carry Christ within himself and that man is responsible only to God, not to any human authority.

Wicked people would upon death transmigrate into higher or lower animals, depending on the magnitude of their sins. Hell did not exist as such but made its presence felt on this earth and in reincarnations. In the end, the tangible world will vanish together with Satan. Christ was assumed to have had the appearance only of a body; thus he actually did not suffer on the cross and die, nor was he resurrected. Having shown his disciples the way to salvation, he reascended into Heaven. The Virgin Mary was never the Mother of Christ; she was an angel with the appearance of a woman. The Cathars, and presumably the Bogumils, required, as a necessary condition of salvation, one act of sacramental nature: reconciliation in the Spirit by the laying on of hands by the "perfect" ones who had already received the Spirit. This rite, the so-called *consolamentum*, was supposed to bring down the Holy Spirit upon the individual. It was their only rite.

The Bogumils and the Cathars rejected Church sacraments and all rites connected with matter, such as bestowal of grace through consecration, baptism with water, marriage, confirmation, communion, confession and the last sacrament. Pointing to the early Christians, they argued that church buildings were unnecessary and condemned them as places of the Devil. They abjured taking an oath and berated the cross—who would adore the wood on which Christ was killed? They also denounced icons as being pagan idols, and statues and church bells belonged to Satan. They abhorred the liturgy and the mass. They made no sign of the cross and knew only one prayer, the Lord's Prayer, explaining that God did not need many words. They also rejected penance, claiming that the Gospel demanded confession only to God; thus absolution could not be given by a priest. They scorned all holidays on the ground that one day is like another. As grave sins the Bogumils and the Cathars considered lying, coveting wealth, eating meat or anything that comes from an animal, including eggs and cheese (but fish was allowed), shedding of human or animal blood, including warfare (though killing of snakes was permitted). They denounced the Church hierarchy, claiming that Christ had not appointed the priests and the bishops, and calling them "pharisees." Neither the Eastern nor the Western Church can provide salvation, for neither is the True Church. The Bogumils and the Cathars regarded themselves as the only true Church of Christ, branding the other two Churches as apostates from the simple faith as preached by Christ and the Apostles, and from the simple organization of the Church during the first three centuries.

In contrast to the splendor of the official Church, the Bogumils and the Cathars distinguished themselves by deliberate poverty. Alms were considered undignified, and members had to work for their essential needs; but to avoid cheating, they did not practice trade, only crafts. The community, however, had its own collective property, coming from contributions and gifts. The "perfect" ones wore black garb, did not frequent inns or attend dances and entertainment. They refrained from anger, did not laugh loudly or raise their voices, never uttered offensive words, never spoke much.

Like baptism in the Early Church, admission to the Bogumil-Cathar Church was granted only to adults and was seldom demanded of the believer except on his deathbed. The sect practiced solemn public confession in front of its "perfect" members. Instead of communion, the Bogumils and the Cathars introduced the breaking of bread, not as the body of Christ, but in memory of the Last Supper. Like the Cathars, the Bogumils held their services in private houses, in the field, in the forest, in a cave. In their service, instead of the altar, they used a simple table covered with a white cloth, on which lay the Gospels opened at that of St. John. Their service consisted of the Lord's Prayer, reading from the Gospel of St. John, a sermon, and the benediction.

Many people liked the strict morality of the Bogumils and the Cathars, as well as the simplicity of their teachings, their service and their organization. The ascetic precepts, however, were not imposed on all the Bogumil-Cathar believers, only on the so-called "perfect" ones. The others could eat meat, marry, accumulate wealth, conduct wars, and so on, but they had at least once a month publicly to confess their sins. For the Bogumils and the Cathars were composed of two groups: the mass of believers (*credentes*) and the small group of the "perfect" or "elected" ones (*perfecti, electi*). The latter were the actual Church and called themselves simply "Christians" or "the Good People." There were no priests, every "perfect" one could perform the functions of a priest. At the beginning of the thirteenth century, the time of its flowering, the sect had sixteen churches between Constantinople and Toulouse, each under a leader called "the Old Man." But while believers were without number, it is thought there were no more than 4,000 "perfect" ones.

The Bogumils scorned the ecclesiastical and the state hierarchy, for it was the work of Satan, not of God, and was characterized by violence and injustice. They attacked serfdom and slavery—service of man to man, they preached, is a sin. Wealth is an evil in itself, and poverty a duty. The long existence of Bogumilism despite all persecution was possible because the peasant masses and the lower clergy wanted a plain human faith at a time when Christianity had already become a complicated theology of dry dogmas long out of touch with the poor and the oppressed. Like Catharism, it explained in a simple manner where the Evil in the world came from, a question the Christian theologians could not easily answer from their monotheistic position. Finally, Bogumilism expressed the democratic protest of the common people against exploitation by the ruling classes. In the West, too, the sect spread mostly because of the moral disgust felt at the wealth and the wickedness of some of the clergy, a feeling which ultimately led to the Reformation.

THE western sect maintained contact with its eastern brethren and looked upon them as the originators of the movement; for instance, at the all-Cathar council near Toulouse, in 1167, it was the head of the Constantinople Bogumil Church, Nicetas, who presided. At the same council, Marcus Lombardus, a Cathar leader from Italy, made a speech on which Dante commented in his *Purgatorio*, "My Marcus ... you have well-pleaded!"

Naturally the religious and political teachings of the Bogumils and the Cathars soon came into stormy conflict with both the Church and the State. The Bogumils were persecuted in a horrible manner. The dazzling Byzantine Empress Theodora alone is credited with more than 100,000 executions. Yet nothing availed. Between the tenth and the twelfth centuries Bogumilism invaded Serbia, where, in the second half of the twelfth century, the ruler, Stephan Nemania, ordered all Bogumil books burned, the tongue of the Bogumil "Old Man" cut off, some adherents burned at the stake, others expelled, and the property of all confiscated. From Serbia Bogumilism moved to Bosnia, where the ruler, Kulin Ban, received the exiles, and the new faith spread so that by the end of the century the ruling family and scores of thousands had embraced it. Soon, in the thirties of the thirteenth century, Bosnia was entirely a Bogumil country, where the heads of State and Church and the majority of the nobles and the population professed the new faith. In Serbia, however, as late as the middle of the fourteenth century the law prescribed the branding of cheeks of the heretics.

The Bogumil cobelievers in Western Europe were exterminated "with incredible ferocity," as Bertrand Russell put it. Pope Innocent III and the king of France both excelled in the brutalities of the Crusade which the Pope called against the Cathars in 1208. It was a massacre of the Waldensians in Piedmont in his time that caused Milton to compose the sonnet, "Avenge, O Lord, Thy Slaughtered Saints!" After the taking of the French town of Carcassonne there was also an appalling blood-letting. In the town of Béziers the Crusaders put to death the entire population of more than 20,000. The Crusaders burned a group of nearly 150 "perfect" ones in Minerve, 400 in Lavour, 60 as Cassès, while at Montségur 200 went to the stake together. Normally only the "perfect" ones were condemned to the pyre, but here ordinary converts who refused to renounce their faith were also burned. Many were sentenced to life imprisonment. At Bram eyes were gouged out, and noses and upper lips cut off, in order to terrorize the populace. Prisoners had their hands, feet or ears lopped off, and there were instances of knights flayed alive. The ravaged countryside was full of hanged men dangling from olive trees, women driven crazy, abandoned children, eviscerated cattle, scorched fields, uprooted vines, castles and towns deserted and blackened by smoke. Chroniclers say that babies lay by the roadside in such numbers that not all could be rescued and that some were eaten alive by vultures. Yet records show that out of more than 800 "perfect" ones sentenced to the stake only three recanted.

By the peace treaty of Meaux, of 1229, the province of Languedoc was brought under the rule of the French king and restored to the jurisdiction of the Catholic Church. Then the reign of terror was introduced to insure the victory. In 1233 Pope Gregory IX founded the Inquisition, with the Inquisitors responsible directly to the Pope, and entrusted its conduct to the newly created Order of St. Dominic. When an accused person was found guilty, he was handed over to the secular authorities, which sent him to the stake. In 1252 torture was sanctioned for the Inquisition. Surprisingly, even St. Thomas Aquinas justified the pyre for heretics.

DURING the papacy of Innocent III, Croatia, Bosnia, Dalmatia and Albania, together with Macedonia, Bulgaria and Thrace, were all countries where Bogumil faith enjoyed exceptional freedom and, in some cases, official state protection. Not only was the Bosnian ruler Kulin Ban with his family devoted to the sect, but his successor Ninoslav supported the Bogumils openly and even appointed one of them to the Catholic episcopal see. In the 1220s thirty-two Dominicans, sent to Bosnia, so exasperated the crowds with their preaching that they were flung into a river and drowned. From 1221 on Bosnia was one of the most important centers of Bogumilism, offering help and asylum to persecuted Bogumils from other countries. In Dalmatia, the Catholic diocese of Trogir was another center of Bogumilism. In the Dalmatian towns of Zadar, Split and Dubrovnik almost the whole nobility, as in Bosnia, was Bogumil. In Constantinople itself an important Bogumil church was connected with the original Macedonian Dragoviti church. Innocent III crowned Kaloian (1197–1207) as tsar of Bulgaria only to find that he protected heretical nobles in his country. His successor Boris II, an enemy of the Bogumils, was dethroned with their help in 1218. And John Asen II (1218–1241) granted the Bogumils complete freedom of worship.

In the fourteenth century Bogumilism became extremely widespread in Bosnia. As the Holy See was informed in 1373, almost all of Bosnia's inhabitants were "schismatics or heretics." The Bogumils could claim the first families and dignitaries of Bosnia in their ranks. In the first half of the fifteenth century, when the Cathars of southern France had long ceased to be and those of northern Italy hid in Alpine valleys, the Bogumil Church in Bosnia was recognized by the State. Their hatred of Catholics finally drove the Bogumils of Bosnia into the Turkish camp. As late as 1459 King Stephen Tomaš complained to the Dominican Barbucci that he was unable to fight the Turks because most of his people were "Manichaeans," who felt friendlier to the Turks than to the Catholics. In 1463 Sultan Mehmed II attacked Bosnia with 150,000 men. The last king of Bosnia, Stephan Tomašević, was captured and executed. The one-and-a-half million Slav Moslems in present-day Bosnia-Herzegovina are the descendants of the Bosnian Bogumils. In Macedonia and Bulgaria, too, the remaining Bogumils adopted the Islamic or the Christian faith.

THERE were certain elements in Bogumil-Cathar thought which contained the germs of the Reformation. It is generally admitted that Bogumilism-Catharism was a seminal movement. Its ways led to Bohemia and influenced the teachings of Johann Huss in the fifteenth century, and in Germany they led, in the sixteenth century, to fruition in the great religious revolution of Europe, the Protestant Reformation.

Tsar Samuel

BULGARIA was the first independent Slav state in the Balkans. Around the year 680 a man by the name of Asperuch appeared on the lower Danube at the head of an Oriental-looking mounted army. They were a Hunnish people, originally from the Caspian Sea, and were called Bulgars. In combat with Mohammed's Arabs, Byzantium could not prevent Asperuch from crossing the Danube into present-day Bulgaria. The disunited local Slav tribes were no match for this not numerous but well-organized invader. When the Arab danger was over, Emperor Constantine V found the intruders firmly entrenched. Incessant wars followed.

A unique process of racial and class amalgamation took place in Bulgaria. Originally the Bulgar conquerors formed the upper class of nobles, while the subjugated Slavs became land-tilling serfs. But, numerically weak, the Bulgars had to draw from the human resources of the Slavs. They freely intermarried with the subject race and were slowly swallowed up by it. By the ninth century they had already forgotten their customs and language and had become indistinguishable from the Slavs. Even the title of Khan changed into the Slav title of *Kniaz* (Prince). The Mongols disappeared in the Slav multitude, and only the Bulgar name remained.

Macedonia was at that time inhabited by a number of Slav tribes—Bersjaks, Dragoviti, Strumjani, Belegiziti, Sagudati, Rinhini, Smoljani, Vojniti, and others. They had already emerged from what Marxist historians paradoxically call "military democracy" and entered the stage of class division through war. The leaders of the military groups had begun to appropriate the lion's share of the plunder, and so a gulf formed between the people and its chiefs, who later assumed the title of princes, soon to become hereditary. The social organization changed from clans, linked by blood, into villages linked by territory, these again combining into provinces. Villages began to distribute the collectively owned land among individuals for tilling and keeping the produce. This, in addition to homesteads that individual families owned, facilitated the growth of economic inequality. Furthermore, large estates created by war and plunder were parceled out to others for tilling with retention of a large share of the harvest. Thus the basis was created for the rise of a nobility. With the gradual conquest of Macedonia by the Bulgars in the middle of the ninth century, the region became feudal in a few decades, and most free peasants were transformed into serfs. The Bulgarian rulers distributed large tracts of land among their nobility and military chiefs, and large estates multiplied among the feudal hierarchy.

The Bulgarian occupation of Macedonia proceeded in swift stages. In 847 Pressian extended Bulgarian rule to Prilep. Boris I (852–884) went beyond. It was under the great Bulgarian Tsar Simeon (893–927) that all Macedonian tribes came under Bulgaria. Under Simeon, Bulgaria was at its zenith—about the time when the Hungarians were settling for good in the middle Danubian plain. Simeon, a man of Greek education and Mongolian dynamism, successfully repelled Byzantium, subjugated the Serb tribes and all of Macedonia, conquered all the territory between the Black Sea and the Adriatic, proclaimed himself Bulgarian tsar, and made the Bulgarian archbishop an independent patriarch. His program was twofold: to help his people toward civilization, and to unite the Balkans under Bulgaria. He came under the spell of that imperishable dream of empire which had motivated Alexander the Great and Byzantine emperors and which was to trouble the nights of various ambitious rulers in the future: to unite the Balkans under the leadership of one nation. Simeon failed for the reason that the Balkans—or any other region—cannot be united by the subjection of all nations to one. Hardly a little more than forty years after Simeon's death, Bulgaria was so weakened under his two unfit successors, Peter and Boris III, that Byzantium easily annexed the country, taking the tsar prisoner (971). But five years later, in the year that Basil II (976–1025) mounted the Byzantine throne, a revolt flared up in Macedonia.

THE uprising of 976 in Macedonia was led by four brothers—David, Moses, Aaron and Samuel. Their father Nicholas had been governor of a Macedonian province and came from the Macedonian Slav tribe of Bersjaks. David and Moses were killed almost immediately in the war. As for Aaron, Samuel killed him and his family, except for one son, John Vladislav. The reason for the murder was suspicion of treason. Samuel remained the sole leader of the rebellion, which broke out when the new emperor, Basil II, was heavily engaged with the Arabs in the east. It is not known when and where Samuel was proclaimed "tsar" or from whom he received the crown. It probably happened in the first decade of his reign.

Samuel's way of warfare was defensively offensive. When he faced a well-ordered big army, he avoided open combat and resorted to ambush tactics. He would take the offensive each time a town or a province was not protected by a large regular army. Samuel was a man of extraordinary vigor who aimed at nothing less than building anew the great empire of Simeon. His first enterprises were all highly successful. As Basil, busy with the Arabs, had to bide his time, Samuel took the offensive, repeatedly invaded Thessaly and even ravaged Greece as far south as the Bay of Corinth. Basil II counterattacked in retaliation but was badly defeated in Bulgaria (986). Encouraged, Samuel took over Bulgaria, and in the 990s secured Epirus and the Albanian port of Durazzo, the terminus of the road known as Via Egnatia. He moved into Thessaly and Attica, and reached the Bay of Corinth. However, on his return, he unexpectedly encountered Basil's commander Uranus's forces at the river Sperchelus in central Greece. Feeling safe behind the overflowing river, Samuel relaxed, but Uranus found where to cross at night and wreaked carnage among Samuel's troops. Samuel and his son Radomir escaped only by hiding among the dead. Undaunted, Samuel moved toward present-day Montenegro, besieged Dubrovnik in vain, advanced as far as Zadar on the Dalmatian coast and returned by way of southern Bosnia and Serbian Rascia. With all these conquests, Samuel moved to the pinnacle of his power. In the 990s he controlled the entire region from the Sava and Danube Rivers in the north to Salonika on the Aegean in the south, from Bosnia in the west to the Black Sea in the east. His state included the Macedonian Slavs, the Bulgars, the Serbs and the Albanians. For a time he became the most powerful local ruler of the Balkans, more powerful than Simeon of Bulgaria had been or Dušan of Serbia was to be. The Byzantine chroniclers called him a "fighting man" of great ability and daring. Like his adversary, Byzantine Emperor Basil II, Tsar Samuel personally led his troops in combat. Samuel was not a mere rebel, he was a capable military man and statesman. Aside from proclaiming himself tsar, he made the Ohrid archbishop a patriarch. He did not persecute the Bogumils but relied on them, his own son being a Bogumil, and he received mass support against the Byzantine Empire. He established his residence at the Macedonian twin lakes of Prespa and Ohrid, inside an intricate system of defenses, where several chains of mountains, strengthened with fortifications, rose around the two lakes. Concealed within this natural stronghold, Samuel's forces could repel anybody and strike out southward against Greece or east toward Constantinople.

But Basil II, also, was an exceptional and robust ruler, patient and not easily broken by misfortune. After the lesson received in 986, he spent years of effort to straighten out the government finances and to make his army competent in every way. Then in a series of drives he systematically pushed back the tsar's armies and reconquered so much territory that only Macedonia remained in Samuel's hands. In 1000 he expedited a large force against Danubian Bulgaria and took it all except for the fortress of Vidin on the Danube in the country's northwestern corner. In 1001 the emperor marched from Salonika to Verria in southern Macedonia, and the town surrendered. Then he stormed Servia, stoutly defended by one of Samuel's ablest commanders, Nikolica, who was taken prisoner. No sooner had the emperor left than Samuel laid siege to the city, accompanied by Nikolica who had escaped. But Basil returned to Servia, lifted the siege and recaptured Nikolica, whom he this time sent in chains to prison in Constantinople. He took all Thessaly, then by assault seized Edessa in southern Macedonia. In 1002 he conquered the Vidin fortress in the far north, then turned south toward Skopje, destroying fortresses along the way. Near Skopje he came face to face with Samuel, who had encamped on the eastern bank of the river Vardar. Here Samuel repeated the mistake he had made years before on the Spercheius River. He thought that because of the rain-swollen Vardar Basil could not cross and relaxed his vigilance. But Basil found a passage across the turbulent river at night, broke up his enemy's camp, captured Samuel's tent, and the city of Skopje surrendered (1004). Basil returned to Constantinople. The four years of encircling strategy had secured for Byzantium Bulgaria, Thessaly and parts of southern and northern Macedonia.

Again Basil II had to call a halt in the Balkans and move against the Arabs in Asia. However, the Byzantine chronicler tells us that in 1005 Basil took Durazzo and that, generally, until 1014 "Emperor Basil did not cease each year to strike... plundering and destroying everything in his way." In fact, no one could have any further doubt about the ultimate outcome of the war. The valiant tsar could not in the long run match the military expertise, organization and technical resources of the old empire.

FINALLY, having temporarily pacified the Near East and put down the revolt in Italy, Basil II resolved to bring the grim long struggle with Samuel to an end by attacking the heart of his domain. In the summer of 1014, he moved with a large army against Macedonia. Samuel went to meet Basil and entrenched himself in a fortified gorge between the Belasica and Ogražden Mountains, near the spot where the frontiers of present-day Bulgaria, Yugoslavia and Greece come together. While Basil pounded at Samuel's ramparts, his commander Xiphias found— with the aid of a traitor, some say—a way across the Ogražden Mountain to fall upon the rear of Samuel's defenders. The lines broke, Samuel's men took to flight, and thousands were captured. Samuel himself would have been taken prisoner if his son Radomir had not quickly hoisted him on his horse and galloped away to the town of Prilep.

Radomir defeated a column of Basil's, and then, to show who the master was, Basil did something that filled even his crude contemporaries with horror. He ordered 15,000 (another chronicler says 14,000, but both figures seem exaggerated) captured soldiers to be blinded, formed them into groups of a hundred under leaders with one good eye, and sent them home on foot. And yet this man, Basil II, wore beneath his embroidered and jeweled robes the coarse garment of a monk! When the ghastly procession reached the capital of Ohrid, Samuel had a stroke at the sight. Water was poured over him and aromatic plants pushed under his nose until he recovered, but two days later he died.

Slav history in general, and the South Slav in particular, offers many macabre scenes and persons, but it is difficult to find something equal to what Samuel watched from the walls of Ohrid in October 1014. In Bari, Italy, the chronicler noted only two events worth recording in the entire year of 1014: "A comet appeared in the month of February, and King Samuel died. . . ." At the end of the big Strumica Valley, in the southeastern corner of Yugoslav Macedonia and Yugoslavia, not far from the Belasica Mountain, lies a hamlet of thatched wattle huts and some stone and brick houses by the name of Vodoča, derived from "eye-poking." Not long ago one could visit an old man there by the name of Nake Mitef, who knew by heart the *predanje*, the orally transmitted folk story of the battle and the putting out of eyes. A little distance away one can visit the *poljanica*, "the little field," all enclosed by low hills, where the gruesome operation was performed. The prisoners had been dragged to this secluded place so their shrieks would not be heard.

Samuel's throne was taken over by his son Radomir. But John Vladislav, son of Aaron whom his brother Samuel had murdered, laid claim to the throne. Basil II secretly prompted John Vladislav to avenge his father and one day in 1015 received a letter from him saying that during a hunt he had killed his cousin Radomir. As in a Greek tragedy, John Vladislav was subsequently blinded by his own eldest son, but kept the throne and continued to resist until he fell during the siege of Durazzo. The peace party now gained the upper hand, counting in its ranks not only most of the nobles but the archbishop and Samuel's widow, Empress Maria. Against these stood the small war party headed by three former commanders of Samuel's—Nikolica, Ivac and Elemag. Basil II now again started with his army for Macedonia. Already in Adrianople he received the first delegation offering submission and informing him that the unassailable fortress of Pernik with thirty-five towns had surrendered. Near Strumica he was met by the archbishop carrying a letter from Samuel's widow promising him the entire land. He proceeded to Skopje, then turned south, everywhere meeting with cheers and congratulations. Finally he ceremoniously entered the capital of Ohrid, where the entire population came out to meet him, "singing, cheering and hailing him." In the town, he opened Samuel's treasury and found "much money, crowns strewn with pearls and embroidered in gold, and 100 centners of gold."

Against all this, the handful of resistance leaders, who had taken to the mountains around the Ohrid and Prespa lakes, could not hold out for long. Basil II sent troops after Nikolica who, encircled, surrendered and was taken to jail in Salonika. Through undercover agents he managed to blind and capture Ivac. In the end, Elemag appeared before the emperor of Byzantium in a slave's clothing, bareheaded and barefooted, a cord around his waist. Pertinacious Basil II had reached his goal. In 1018, the rebellious country of Samuel's, against which he had struggled for more than forty years, lay at his feet and was annexed. The whole Balkan peninsula once again belonged to the Byzantine Empire, for the first time since the Slav occupation.

Basil then went to Athens, where in the Parthenon, converted into a church dedicated to the Mother of God, he offered solemn thanksgiving for the successful conclusion of an almost endless war. He then returned to Constantinople. Adorned with a plumed golden crown, he entered the city triumphantly, with Samuel's widow, daughters and commanders marching in front of him. "In this manner, accompanied by the shouts of congratulations on the victory, he walked into the great church; and after offering thanks to God, turned toward his palace."

THE peace policy of Basil II toward the subjugated country was as tolerant as his conduct in battle had been inhuman. He exempted his new subjects from paying taxes in gold, which was the obligation of the more developed parts of the empire, and let them continue with payments in kind in the proportion of one measure of wheat, one measure of millet and one jar of wine for every team of oxen. He reduced the Ohrid patriarchy to an archbishropic but maintained its autonomy vis-à-vis the patriarch of Constantinople, retaining for himself the right to appoint the archbishop. And he appointed the head of a Macedonian Slav monastery. He wooed the local aristocracy by distribution of titles, favors and honors. The widow of Tsar Samuel received one of the highest titles in the court hierarchy, while her sons became distinguished imperial administrators. A daughter of Tsar

Samuel married a Comnenus who later became emperor. Another Macedonian-Slav lady became the wife of the first Greek governor of the conquered country, Duke Constantine Diogenes, and was to be the mother of another emperor.

But after the death of Basil II, Greeks began to be appointed to the Ohrid Archbishropic in an attempt at Hellenization. Constantinople also began to insist on bringing Greek priests to Macedonia and excluding the Slav language from the church service. Other races—Jews, Armenians, Vlachs, Tartar Pechenegs—were settled among the Slav population of Macedonia, while natives were often resettled in Thrace or Asia Minor. Also, feudal exploitation increased after Basil II's death because of Byzantium's constant wars.

There were three catgories of peasants. The few free peasants owned small plots of land. The *pariks*, or the serfs, were "attached" to the land, bought and sold with it. The *otroks* were slaves pure and simple, usually war prisoners. All peasants became subject to many and varied taxes and levies, such as the tithe (one-tenth of the annual produce of the land on which they lived), the chimney tax and a levy on the plough; all these taxes were paid only partly in kind (grain, wine, meat) and ever more in money. Then there was a tax on salt, market and bridge tolls, and many other levies. The serfs were bound to work for the government, building towns, fortresses, bridges, roads. They had to work a number of days a week on the master's estate, supply him with firewood and straw, and feed his horses and dogs. The military service forced on all peasants was harmful to society; because of incessant wars much land remained uncultivated. A great part of the land belonged to the emperor or the treasury. Churches and monasteries also owned a large number of estates. The remainder belonged mostly to the nobility or to the uninheritable fiefs, whose holders only owed military service. The bigger feudal lords soon surrounded themselves with their own instruments of power, such as armies and courts of justice, thus undermining the central authority of the state. Finally there were the ever fewer free peasants. The increasing hardships aroused a universal discontent among the peasantry. It was soon not uncommon for the peasants to regard the coming of a foreign master almost as a deliverance. As early as the eleventh century, provincial peasants sometimes appealed to the enemy or joined forces with the rebels. Often they fled into the mountains, and vast tracts of land lay deserted.

THERE were two more uprisings in Macedonia in the eleventh century. In 1040 a rebellion flared up under Peter Deljan, a grandson of Tsar

Samuel. The solid walls of Salonika were too much for Deljan. But then he dispatched his troops in three directions: toward Durazzo which was conquered, toward fortifications in the Ohrid-Prespa regions which also fell, and toward central Greece where his commander Antim defeated the Byzantines and penetrated to the Bay of Corinth. The uprising assumed dangerous proportions, for large parts of the Balkans were liberated, from the Danube to Attica and from Durazzo on the Adriatic to Sofia and almost as far as Salonika on the Aegean. It began to look like an all-Slav liberation war. But Emperor Michael IV mobilized a large army, while division and treason undermined insurgent unity. The main instigator for this seems to have been Alusian, grandson of Samuel's murdered brother Aaron. When the revolt started to take on an antifeudal character, Slav feudal barons began to defect or go over to the enemy. Their representative, Alusian, invited Deljan to a banquet, had him blinded, then joined the enemy camp. After this, the rebels kept retreating and surrendering to the superior forces. Finally at Lake Ostrovo (in present-day Greek Macedonia), the insurgents were completely defeated, with the blinded Peter Deljan himself taken prisoner (1041).

After the catastrophic defeat of the Byzantines by the Seljuk Turks under Sultan Alp Arslan at Mantzikert, in Armenia, in 1071, there was no way of preventing them from taking over most of Asia Minor. The main economic burden now fell upon the Balkan peasantry. These peasants had to feed not only Byzantium's soldiers but the inhabitants of the big Byzantine cities. For example, the one million people of Constantinople could no longer be supplied from Asia Minor, only from the Balkans. In addition, the government made the grain trade a state monopoly, which meant that neither the feudal landowners nor the free peasants could sell on the free market.

All this led to another uprising of the Macedonian Slavs, in 1072, under Georgij Vojtech. The nobility of Macedonia was at the head of the insurrection, Vojtech himself was a local nobleman, and the center of the uprising was the Skopje region. In a battle near Prizren (on the present-day northern Yugoslav-Albanian frontier), the Byzantines suffered a defeat, and Bodin of Zeta (present-day Montenegro) was proclaimed tsar. The rebels took Skopje, and Vojtech divided his forces into two armies, one to march northward toward Niš in present-day Serbia, the other southward toward Kastoria in present-day Greek Macedonia. The southern army was badly defeated. The northern army under Bodin took Niš, but Vojtech, unable to defend Skopje, surrendered both the town and himself and died while being escorted to Constantinople. Bodin, too, was defeated and taken prisoner but managed to escape back to Zeta.

After this, there were no more rebellions of the Macedonian Slavs for six centuries; when they were resumed, the enemy was the .Turks.

Soon after the Vojtech uprising, the Normans briefly (1081–1083) conquered the greater part of Macedonia. Then the country went from hand to hand. It reverted back to Byzantium, came under the domination of the Latin Empire created by the Fourth Crusade on Byzantine soil (1204–1261), and back to Byzantium again. After nearly two hundred years under Byzantium, the Bulgars and the Vlachs revolted against exorbitant taxes (1186), and Kaloian (Handsome John) was made tsar (1187–1207). In the second half of the thirteenth century, Macedonia, with the exception of Salonika, formed part of the Second Bulgarian Empire. In 1285 Byzantium strengthened its hand in Macedonia. This was under King Milutin (1282–1321), who conquered Skopje and what is now western Yugoslav Macedonia. Tsar Dušan of Serbia (1331–1355) occupied all of Macedonia, with the exception of Salonika. After Dušan's death, Macedonia was partitioned between several Serbian and local feudal princes. Then came the Turks.

WAS Samuel's tsardom a Bulgarian or a Macedonian state?

According to some Bulgarian, Yugoslav, Russian and most Western scholars, it was a Bulgarian state, sometimes called the Western Bulgarian Empire. They also argue that Samuel's title was "Tsar of the Bulgars." Macedonian, some Russian and most Yugoslav historians deny that Samuel's tsardom was a Bulgarian state. Although some Macedonians, influenced by the patriotism of a new nation in search of its roots, will exaggerate and claim that Samuel's was a Macedonian state, responsible Macedonian scholars do not go that far. They acknowledge that Macedonian national consciousness did not exist at the time and that there was only an association of non-Bulgarian Slav tribes living in the territory of Macedonia. They point out, however, that Macedonia was the birthplace of Samuel's state, and at all times its pillar; that the popular force Samuel was leaning on were Macedonian Slavs, the people of the country called "Sclavinia" by the ancient chroniclers; and that Samuel's title of the "Tsar of the Bulgars" did not imply recognition of Bulgarian nationality but merely the right to claim all the lands which once belonged to Simeon's Bulgarian empire. After all, Bulgaria's Simeon and Serbia's Dušan called themselves tsars of their nations and of the Greeks, which did not mean that they were Greeks but that they claimed title to all Byzantine possessions with the idea of replacing the Byzantine empire.

Actually, all these Balkan "tsardoms" were ephemeral local imitations of the Byzantine Empire; the only real and lasting tsar was to be the Russian.

As for Samuel's empire, it was the one flash of lightning in the long Macedonian night.

The Grandeur of Byzantium

ALWAYS underestimated by the West, Byzantium has been undergoing a thorough reevaluation since before and after the Second World War by Western scholars. After all, this was one of the most stable states and civilizations in Europe between the fifth and the eleventh centuries, surviving the Great Migrations and tenaciously repulsing powerful enemies. Byzantium painted while the West could hardly write, It held commercial routes to the East long before Venice stepped in. It had a strong bureaucracy at a time when the rest of Europe seethed in feudal anarchy. Its Emperor Justinian codified Roman Law when there was practically no law in the West. At the pinnacle of Byzantium's edifice sat a Sacred Emperor to whom even the Church was subordinated.

Five features distinguished the Byzantine Empire. It was the most absolute monarchy ever known except for the Sultan's. It displayed dazzling pomp and splendor. It created great art. It practiced a multi-racial policy. It decayed.

IT was not only that the Eastern Empire was economically more resilient than the Western; that it contained rich and cultured provinces; that it had many big cities outside Constantinople, such as Salonika, Corinth, Ephesus, Smyrna, Antioch, Alexandria, where crafts and trade flourished with connections to India, China, Arabia, Ethiopia; that free peasants were numerous during the first centuries. Beyond all this, Constantinople or Tsarigrad—the "Emperor's City," as the Slavs still call it—haunted the imagination of the East and the still barbarian medieval West. Byzantium gave the Bulgars, the Serbs, the Macedonian Slavs and many others a whole world of ideas, sentiments, faith, arts and customs, a whole new civilization on which to build their own. Above all, it was the form of government, and the style of the "tsar" in Constantinople, that every Slav potentate from the Russian plains to the Balkan mountains tried to adopt or imitate. Even in the twentieth century Russia attemped to be the "Third Rome." Russia of the Tsars remained to the very end the most faithful successor to the vanished Byzantine Empire, in its autocratic despotism, its Orthodoxy, and its belief in having a religious and political mission in the world. Lenin's

Moscow became fired with the image of a Third Rome on a global scale.

Pomp and splendor were a deliberate Byzantine policy. In the heart of it all, the emperor, the Basileus, sheathed in gold, sat upon his throne like a holy icon. Amidst chants, rhythmic acclamations, processions and solemnities, his every act, every gesture, was regulated by the Book of Ceremonies, the only parallel being the Mikado prior to the Second World War. Pomp and splendor were especially lavished on foreign ambassadors and visitors. Received with fanfares and flying flags, they were shown the churches, the palaces, the bazaars, they were feted and showered with presents. As Charles Diehl said, men of the Middle Ages dreamed of Constantinople as a city of marvels, glimpsed through a haze of gold. They dreamed of it along the fjords of Norway and along the rivers of Russia; in the castles of the West, where tales were spun about the blazing gems that lit the apartments at night; and in the banking houses of Venice where clerks calculated the annual revenue of the fabulous emperor.

In church architecture, Byzantium soon evolved its own style, easily recognizable by the characteristic cupola balanced over a quadrangular basis with lateral semi-cupolas. Byzantine churches were imitated both in Russia and in Italy. For example, St. Vitale of Ravenna, with its mosaics, is Byzantine in style. So is St. Mark's in Venice. Of course, the Byzantine form was most superbly achieved in the church of St .Sofia, in Constantinople. Actually, the builders of this marvelous dome were universally believed to have been assisted by angels. The dome was so ethereal that, in the words of Procopius, it seemed "suspended from the heavens by a golden chain." Amidst all this spaciousness and resplendent mosaic, in front of and behind the silver-wrought iconostasis, the night services were performed by the light of the hanging silver lamps and lanterns and the sparkling candelabra, so that the entire church seemed on fire, while incense curled aloft and silver organs accompanied the voices of the choir. When the envoys of Prince Vladimir of Russia attended the liturgy in St. Sofia they had a vision of young men floating in the air and singing amidst the clouds of incense and the radiance of candles, and were told that angels themselves descended from heaven to take part in the service.

IT was an interesting composite. Byzantium had Roman conceptions of government and law. But in art, literature, trade and mode of living it continued the Hellenic tradition mingled with Christianity and with Oriental influences from Persia, Syria, Armenia and elsewhere. The Hellenic strain brought a taste of measure and simplicity; the Oriental trait introduced liveliness, movement and the picturesque; while the

Church never forgot to superimpose austerity. This blend of rival influences explains the realism, the fantasy and the immobility of Byzantine art. This also explains why Byzantine art, although under the thumb of the Church, which abhorred all references to the flesh, never became pure decoration. Also, Byzantine workmanship in mosaics, altar pieces, icons, enamel, ivory and illuminated parchments has hardly ever been equaled. A Byzantine painter would rather work on a mosaic than on a canvas or wet plaster. Whatever he did, he preferred a gold background. Gold also predominated in illuminated manuscripts. In textiles it was the silk, the brocade and the gold thread that stood out.

Oriental-type bazaars occupied an entire quarter of the city and filled the air with clamorous bargaining. Here were stalls and booths for goldsmiths, money changers, merchants of provisions, sellers of silks and cottons, while traders of sheep, pigs and horses had their own allotted places. The big harbor with its quays and warehouses, again in C. Diehl's description, swarmed with hooknosed Asiatics with pointed beards and black hair falling to their shoulders; turbaned traders from Babylon, Syria, Egypt or Persia; Bulgars with shaven skulls, wearing iron chains instead of belts; Russians with long drooping mustaches, snub-nosed, and dressed all in furs; Tartars; men from Spain; merchants from Genoa and Venice, who had their own quarter.

As early as the fifth century, the population of Constantinople may have numbered one million and probably remained as high until the Latin conquest (1204), after which it began to fall off rapidly, so that at the time of the Turkish conquest (1453) it was much less than 100,000. No wonder the hippodrome for sports events in a city of this size contained seats for 40,000 people. Nor could a city of this size be without its poor. They lived in great dirt, and their dens often leaned on the palaces of the rich. In contrast to the wide avenues and resplendent buildings, there were noisy, narrow, stinking and filthy alleys, where mud sometimes lay knee-deep and bedraggled humanity teemed in low, cramped hovels, where the sun seldom shone, and where at night no lamp showed the way and the only passersby were stray dogs and robbers. Yet the poor of Constantinople fared better than the poor of most other countries. True, free distribution of bread was abolished in the seventh century. But the circus, their only amusement, was free. And there were many institutions for the poor, in addition to hospitals, maintained by the monasteries, of which Constantinople had many in its shady gardens.

BYZANTIUM has of late been defined as a commonwealth rather than an empire. It was a community of some twenty nationalities, with the

Greeks predominant and the Greek language being the official language, superseding Latin in the seventh century. The commonwealth had one emperor and one faith, but also cultural tolerance and decentralization. A tenth-century Basileus (emperor) stated, "Any nation having customs which differ from the rest must be left in possession of its own."

At times, the Byzantines brutally persecuted religious dissenters, like the Paulicians in the ninth century, the Armenians in the eleventh, and the Bogumils in the twelfth. Thousands upon thousands of heretics perished by steel or fire. On the whole, however, the Bzyantines displayed tolerance and persuasion in the winning of souls.

To the Slav world and the East, Byzantium was the great educator, the champion of civilization and Christianity. To the nations it converted, Byzantium introduced the concept of government, the principles of law, a more civilized way of life, and an intellectual and artistic culture. Its architects built churches for the Russians; its chroniclers provided models for Slav annalists; and its folktales captivated the imagination of all these less cultured peoples. Most important of all, unlike Rome which imposed Latin on those it converted, Byzantium gave the Balkan and Eastern Slavs their alphabet and their own literary language. This was perhaps the greatest of all Byzantium's achievements.

NOT until feudalism after the eleventh century began to undermine imperial authority and the class of free small landowners was eliminated by the large serf-worked estates in the hands of absentee nobles did Byzantium embark upon the road of political demoralization and social corruption. Of 107 emperors in a thousand years, only 34 died in bed, 8 died in war or by accident, and 65 were murdered. With a restless peasantry, the empire continued to be plagued by wars within and without, along with financial decline to such an extent that Emperor John V, while on a journey to the West, was arrested in Venice for nonpayment of a debt. In the middle of the fourteenth century, a chronicler reported about the treasury, "Nothing was to be found there but air and dust."

The Byzantine had a cruel streak in him. Punishments were ferocious, and examples are plentiful of noses cut off, eyes put out and ears torn off. Voluptuaries with a taste for blood, the Byzantines were merciless when their passions were aroused. Yet the same people were charmed by the things of the mind, sensitive to subtleties and keenly intelligent. But their character did not match their intellect. They knew no scruples in self-seeking and were unreliable in personal relationships. The wily Byzantine delighted so much in feats of cunning and nicely calculated deceits that he could not resist indulging in them. This explains why, despite very real virtues, the refined Byzantine always disconcerted the blunt, straightforward Latin, and why the term "Byzantine" has acquired unpleasant connotations.

Already in the sixth century, the Byzantines were regarded in the West as crafty and untrustworthy people. An instinctive aversion has always existed between the two. Said Gregory the Great about the Byzantines, "We have not your finesse, but neither have we your falseness." To the elegant, sophisticated society of Byzantium, the Latins appeared somewhat boorish. Anna Comnena called the Westerners "by nature brazen-faced and immodest, greedy for money, and above all more talkative than any other men on earth.

AT the end of the twelfth century the Bulgars under the Asen dynasty built up their second empire, which lasted one century. In the same century, under the rule of Stephan Nemania, Serbia—long a vassal—became completely independent. It expanded in the thirteenth century to the extent that these two states deprived Byzantium of the entire northern part of the Balkan peninsula. In the fourteenth century, Tsar Stephan Dušan of Serbia was able to dispute hegemony in the Balkans with Byzantium.

The Western Crusades against the Moslems particularly contributed to the downfall of the Empire. Each was exploited by the Venetians to take over more and more of the Byzantine trade in the eastern Mediterranean. The Fourth Crusade especially, stripped of any religious slogans, was clearly an imperialistic war of an international army of Western knights under the leadership of the grim, ninety-year-old doge Enrico Dandolo. The Christian soldiers, having captured Christian Constantinople in 1204, showed no intention of advancing against the infidels. Instead, they plundered the Orthodox churches so outrageously that even the Catholic West was scandalized; they divided Byzantium among themselves in a swarm of little states, including a farcical Latin Empire on Greek soil. It is true that in 1261 the Byzantines drove them out, but with Serbia and Bulgaria being independent, and the Turks in Asia Minor, what was brought back to life was hardly bigger than present-day Greece with Constantinople and a strip of land across the Straits. The Eastern Empire vegetated, becoming smaller and smaller, until only Constantinople remained.

It was the arrival of the Seljuk Turks that ultimately sealed the fate of the Byzantine Empire. It is not widely known that in the sixth century A.D. the Turks were the masters of an empire stretching from the Caspian Sea to the Pacific and lasting two centuries. In the eleventh century—to be exact, in 1054, the year of the final schism between the Western and Eastern Churches—a Turkish tribe called the Seljuks moved from Turkestan in Central Asia toward the south, crossed the Euphrates and settled in Asia Minor. By the end of the same century, Byzantium possessed no more than a strip of territory along the shores of the Black Sea and northwestern Asia Minor. Whether the Turks embraced Islam before or after they settled in Asia Minor is uncertain. But the Greeks of Asia Minor went over to the new religion in masses, because the Koran, prohibiting class exploitation among Moslems, was obeyed at the time.

The Turks turned their eyes toward Europe in 1326 when they captured the fortified city of Brussa, opposite Constantinople, and made it their new capital. In the middle of the century, agriculture and commerce were in critical decline in the weakened empire of Byzantium, now deprived of its last possessions in Asia Minor. This was precisely the time the rulers of Byzantium chose for civil strife. John Cantacuzenus, guardian of the young Emperor John Paleologus, undertook to remove his imperial ward from the throne and asked the Turks for help. Thus it was at Byzantine invitation that the Turks first set foot on European soil. As a reward, the Turks obtained a stronghold on the European side of the Dardanelles. They swiftly spread over the entire peninsula of Gallipoli, converting it into a military base against Byzantium. In 1361 the Turks were in Adrianople.

The campaign that followed was ingeniously conceived. The Turks patiently spent a full hundred years encircling impregnable Constantinople by first conquering and consolidating the rest of the Balkans. From Adrianople they made a thrust into Bulgarian Thrace and in 1371 defeated a Serbo-Bulgarian coalition at the river Maritsa. In 1382 Sofia fell after a siege of two years. Then Sultan Murad I hurled his troops against the Serbs. The two armies met in June 1389 on the Kosovo (Blackbird's) Field, under the snowcapped mountain of Šar just north of present-day Yugoslav Macedonia. The Sultan fell in battle, but the Serbs were routed and their Prince Lazarus was captured and beheaded. The Serbian state did not disappear at Kosovo. It became a vassal and was wholly incorporated into the Ottoman empire seventy years later. For the time being, Murad I's son Bayazid the Thunderbolt rushed to give the final blow to the Bulgars. Salonika fell in 1430, and in 1446 Murad II overran the Peloponnesus. Constantinople, an island in the Turkish sea, was now all that remained of the Byzantine Empire.

Only when the Turkish groundwork in the Balkans had thus been thoroughly prepared did Sultan Mohammed II the Conqueror attack Constantinople with a formidable army of 150,000 men and a fleet of

400 sails (1453). Constantinople boasted the most impregnable fortifications in all of medieval Europe. Its phenomenal wall was actually three in one, the second alone being twenty feet high, the third having towers of forty feet in height. But the Turks had cannon, sixty of them, a weapon unknown to the Byzantines. One pulled by thirty pairs of oxen, was three feet in diameter and projected a ball of 1500 pounds the distance of a mile. Frantic pleas to the Christian states for help were of no avail, even when the Patriarch offered a reunion of the two Churches to the Pope. The defending force numbered a bare 8,000 men, but they held out for seven long weeks. And when Mohammed II finally entered the great city, the body of the last emperor of Byzantium, Constantine XI, was found under a heap of dead soldiers.

The first thing Mohammed II did was to go to admire the famous church of St. Sofia. He ordered an *imam* to mount the pulpit and give a prayer of thanks to Allah, thus converting the church into a mosque. Next he summoned the Patriarch and asked him to explain his faith. Perceiving in an unfettered Orthodox institution an excellent instrument for ruling his Christian subjects, he confirmed the Patriarch in his office. Thus the Greek Church survived the Greek State.

FOR a number of reasons, the West was implacably hostile to Byzantium. The Papacy felt antagonized. The Latins were intent on exploiting the Near East commercially. The Crusades, instead of making contact between the West and the East, promoted nothing but mistrust and hatred. Thus it happened that the imminent danger of the Turkish advance was lost on the West. Responsible historians have stated that, less concerned with the present danger than with past enmity, Western Christendom allowed Constantinople to fall before the Turkish assault.

It would seem unrealistic to argue that the Byzantine Empire might have been saved in the eleventh hour by Western intervention. The downfall of Byzantium can be fully accounted for by Byzantine weaknesses and Turkish might. One can only say that Western aid would have delayed the fall of Constantinople; and that, conversely, Western negligence hastened this fall.

The Long Turkish Night

THE Seljuk Turks developed an institution uncommon to Europe of the time: the Orders. These were groups of selected men, at once Moslems and trained soldiers, organized under the severe discipline of Leaders. In the twelfth and thirteenth centuries, Asia Minor was full of such Seljuk élite corps. Toward the end of the thirteenth century there was a Seljuk Order called the Swift Young Men. Its Leader was Osman, or Othman, an exceptional man who was able to bring all the other Orders under his command. Starting out as the chief of no more than four hundred families, he organized the entire Seljuk nation into a believing and fighting unit. Since his time the Seljuk Turks have adopted the name of Osmanlis, and the realm for which he laid the foundation was called the Ottoman Empire until 1922.

It was Osman's grandson Murad I—the one who fell in the victorious battle against the Serbs—who hit upon the strange idea of recruiting the Moslem crack infantry from among the conquered non-Moslems. Thereafter, at intervals of four years, the sultan's commissioners roamed through the Balkan Christian villages. They conscripted the soundest boys of from six to ten years, took them to Istanbul, converted them to Islam and put them into special schools. There, upon receiving intensive physical and moral training, the youths joined the formidable corps of the Janissaries.

Well-clothed, well-fed and paid in cash, the Janissaries were the first standing crack infantry in Europe since Roman times. Living in barracks, in inviolate celibacy and seclusion, they were bound by a rigid esprit de corps, and wore insignia and uniforms topped by the familiar tall white caps with hanging folds. They numbered 60,000 to 70,000 men, exceeding any professional army in Western Europe. The unparalleled novelty of the Janissaries was that no born Moslem could belong to them. It was a fighting organization of converted and indoctrinated infidels exclusively. By exception, the Sultan was an honorary member of the Janissaries.

The Turks were culturally inferior to the Balkan peoples they conquered. Their empire lasted for so many centuries because of their simple fanatical faith, the effectiveness of their military organization and the division of European powers.

Macedonia fell to the Turks toward the end of the fourteenth century. The Ottoman Empire reached the peak of its might in the middle of the sixteenth century. It then held the entire Balkan peninsula, present-day Rumania, most of Hungary, all the Aegean Islands, Cyprus, Algeria, Tunisia, Libya, Egypt, Syria, Arabia, Mesopotamia, Asia Minor, Georgia and Crimea.

FEUDALISM continued under new masters, with some differences. All non-Moslems were called *rayah*, the Herd. The Herd was considered morally inferior to the believers in the Koran. The *rayah* were not permitted to bear arms or ride a horse; they could not live in towns; they had to move out of the way of a Turk on the road; their churches could not ring bells to offend the believers' ears; they were more heavily taxed than the Moslems; they were subject to the "blood tax," the periodic levy of healthy children for Janissaries, which took one-fifth of the Balkan male population every four years (from this duty only Jews and Armenians were exempted). The function of the Herd was to provide the Turks with the material amenities of life; while the Moslems served the Ottoman Empire with the sword and the Koran, the *rayah* maintained it with labor and taxes.

According to Islam all conquered land was the private property of the Sultan. He kept part of it for himself as state domains, gave some away to Beys as estates, donated others to mosques and Moslem schools as endowments, and distributed the largest portion among his cavalry, the Spahis, as inalienable and uninheritable fiefs. On all of these estates, the *rayah* worked as serfs or tenants. Thus, while the Moslems were landholders, and the Christians land-workers, there was no class distinction among the Osmanlis. Rich or poor, they were all equal before the Holy Law. The Osmanli land system differed from European feudalism most sharply in that the landlord had no power of jurisdiction, and the peasant was free to move elsewhere, just as he could be bought and sold without the land. All public functions were exercised by the Sultan's officials and judges.

The land-tilling *rayah* gave one-tenth of their produce to the landlord. All had to pay the *harach* to the state, a special head tax on every non-Moslem male over ten. Then there was the ransom tax to pay to the state for military duty, from which the *rayah* was exempted. There were altogether some eighty imposts and duties levied or performed for the Ottoman state and the Turkish feudal lord. The fief-holding Spahi, on the other hand, was obliged to take to the field on horseback in times of war and bring with him a number of cavalrymen proportionate to the size of his fief. The total number of Spahis, at the height of the Turkish might, was calculated at 80,000 not counting the 10,000 to 12,000 special Spahis of the Sultan.

The unbearable oppression suffered by the Christian peasantry under native rulers had been the best ally of the Sultans. The serfs did not overzealously defend their masters against the Turks; they often made common cause with the Osmanlis and even rose against their own feudal barons. This was also often true of the petty nobles. Tvrtko, king of Bosnia, wrote to Pope Pius II, "The Turks in my kingdom show smiling faces to the peasants and promise freedom to all who go over to them. . . ."

It is difficult to know how the peasants lived during the early Turkish reign. The fact is that for the first hundred years the peasants made no attempt at rebellion. Apparently they were relieved to be rid of the Balkan feudal barons. There was as yet little reason to regret the loss of national independence. As long as the peasant paid his taxes in naturalia, the Turks did not bother him. With the Turks living mainly in towns, the life in the villages went on untroubled and unchanged. In the early stages of the Turkish rule, the situation of the peasant was undignified but materially not difficult.

The most drastic and far-reaching change which the Turks made in the Balkans was the liquidation of the native aristocracy. The nobles who did not escape were dispossessed, expelled to Asia Minor, or simply executed. Only those who embraced Islam saved their property rights. Without any nobility and for a long time with hardly any bourgeoisie, the Balkan Slavs consisted for more than four centuries of only a peasant class. When national independence was regained in the nineteenth and twentieth centuries, all new classes sprang from this basic stock.

During the first generation, the Turks accepted submission without Islamization from the Macedonian Slav feudal lords. This left them with limited independence in local affairs on the condition of serving with prescribed contingents in Turkish wars. Such was, among others, the case of the Macedonian and South-Slav folk-poem hero Marko Kral or Kraljević, of Prilep, who was killed fighting on the Turkish side against Prince Mirče of Rumania. But in the second half of the fifteenth century Christian Spahis were rare. How does one explain this sudden disappearance of the Christian Spahis? By their mass conversion to Islam, to preserve their estates after the first generation's demise.

In addition to the voluntary Islamization of the nobles, there was a rare Turkish attempt at forcible mass Islamization in Macedonia in the fifteenth and sixteenth centuries. Whole villages at one point went over to Islam, but altogether only one-tenth of the population of Macedonia was Islamized. Thus one will still find the so-called Pomaks in Macedonia; they are Slavs who, like the Bosnian Moslem Slavs, consider themselves an Islamic nation without being able to speak a word of Turkish or Arabic.

In addition to partial Islamization, there was the gradual settling down in the Balkans of the Turks and others (Tartars, Armenians, and so on). Murad I started colonizing strategically important regions in the Balkans, including Macedonia. The Turks mostly lived in towns and in the fertile valleys of Bulgaria, Thrace and Macedonia—the 130,000 Turks in present-day Yugoslav Macedonia are their descendants.

The Turkish conquest interrupted the normal development of the Macedonian and other Balkan peoples, arrested and even reversed their growth in every field, by depriving them of their upper classes and of urbanization, and by reducing them to a uniform backwoods peasantry among whom only a few priests and monks could read and write. Along with the Albanians, the Macedonians were the longest under Turkish rule (until 1912) and, after the Albanians, came to be the most backward Balkan nation, although the Cyrillic alphabet had been born in their land. In Macedonian towns the Slav element never quite disappeared. With the development of crafts and trade, a few Christians were permitted to settle in towns. Churches, too, were occasionally allowed in towns, but behind high walls, half buried, and with a separate rattle tower instead of the steeple as one can still observe in the Church of the Holy Salvation in Skopje. In the seventeenth century, Slav settlements in Macedonian towns began to increase, leading in the nineteenth century to a rebirth of the cultural and national spirit of the people.

TURKISH towns, displaying an ancient oriental atmosphere, exist even today as backyard sections of Macedonian and other Balkan cities. The incongruous architecture with modern skyscrapers next to oriental houses with jutting-out second storeys, the contrast of two ways of life, derive from two mutually alien civilizations, future and past. Only Turkish officials, shopkeepers, artisans and Spahis lived in these towns, mixing eventually with Greek, Armenian and Jewish merchants, and maybe a Slav craftsman here and there. One can still ride on horseback through narrow, cobblestoned streets and pass by minareted mosques, or open bazaars, or small shuttered shops with baggy-trousered men squatting in the doorways, waiting for customers. Sometimes, as for instance in the Macedonian town of Tetovo, one can still see only a wall winding along the roadway. Behind it are concealed green gardens and courtyards with fountains and houses with airy verandahs flooded with bright light. Symbolically, the Moslem's house has its face turned away from the road and the world.

In the sixteenth and seventeenth centuries Skopje was one of the well-to-do towns in the peninsula. In the second half of the seventeenth century the town had 10,000 to 12,000 houses, forty mosques and seven or eight beautiful shops. Mostly only the ground floor of the houses were made of stone or brick, the rest was wood. Skopje had about 60,000 inhabitants, including 3,000 Jews. Travelers of the sixteenth century reported all kinds of expensive goods in Skopje. Many Dubrovnik and Italian merchants were attracted to the city. Dubrovnik people founded colonies in Skopje, as well as trading posts in a number of Macedonian towns. They lived in the better parts of the towns, had the privilege of immunity, and had their own courts and churches in Skopje, Drama and Kratovo. The English traveler Edward Brown noticed, in 1673, much manufacture of furs, hides and leather. There were many rich and well-furnished homes. The population was mainly Turkish. Only an insignificant part were Slavs, mainly busy in crafts as tanners, cobblers, bakers, boilermakers. A famed Turkish traveler through the Balkans of the time, Evli Čelebi, visited Skopje in 1669, observed many master smiths and pointed to the production of cloth, silk kerchiefs, hand embroidery, gloves, pillows, braided curtains, and many other goods not below the quality of Persian wares.

Bitola was also a big town in the sixteenth and seventeenth centuries. Čelebi portrays it as beautiful and vivacious, traversed by a river spanned by many wooden and stone bridges, with 3,000 tile-roofed one- and two-storey houses, two hundred shops, forty cafés, twenty pretty promenades, seventy mosques, forty-seven poorhouses, a fortress, and thousands of handsome trees in the parks around the city where one can still take a peaceful walk under the flocks of cawing crows. As for the town of Voden (Edessa, in present-day Greek Macedonia), perched above a string of waterfalls, the Turkish traveler Hadži Kalfa considered its promenades the most beautiful in the entire world.

The Turks continued to exploit the old Macedonian mining centers of Kratovo, nearby Zletovo, Kočani, Ovče Pole, Kriva Palanka, Kumanovo, known for their copper, lead, silver, iron and gold; these mines had formerly been worked by the Serbian kings with the aid of miners from Saxony. Turkish methods of extraction were quite primitive, all work being done by hand, so that in one pit usually fifteen to sixteen men worked without any labor-saving devices. But Christian miners were exempted from all taxes, and Christians were allowed to be managers. The mines of Zletovo are still important for their copper, lead and zinc.

ANOTHER interesting facet of the Osmanli mentality was tolerance toward other religions. Except for the prospective Janissaries and a passing early Islamization drive, the Turks cared amazingly little about proselytizing among the masses. This chiefly resulted from the Islamic idea that a nation was identical with its religion. To the Turks their empire was an assemblage of religions of which the Moslem was supreme. This explains their system of *millets* (an Arabic word meaning nation): throughout the Ottoman empire religious autonomy was conceded to groups of non-Moslems. The law of Islam ordered freedom of belief for all who willingly submitted to Moslem rule; and all religions, even the Jewish, were formally recognized by the Sultan as long as they acknowledged his sovereignty. The Greek Orthodox Patriarch continued to perform his duties in Istanbul.

Thus it happened that under the guise of religious liberty the Slav villages in the Balkans were ruled by chiefs of their own blood and choice, responsible to the Turkish governors mainly for tax collection. However, village self-government and a free soul were all that was accorded the subject Christians. Political rights were reserved for the Osmanlis, the believers in Islam. Nevertheless, religious toleration made possible the self-perpetuation of national consciousness.

THE Osman dynasty, the longest-ruling in Europe next to the Habsburgs, gave the Ottoman empire thirty-five monarchs between the thirteenth and the twentieth centuries. All but one of the first ten were vigorous, forceful personalities. But with Selim the Sot (1566–74) began a series of degenerates, which lasted until 1922.

The trouble with the Turks was that they were a fighting, not a working nation. When the conquests and amassment of war booty stopped, the only way they knew how to make a living was to tax the last penny out of the *rayah*. Thus production decreased, the land was deserted, and depopulation and poverty resulted. The Turkish administration began to fester with corruption, and the bribe—*baksheesh*— became the custom. The two chief offices—that of the *Pasha*, the provincial governor, and the *kadi*, the judge—could be obtained only for money; and the Armenian bankers, buying patents for these appointments, sold them at large profits. Infected by depravity from above, the smallest local official behaved like a little tyrant and fleeced the people. One needn't emphasize the laziness and the rapacity of the Turks during this long agony of dissolution.

The Spahi cavalry, formerly one of the pillars of the empire's military might, lost its fighting spirit. The Spahis ceased to be interested in the military service because the wars did not bring much profit any longer. More often than not, the Spahis sent mercenaries into battle. Becoming used to luxury, Turkish feudal masters began to fall ever more deeply into debt. They inordinately raised the taxes and obligations of the peasants. According to Turkish documents of the sixteenth and seventeenth centuries, many peasants began to flee into the woods.

The Janissary ranks became swelled with Moslems. The enlarged troops failed to maintain the discipline which had made the old Janissaries the most feared foot soldiers in Europe. The requirement of celibacy was relaxed. There was soon no reason to exclude anybody with cash in hand. The levy of Christian boys was gradually abandoned because of the mounting clamor of the born Moslems to be admitted to the benefits of the favored corps. The last record of the levy of Christian boys is dated 1676. The new and corrupt Moslem-born Janissaries made riots their pastime, demanded more pay, plundered the Istanbul shops. Occasionally they rose in rebellion, murdered a Grand Vizier or even a Sultan.

The second siege of Vienna, in 1683, where the Osmanlis were disastrously routed, marked the turning point in Turkish military history and the beginning of Turkish decline.

UNDER the growing Turkish oppression sporadic revolts began to take place in the Balkans. Guerrilla bands appeared in the woods and mountains of Serbia, Bulgaria, Macedonia and Greece. They were called *hayduks,* based on the Turkish word *haydud,* meaning a man who has turned against authority and lives in the mountains. The *hayduks* plundered merchant caravans on the highways, attacked Turkish feudal estates, murdered their owners, seized their stocks, set fire to their buildings, barns and harvests, killed their livestock, and occasionally raided Turkish villages and towns. The outlaws were at first armed only with cudgels and axes—one such uprising was recorded in the 1560s in the wild Mariovo region in the south of present-day Yugoslav Macedonia. During the seventeenth century an increasing number of people left for the woods as *hayduks.*

A hierarchical order pervaded the *hayduk* bands. At the head of the band stood the chief, usually elected for bravery, experience and a sense of discipline and justice. He was called *harambasha* or *vojvoda.* The first word is a combination of the Arabic *harami,* "he who does unlawful things," and the Turkish *basha,* the chief *Vojvoda* is a Slav word meaning "war leader." The *hayduk* leaders wore plumes in their caps.

Some *hayduks* worked like lone wolves. Others operated in groups of from three to two hundred. Most frequent were bands of from thirty to forty men. There were cases of bands of two hundred men attacking Turkish settlements with flags unfurled and bugles sounding. The *hayduks* would regularly disband on the Day of St. Demetrius in November for the winter, which they would spend separately in the homes of underground friends; they would reassemble at appointed places on St. George's Day in May.

The *hayduk* activities were the only possible form of lasting peasant armed resistance to the Turkish government and feudalism. It was the longest—practically permanent, of lesser or greater intensity—form of warfare of the Balkan Christians against the Turks prior to the national liberation wars of the nineteenth and twentieth centuries.

Turkish authorities used a whole network of spies and infiltrators in the fight against the *hayduks*. The latter, however, also used counter-guerrilla tactics and often managed to be *hayduks* at night and members of the *martolozi* (Turkish field gendarmerie) in the daytime. Sometimes the Turks had to send large army units to combat the *hayduks*. As always in war, they would spread devastation, burn down villages and entire forests, especially in the Babuna Mountain area, and deport whole populations to Asia. An old folk saying has it that "grass does not grow where the Turk passes." Penalties for the *hayduks* were hanging, decapitation, the firing squad, the cutting off of a part of the body, impaling or life-long service as galley-slaves. At times a victim would have his arms and legs tied to horses' tails and be torn apart.

There are no Turkish documentary sources about the *hayduks* in the fifteenth century. But in the second half of the sixteenth century, the *hayduk* actions were fully recorded. And several hundred Turkish court documents deal with the widespread *hayduk* activity in Macedonia in the first half of the seventeenth century. From these documents, reports of travelers, folk poems and tales we learn about the names and activities of many *hayduk* leaders throughout Macedonia—of the legendary Čavdar and his sister Laluša; of Ivan of the Sheep's Field; of the elder and the younger Korčo of Strumica and Voden; of Pejo, Radojko and Toma, the latter specializing in raiding the Spahi estates; of Stojan and Dimov of Prilep; of the celebrated Babo of Bitola; and of many others. We learn that a detachment of 500 to 600 *hayduks* operated near Skopje, keeping the entire population terror stricken. We learn of *hayduks* led or harbored by priests and monks. We learn that in 1635 a fortress equipped with ten artillery pieces was erected in Kriva Palanka, in present-day eastern Yugoslav Macedonia, to protect the nearby iron ore mines from the *hayduks*; and that in 1651 Malek Ahmed Pasha of Sofia led 10,000 men on a punitive expedition against the Macedonian *hayduks*. Evli Čelebi, the above-mentioned Turkish traveler, reports that in town fortresses of Macedonia one could often see severed *hayduk* heads planted on upright spears. He was present in Bitola, in 1661, when the famed Babo with 500 *hayduks* invaded the town and in broad daylight raided the warehouses and the *bezisten* (the roofed marketplace).

The Turkish documents also tell of the peasant uprisings in the second half of the sixteenth century. Uprisings occurred also in towns—for instance, in Ohrid and Skopje in 1572, and again in Skopje in 1584, 1585 and 1595. In the latter two uprisings the *hayduks* joined in and the town was partially burned and destroyed. Already in the forties of the seventeenth century, the Macedonian *hayduks* became so emboldened as to attack heavily populated settlements, and the Turkish authorities made the villages collectively responsible for the actions of the *hayduks*. In the Bitola region alone 131 villages were made hostage in this way. From the middle of the seventeenth century on, *hayduk* activities were part of the normal state of affairs in Macedonia and, according to the Turkish documents, assumed the character of an insurrection. The *hayduks* at that time mostly operated in units of from seventy to eighty men, were interconnected, and were aided by the *rayah* in matters of signaling, provisioning and shelter.

MANY ecclesiastical representatives of the Balkan peoples believed that liberation from the Turks could come only with the aid of the Western states. One of the most persistent advocates of the Southern Slavs before the Western world was Archbishop Athanasius of Ohrid. He devoted the greater part of his life to preparation for a general uprising of the Balkan Christians with Western help. Athanasius solicited the whole Catholic world for aid. In 1596 he set out for Italy, met with the Venetian ambassador on the island of Corfu, told him that an insurrection had flared up in Albania and asked for Venetian support. Venice refused. Athanasius then sent a message to the Neapolitan vice king, De Olivares, saying that Albania and Epirus had risen and that Bulgaria, Serbia and Macedonia were ready to join them. De Olivares forwarded the message to Pope Clement, but again Athanasius's efforts were of no avail. He then betook himself to the Austrian emperor, Rudolph II, in Prague, arguing that 3,000 soldiers would be enough to seize the more important Macedonian and Albanian towns with the help of 10,000 native fighters. Rudolph II sent Athanasius to Philip III, king of Spain, who finally promised aid. Athanasius returned to Ohrid and waited.

In 1611 a second Macedonian delegation appealed for aid, this time from the duke of Tuscany. The delegation assured the duke that the people of Macedonia were ready to rise and that the rebels could muster 50,000 to 60,000 fighting men. There was no answer.

At that time Athanasius, through the Spanish ambassador in Naples, informed Philip III that the Christians were ready to rise and could mobilize 12,000 fighting men. But at that moment Spain did not care for a war with Turkey. Athanasius, accompanied by a number of Balkan Christian representatives, again went to Naples (1615) and explained the Balkan situation to the Spanish ambassador. He said that he personally had made the rounds of Serbia, Bosnia, Dalmatia, Macedonia,

Greece, Thrace and Bulgaria, and that the majority of the Christians, controlling mountain passes and many strongholds, were ready to fight the Turks. From Spain and Venice he requested 5,000 to 6,000 infantrymen, arms and supplies for 15,000 rebels, and saddles and harness for 4,000 horses. In return Athanasius promised the submission of Macedonia to Spain, payment for all arms and supplies, and maintenance of the entire Western army. The signal for a general uprising in the Balkans would be called by the archbishops, bishops and priests, and with the requested help he felt certain of success. This plan received a sympathetic hearing, and in 1619 a coalition was formed. It soon fell apart, and the war on the Turks never got started. The disconnected, badly organized revolts that followed were crushed by the Turks, and many Christians were relocated elsewhere.

IN 1683 the Turks were for the second time defeated at Vienna. An essential element in the Habsburg victory was support given by the Poles under Jan Sobieski. In 1684 Austria and Poland were joined by Venice, and in 1686 by Russia. In the course of the long war, the Austrian army captured Belgrade and in the following year, 1689, started to push south through Serbia toward Macedonia under Margrave Ludwig of Baden. The second-largest Serbian town of Niš fell in September of the same year. Then Count Silvio Piccolomini received orders to head farther south toward Kosovo on the Macedonian border and, according to the plan of the Austrian General Staff, was to strike out "for an exit to the Adriatic Sea near Herzegovina and Albania, with the whole of Bosnia cut off from the remaining Turkish regions, as was the wish of His Majesty." Nothing but a major Macedonian tragedy came of the plan.

Austrian military successes against the Turks strengthened the hopes of the Serbs and Macedonians that the hour of liberation was near. As it penetrated more deeply into the south, the Austrian army addressed appeals to the Christian population for help and, indeed, was joined by numerous organized armed units.

According to Turkish documents, the *rayah* of the Mariovo wilderness revolted even before the fall of Niš. Everywhere the *hayduks* were on the move, no longer acting in isolation but concerting their efforts with the general uprising. The center of the insurrection was in the Kratovo and Kriva Palanka region (present-day northeastern Yugoslav Macedonia); heading the peasants were craftsmen, monks, miners and *hayduks* under the leadership of Peter Karpoš. The insurgents showed the way to the Austrian detachments and attacked Turkish villages.

They took the towns of Kratovo, Kriva Palanka and Kumanovo, as well as the Kačanik pass into Serbia.

Peter Karpoš had at first been a *hayduk*, who later accepted amnesty and then became the commander of the Turkish *martolozi*. To Macedonian historians it is not clear whether Karpoš's collaboration with the Turks was genuine or a *hayduk* feint. With the Austrians on the horizon, he became a *hayduk* chieftain again and a popular rebel leader. On the whole, there is little documentary material on Karpoš. According to the orally transmitted folk legend, he was the son of a poor miller. His last name comes from *karpa*, a nickname a Greek gave him because of his great physical strength. Also according to the folklore, Karpoš went to work in the Kratovo mines. After a while he returned to his village, married and had two children. Then he went to Vallachia looking for work. He made money, but on his way home he was waylaid by Turks and robbed of all his earnings. He never returned to his village but once more went to work in the mines near Kratovo. When word came of the approach of the Austrians, he mobilized the peasants who worked in the mines, gradually expanded his forces, and soon was in control of present-day north-central and northeastern Yugoslav Macedonia.

According to Austrian documents, when Piccolomini in 1689 entered Priština, just across the Macedonian border, he was met by some 5,000 rebels, among whom the biggest unit was Karpoš's. He had already proclaimed himself "King of Kumanovo," a title later recognized by Emperor Leopold I. A version has it that Karpoš received a royal hat from the emperor, a crest, a decoration, plus an imperial patent (certificate) recognizing his rule over the domains in his possession; he was also given the rank of general.

The plague reigned in Skopje. Piccolomini sent in only units for reconnaissance and for collecting supplies. The town was almost deserted. Most of its 60,000 people had fled because of the Austrians and the plague. Piccolomini set fire to Skopje—whether because of the plague or because it was a Turkish stronghold has never been explained. In a letter to Emperor Leopold I he expressed his regrets for doing so since the city was as big as Prague, though being without outside walls and moats. He also regretted his action for the reason that Skopje's mosques were of the finest marble and porphyry with thousands of lamps, and the city had such beautiful gardens and places of entertainment. Austrian soldiers with torches were placed at street corners, and at the sound of three cannon shots fires blazed up, the more rapidly as the houses were mostly of wood above the first storey.

Upon setting fire to the city, the Austrian army withdrew to Priština.

From there Piccolomini went to Prizren, the heart of medieval Serbia, to arrange with Patriarch Arsenije II Čarnojević about the emigration of Serbs from the area to southern Hungary. On his way Piccolomini was stricken with the plague. He died in Prizren on November 9, 1689.

In January 1690 the Turks defeated the Austrians on the Kosovo Field. Among the fallen were Prince Charles of Hanover and the Counts Sturm, Kronsfeld and Auersperg. In August 1690 the Austrian army had to abandon Niš and withdraw from Serbia and the Ottoman empire altogether.

That was the end of the Macedonian uprising. The task of suppressing it had been given by the Sultan to the governor of Greece, Halil Pasha. Turkish documents do not tell us much about the time the offensive against the rebel-held territory began, how it progressed, or what resistance it met. We know that the rebels burned Kriva Palanka and retreated to Kumanovo. There a fierce battle ensued in which the Turks were victorious and captured a number of insurgents, including Peter Karpoš. The Turks proceeded toward Skopje, but when the rebels heard of the defeat at Kumanovo and the capture of Karpoš, they broke ranks and fled without offering resistance. The Turks impaled Peter Karpoš on the Stone Bridge in Skopje, and the Tartar soldiers repeatedly speared his still live body, then threw it into the Vardar. A large portion of the rebel population retreated northward with the Austrian army and with Patriarch Arsenije III Čarnojević, who led 37,000 Serbian families under the protection of the Austrians to southern Hungary (the present-day Yugoslav autonomous province of Vojvodina). The Sultan promised no taxation for five years to those who returned, but the deserted and devastated lands were largely resettled with Turks and Albanians.

The Nineteenth-Century Awakening

Rebirth of the Written Language

THE ever-growing lawlessness in European Turkey finally led to the first successful national uprising, fifteen years after the French Revolution (1804). It took place in Serbia and was led first by Karageorge, then by Miloš Obrenović. Serbia was granted autonomy in domestic affairs in 1829. In 1821 occurred the successful Greek revolt. According to Turkish documents, *hayduk* activities also increased in the Balkans, including Macedonia. We know, for instance, of the bands under Baneš and Nurikeš in the Prilep region. Further west toward the Albanian frontier a famous Macedonian leader was Vojvoda Sirma, and the band for a long time did not know that this was a woman. Reports have also been preserved of inhabitants of northern Macedonia taking part in the Serbian uprising, and the inhabitants of southern Macedonia in the Greek uprising.

But the sword would not have been enough even if the Macedonians—like the Serbs and the Greeks—had been able to liberate themselves. More backward than the others, the Macedonians faced a greater task than the other Slav nations in throwing off the centuries-long cultural stupor under foreign domination and establishing their own literary language. All the Slav nations in the Balkans achieved national revivals with the pen. And the leaders in each one—the Czech, the Slovak, the Croatian, the Serbian—were the new bourgeoisie and the intellectuals.

The first national renaissance was the Czech. It started as a purely literary movement among a group of intelligentsia, called Buditeli, the Awakeners. In the middle of the last century a Slovak newspaperman and professor, Louis Stur, composed a grammar of the as yet unwritten Slovak language, founded literary clubs, edited newspapers, and collected folk poems and tales. The Croatian cultural pioneer, Louis Gaj, in 1835 started a campaign for the founding of Croatian-language newspapers, and within a decade there arose a floodtide of literature and writers. The Serb Vuk Karadžić settled in 1814 in Vienna, where he wrote the first Serbian grammar and dictionary, and succeeded in making Ranke, Goethe, the Grimm brothers, Pushkin and Walter Scott interested in his collection of Serbian folk poems, tales and proverbs.

Up to the end of the eighteenth century, the only Macedonian literary work was done by monks, who in the cells of their monasteries translated religious books for the needs of the Church. The schools were Greek. The people were illiterate. Until well into the nineteenth century they did not call themselves "Macedonian" but "Christian" or "Slav."

Long before Father Hadži Theodosius of Doiran opened the first Macedonian printing shop in Salonika (1838), before the first Macedonian-language schools were opened in the 1840s, and before the appearance of the first Macedonian-language textbooks (1857), some hardy Macedonians took steps to bring about the reawakening of their people. Thus Marko Teodorovič printed a primer in Vienna in 1792, the first in the Macedonian-Slav language. In 1814 Joachim Krčevski printed in Budapest a book in his native language. In 1816 Cyril Pejčinović published in the same city his book *Mirror*, based on folklore. Both books were made possible by financial help from the economically well-off Macedonian burghers. The authors wrote in their local dialects

107

and must be considered precursors of the Macedonian cultural renaissance in the nineteenth century.

Ironically, the Macedonian struggle for the mother tongue was not against the Turks but against the equally subjugated Greeks. At the end of the eighteenth and the beginning of the nineteenth centuries, when the might of Turkey was waning, the Greeks began to take into their own hands important positions in the Ottoman Empire. Together with the Greek Patriarchy in Istanbul, which had assumed ecclesiastical control over all the Slav territories following the abolition of the Serbian Peć Patriarchy and the Macedonian Ohrid Archbishopric (1767), the young Greek bourgeoisie undertook to expand their domination of the Balkan Slavs in the fields of business, education and religion. As late as the first half of the nineteenth century, the ruling business language in Macedonia was Greek, as may be observed in the Ohrid town archives. The Greek bourgeoisie and the Church began to impose Greek schools on Slavs in towns and monasteries and to introduce Greek in the church service, a language not understood by the Slav people. The Greek clergy acted drastically. In a number of monasteries on the Holy Mountain of Athos, quantities of old Slav parchments filled the furnaces or were thrown into the sea. In the venerable monastery of St. Naum, on Lake Ohrid, the Greek prior Dionysius burned all Slav manuscripts. Mackenzie and Yearby, in their *Travels in the Slav Sections of European Turkey*, noted that in Prilep the Greeks destroyed and burned all Slav books and that in Veles's bazaar avenue valuable Slav documents were thrown into a huge bonfire. Thus the conflict with the Greeks centered around the right of the Slav people to use their own language in their churches and schools.

IT is true that rich Macedonians believed that they could express themselves in a "cultured" way only in Greek, and that the native language was regarded as "common" and not proper for a cultured man. Education in Greek schools often led to Hellenization, with the pupils apt to forget their mother tongue or using Greek letters when writing it. But it is also true that Hellenization affected only a small minority among the well-to-do Macedonians and that the infant Macedonian bourgeoisie on the whole joined the fight for the Macedonian language.

At the beginning of the nineteenth century, with the development of capitalism, the merchants and craftsmen of Macedonia started to open agencies in Budapest, Vienna, Munich, Leipzig, Lyons, Geneva, all the way to Berlin and London. There was also contact with the West via Salonika, the second largest city in the Ottoman Empire. In the thirties of the last century, the port began to flourish, being filled with French, British, Italian and Austrian ships. The warehouses began to be stocked with wool, tobacco, copper, wax, rabbit skins and grain for export. And from Salonika camel caravans transported linen, coffee, sugar, dyes, lead, tin, paper, metalwares, glass throughout Macedonia and beyond. One must remember, however, that trade in Macedonia lay mainly in the hands of Greeks, Tsintsars, Armenians, Jews and Turks, of whom the Greeks and the Tsintsars in particular were the more agile and had the most connections abroad. The Slav commercial circles saw in the Greek attempt at Hellenization an infringement of their economic interests. They began to realize that the old-fashioned monastic schools could not satisfy their new needs. Facing the danger of Hellenization in Greek schools, they attempted to get into their hands the management of the church-school communes, within which they could open their own schools. These communes were in charge of the building of churches and schools, the hiring of teachers, and deciding on school programs. There were not many literate men among the Macedonian businessmen, and an unhampered development of the people's language was considered absolutely essential.

Gradually, along with the printing of books went the establishment of Macedonian schools, in which ecclesiastical matters were replaced by secular subjects required in commercial life: mathematics, geometry, physics, zoology and, above all, the native Slav language and grammar. The schools were mostly founded as annexes of newly-built churches or in private homes. Teachers were not ecclesiastics but laymen.

The teachers were the sole Macedonian intelligentsia at the time. Few of them could boast a good education or a cultural background. The majority, except for their being barely literate and possessing an elementary knowledge of the sciences, had nothing to pass on to their pupils. Teachers were in continual trouble trying to find or keep a teaching post. It was not good for the learned to be looked upon as very learned, for they were apt to be denounced as Russian spies. If a teacher was not patronized by a rich person, he was often left without work. But in the fifties and sixties of the last century there came a new generation of teachers, educated in Russia or the neighboring Slav regions. The most prominent teacher of this time was Dimitar Miladinov. Almost all the Macedonians from the middle of the last century who earned literary laurels were pupils or collaborators of D. Miladinov. They were Konstantin Miladinov, Rajko Žinzifov, Parteni Zografski, George Prličev and Kuzman Šapkarev. From outside this group we have only J. H. Konstantinov-Džinot, who opened the first Slav school in Macedonia, in 1840.

DIMITAR Miladinov (1810–62) and his younger brother Konstantin were born in Struga, at Lake Ohrid. Dimitar chose to be a schoolteacher. Turkish censorship was most severe. The teacher could read no newspapers. His correspondence was opened. There was not one teacher in Macedonia who within three or four years would not land in jail. Dimitar Miladinov taught school in various towns, though not without interruptions. In the winter of 1855–56 he was removed from his post, whereupon he took a trip through Herzegovina, Bosnia and Serbia. He returned full of exuberant patriotism. He secured a teaching position in Prilep, where he taught Macedonian subjects—history, folklore, language—in the Macedonian Ohrid dialect. The Greek bishop of Bitola promptly forbade his teachings and had him arrested as a Russian agent. Dimitar was released but not permitted to teach in Prilep again.

As far back as 1845, the great Russian Slavist and professor at Kazan University, Viktor Grigorovich, visited Macedonia and advised Dimitar Miladinov to start collecting Macedonian folklore. During his journey in Serbia, Miladinov was also strongly urged to do so by Vuk S. Karadžić, who through his famous collection of Serbian folk poems, tales and proverbs had made his people known to Europe. The Balkan Slav regions are probably still the richest source of folklore in Europe. This folk poetry, especially the Serbian, of Shakespearean majesty, had been created through slow, centuries-long labor of the mind and imagination of the oppressed peasants, and described the history, the land, the life and the character of the people. Both Goethe and Herder were fascinated by this folk poetry.

With his brother Konstantin, who was a poet and studied history and philosophy in Athens and Moscow, Dimitar Miladinov could be seen walking along the streets of Macedonian villages, noting down folk poems, legends, proverbs, riddles, popular beliefs, descriptions of weddings and other customs. This was difficult work because it had to be done unobtrusively, often surreptitiously in the underground manner, in order not to arouse the suspicion of the Turkish authorities or of the Greek clergy.

When Konstantin Miladinov went to Russia he took with him his collected folklore material. But in that great country he could find no publisher. Significantly, it was a Croatian Roman Catholic bishop and promoter of South Slav unity, Josip J. Strossmayer, who in 1861 sponsored and financed the publication in Zagreb of Miladinovs' collection of Macedonian folk poems. There were altogether 600 poems. They were divided into ecclesiastical, heroic, pastoral, *hayduk*, mourning, humorous, love, nuptial and harvest poems as well as poems about fairies.

The most prominent were the poems about the Balkan, more especially Serbian, folk hero Marko Kral or Kraljević. Some other folk heroes were also shared with the Serbs. The *hayduk* poems exalted the fighting spirit, not by glorifying violence as such but by showing that those who did injustice to the people must be punished.

Strangely, the Miladinovs gave their collection the title of *Bulgarian Folk Poems*, although only one hundred were designated as Bulgarian. One explanation is that at the time the Bulgars were a better known nation. But this is only a conjecture.

Stefan Verković published in Belgrade, in the same year, his own, smaller, collection of Macedonian folk poems under the title *Folk Poems of the Macedonian Bulgars*, pointing in the preface to the absence of Macedonian national consciousness at the time. This may have been the true explanation of the title of the Miladinovs' collection: the Macedonian national feeling was not yet strong enough to assert itself beside the Bulgarian in the common struggle against domination by the Turks and the Greek Church.

The brothers Miladinov achieved their triumph in the eleventh hour. In the very year of the publication of their collection, Dimitar Miladinov was accused by the Greek bishop of Ohrid, Meletius, of being a Russian agent dangerous to the security of the Turkish state. He was arrested, put in shackles and charged with high treason. He spent some time in the Bitola jail, then was sent to the Istanbul prison. Nobody was allowed to see him except an emissary of the Roman Catholic Church who promised help if he would embrace the Catholic faith. Young Konstantin Miladinov, ill with tuberculosis, went to Istanbul to see what he could do for his brother but was himself arrested. Both brothers died in jail in early 1862.

IN the 1860s two kinds of textbooks were used in Macedonia: those written in a mixed Macedonian-Bulgarian language; and those in a pure Macedonian language, which had to be one of the spoken local dialects. The first kind was supported by those Macedonians who considered it useful to go along with the Bulgars; the second kind was promoted by those who thought independence was the only true solution for the Macedonian people. Three figures from the Miladinov circle are worth mentioning in the first group.

At the age of seventeen, Rajko Žinzifov began his teaching activities in Macedonia. He then spent half of his life in Russia, where he became a renowned writer and poet. At Moscow University he became acquainted with the young Bulgars and through them established contact with the Russian Slavophiles. At the All-Slav Congress in 1867 he expressed the hope that the Russian people would extend a helping hand to the Bulgarian people. In his poetry he attempted to create a common Bulgarian-Macedonian language.

Parteni Zografski, a pupil of Dimitar Miladinov, studied in Russia but previously had taken advanced courses in Athens and again in a Bulgarian environment where he had become very pro-Bulgarian. In Russia, Zografski graduated from a seminary and was for a time religious instructor to the Tsar's children. In the late 1860s he established himself in Istanbul and edited his Macedonian textbooks. Zografski, too, worked out a language in common with the Bulgarian, a compromise between the western Macedonian dialect and the Bulgarian language.

The most prominent of this group was Kuzman Šapkarev (1834–1908), a famous collector of Macedonian folklore. He published eight textbooks, but there was a fundamental contradiction in his attitude. He shared Zografski's views on a common Bulgarian-Macedonian language. At the same time he was a fervent Macedonian, who considered the Macedonians a separate people which had to be provided with a special literary language. He wavered between the pro-Macedonian and pro-Bulgarian ideas, trying to keep on good terms with either group, an attitude frequently observable in Macedonian life in his time.

Part of the Macedonian bourgeoisie accepted the Bulgarian cause but wished to be treated as an equal partner. These men wanted to collaborate with the Bulgars, they agreed to have the struggle against Hellenization being part of a common Bulgarian cause, but after having pushed the Greek merchants out they did not desire to see their place taken by the Bulgars. The "common" Bulgarian-Macedonian language was a projection of what was wanted in the marketplace.

The actual choice was either to accept the Bulgarian or the Serbian language or to construct a Macedonian literary language. The second alternative was the one adopted.

Along with the fight of the Macedonian bourgeoisie for a greater share in commerce and trade and for an independent church and bishops went the struggle for the introduction of the Macedonian language and textbooks into the schools. This struggle was conducted by the so-called "Macedonists," who as early as the 1850s declared that the Macedonians were a separate Slav nation. Two "Macedonist" assertions stand out: (a) The Macedonian people are descended from the Macedonians of Alexander the Great; (b) the Macedonians, in contrast to the Bulgars, are pure and unmixed Slavs, into whose language the religious works of Cyril and Methodius had been translated. These two assertions were not complete nonsense, since the "Macedonists" regarded Alexander the Great and his Macedonians as Slavs (as do some uneducated, Macedonians even today). This opinion was not particularly "Macedonist," because it was widespread and had been handed down in certain old history books.

The most prominent "Macedonist" was George Pulevski. A migrant bricklayer by trade, he worked in Rumania, and in the early 1870s published two dictionaries in Belgrade. Later he took part in the famous Battle of Šipka in the Russo-Turkish War of 1877–78, leading a squad of Macedonian volunteers, and was decorated by the Russians for bravery. In 1879, in newly liberated Sofia, he published his *Macedonian Song Book*. His Macedonian grammar appeared the following year. Pulevski most decidedly expressed the Macedonian consciousness. In his dictionary he asks, "What is our country called?" The answer, "Our country is called Macedonia and we are called Macedonians."

Between Zografski and Pulevski, both from the picturesque village of Galičnik in western Macedonia, there is a considerable line of development. Pulevski was not educated like Zografski. He was a self-taught man who did not understand much about grammatical rules and punctuation, though he talked about them. This may be exactly what made Pulevski a better interpreter of the thoughts and the aspirations of the people than were some of the Macedonian intellectuals of the time.

The last major work affirming the right of the Macedonian language to a separate existence was Krste P. Misirkov's *On Macedonian Affairs*, published in Sofia in 1903. The book was promptly banned by the Bulgarian authorities. In the book Misirkov wrote, "My views are not new . . . they constitute a step forward in the development of our national self-awareness. . . ." Misirkov maintained that the Macedonian literary language should adopt the central-Macedonian speech forms. He strongly emphasized that a Macedonian literary language should be created to ensure the very survival and further development of the Macedonian people.

SERBIAN influence in Macedonia was also of great significance. Serbia was an autonomous Balkan state, and as a Slav country was bound to inspire hopes of liberation. Together with Serbian textbooks, Serbian teachers came down to Macedonia between the 1840s and 1860. Serbia could not for long allow the strengthening of Bulgarian influence in Macedonia without counteraction. Thus already at the time of the publication of Slav textbooks for Macedonia all three neighbors clashed over the region, a clash ultimately leading to a partition of Macedonia among Serbia, Bulgaria and Greece in 1913.

In the three-cornered battle for future spoils, the Bulgarian position was soon strengthened by the Bulgarian church. In the 1860s town after town in Bulgaria submitted to the Turkish government a plea for the establishment of a separate Bulgarian Church for all the Slavs in the Ottoman Empire. Yielding to the tremendous pressure, the Sultan in 1870 published a *firman* setting up an independent Bulgarian Church, to be called Exarchy. Not only did this act assign the entire province of Bulgaria to the Exarch but it gave the Christian parishes in Macedonia the right to join the Exarchy whenever two-thirds of the population expressed a wish to do so. All the Macedonian eparchies expressed this wish. The Greek Patriarch of Istanbul immediately proclaimed the Bulgarian Church schismatic and anathematized the Bulgarian Exarch. However, politically this meant nothing.

The Macedonians conducted their cultural struggle jointly with the Bulgars. It could not be otherwise. The two nations had common enemies in Turkey and the Greek Patriarchy. Both had to rely on their one friend, Slav Orthodox Russia, which in its thrust toward the Aegean Sea sought to have all Slavs east and south of Serbia in one church organization as the basis for the future "Trans-Danubian *gubernia.*" Since the Macedonian bourgeoisie was weaker, the leadership was kept in the hands of the big Bulgarian merchants in Istanbul and the associated intelligentsia. This alliance made possible the spread of Bulgarian textbooks and influence in Macedonia, to such an extent that in the 1860s a part of the Macedonian intelligentsia on the basis of common interests began to orient itself toward Bulgaria.

With the establishment of the Exarchy in 1870, a joint Bulgarian-Macedonian victory was won in Istanbul. But soon the Bulgarian bourgeoisie, more numerous and richer, obtained commanding positions in the Exarchy, which thereupon assumed the tutelage over Macedonia formerly exerted by the Istanbul Patriarchy. The Exarchy, of course, appointed Bulgarian bishops in Macedonia, and these in turn installed Bulgarian clergy and set up Bulgarian schools in the territory where the Greek Patriarchy formerly had reigned supreme. This became a systematic policy after the liberation of Bulgaria in 1878, when the Exarchy became an agency of the Bulgarian government. The Macedonian people did not begin a struggle against the Exarchy until the end of the nineteenth century. Paradoxically, the Turkish act of recognizing a Bulgarian Church to which the Macedonian eparchies voluntarily acceded, is today considered to be one of the legal grounds for the claim of Communist Bulgaria to Yugoslav Communist Macedonia.

AFTER the First World War Macedonia found itself divided among Yugoslavia, Bulgaria and Greece. The official languages were the Serbo-Croatian, the Bulgarian and the Greek. These were also the official school languages. It seemed as if the authorities denied that the Macedonian language existed. The Serbs considered it to be Bulgarian, the Bulgars called it a Serbian dialect. In Greece, during the dictatorship of General Metaxas, the Macedonian language was forbidden by law to be spoken even in one's home.

In the kingdom of Yugoslavia, conditions for the cultural development of the Macedonians were somewhat better. The people used their native language in conversation and even occasionally in literature. In the late twenties and in the thirties several plays were performed in Macedonian. From time to time newspapers and magazines published verse and prose in Macedonian, and finally collections of modern Macedonian poetry saw the light of day. The most outstanding was the verse of the prominent Macedonian poet and subsequent Second World War martyr Kosta Racin. It was published in 1939 under the title of *White Dawns*. The prewar Macedonian writers laid the foundation for the literary language.

During the Second World War there was a Partisan printing press in Macedonia, which printed leaflets, proclamations, army newspapers, political brochures, apart from poetic and prose works. Partisan units and organs of authority and command were composed of people from various regions and became "workshops" hastening the formation of a common Macedonian literary language. The Macedonian language is divided into many spoken dialects, and the wartime printed material shows a mixture of dialects; there was a prevalence of the central dialect, and on it was based today's literary language.

In the summer of 1944, Macedonian was proclaimed the official language of Macedonia. In the summer of 1945, a group of scholars adopted the modern Macedonian alphabet and grammar, based on the central dialect. In the development of the language, the folklore stage of writing was soon abandoned, although Macedonian literature had begun with it. Many words had to be borrowed from world languages, many from other local dialects or other Slav languages, and many had to be coined. Once the most literate Slavs in the Balkans, the Macedonians a little more than a hundred years ago had the fewest literate men of any Balkan nation. And their language took its proper place among other literary languages no more than thirty years ago.

Volumes have since been translated from the Russian, West European and American literatures into the Macedonian literary language. The wide network of schools, from the elementary to the university; one daily and several weekly newspapers; numerous magazines, popular, literary and specialized; several publishing houses; a radio station; administration in Macedonian—all these help the Macedonian literary language to grow and penetrate the life of the Macedonian people.

An Imperialistic Interlude

IN the spring of 1875, in the rocky South Slav province of Herzegovina northwest from Macedonia, the Turkish tax collectors went from house to house as usual, demanding the *harač* head tax despite the complete failure of the crops. On July 1, the inhabitants of the town of Nevesinje, on a high plateau not far from the Herzegovinian capital of Mostar, took to arms. Other villages joined them, and soon a serious rebellion spread into Bosnia and led to a war between Serbia and Turkey.

The following year another uprising flared up under Dimitrije Pop-Georgiev Berovski in the Macedonian mountain area of Maleševo, but it was soon suppressed. Vassal Serbia, with independent Montenegro, persisted in the war on Turkey in support of their racial brothers in Bosnia and Herzegovina. The Serbs had adopted a too ambitious invasion plan and after a few initial successes were thoroughly defeated, but then a Russian ultimatum stopped the Turkish advance. Little Montenegro gave a much better account of itself, and when the Montenegrins signed the truce they were well inside enemy territory.

In the same year of 1876 a large-scale insurrection broke out in Bulgaria. Directed by Bulgarian leaders from abroad through underground channels and headed by Christo Boteff, a temperamental poet educated in Russia, the uprising was badly organized. The Turks soon crushed it, but then their irregulars, the dreaded *bashibozuks,* swooped down upon a number of villages in the Rhodope mountains and put them to fire and sword, massacring some 15,000 men, women and children. When the correspondent of the London *Daily News* revealed the deed, horrified voices were raised all over Western Europe. Victor Hugo protested eloquently, and a wave of indignation swept the press. Even in pro-Turkish Britain, William Ewart Gladstone left his theological studies to write his famous pamphlet on *The Bulgarian Atrocities* which sold in the tens of thousands. The official Turkish reply to diplomatic inquiries was that irresponsible Bulgarian *hayduk* bands had had a dispute which ended in mutual extermination.

Then Russia boldly intervened (1877). Her armies, after stubborn Turkish resistance and a heroic defense of Plevna, crossed the Balkan passes, entered Adrianople and appeared on the shores of the Sea of Marmora in plain view of Istanbul. Frightened, the Turks signed at San Stefano a treaty which made sweeping changes in the Balkans. Rumania was declared independent and Bosnia autonomous; vassal

116

Serbia and independent Montenegro were enlarged; and an enormous independent Bulgaria was created, embracing entire Macedonia, some territories inhabited by Serbians and Albanians, and parts of Thrace, altogether covering almost one-half of the Balkan peninsula.

When the terms of the San Stefano treaty became known, Britain made it plain that she would go to war if Russia took Istanbul. The British and the Austrians quickly saw that the treaty meant the end of Turkish rule in the Balkans and the establishment of Russian control of the peninsula through a subservient oversized Bulgaria. Disraeli railed at the Russians and said that they had created a Greater Bulgaria uninhabited by Bulgars. British dissatisfaction with the Treaty of San Stefano was also pressed by the Liberals, who at the time of the "Bulgarian atrocities" had defended the Bulgarian cause. Their leader, Gladstone, declared that many countries had been given to Bulgaria. He thought that the European portions of the Ottoman Empire should be divided equitably among the Christian populations of the Balkans according to the principle "the Balkans for the Balkan peoples." This stand he repeated in 1897 when he proposed the solution of the Macedonian question within a Balkan federation, under the slogan of "Macedonia for the Macedonians."

Serbia and Greece also protested against the Treaty of San Stefano, in particular against the expansion of Bulgaria and the occupation of Macedonia. The answer of the Russian Foreign Ministry to the Serbian protest was typical: Russian interests came first, then came the Bulgarian interests, then the Serbian, and there were occasions on which some Bulgarian interests were on a par with the Russian.

The British government in the person of Benjamin Disraeli rallied other European powers to prevent Russian expansion. An international congress was held in Berlin (1878), composed of the representatives of Great Britain, Russia, Austria-Hungary, Germany, Turkey, France and Italy. Otto von Bismarck of Germany, presiding, played the self-styled role of "the honest broker." None of the Balkan nations was invited. Under vigorous British leadership the Congress practically nullified the Russian victory and reemphasized the principle of "the territorial integrity of the Ottoman Empire" as the cornerstone of European peace. A Greater Bulgaria was ruled out. Only a small Bulgaria was permitted to be established between the Danube and the Balkan Mountain, and only as a vassal princedom paying an annual tribute to the Sultan. The adjoining Turkish province of Eastern Rumelia, also inhabited by Bulgars, was to have a Christian governor under the Porte (in 1885 Eastern Rumelia was united with vassal Bulgaria). The strategically invaluable province of Macedonia was handed back to the Sultan. Serbia and Montenegro received some increase in territory. Both Serbia and Rumania were declared independent, and both proclaimed themselves kingdoms. In the case of Montenegro, a declaration of independence was not necessary. Greece was promised an increase in territory and in 1881 she took Thessaly and a part of Epirus. As for Russia, she was permitted to retake Bessarabia from Rumania in exchange for Bulgarian Dobrudja; in Asia Minor she obtained a strip of territory in Armenia with the towns of Kars and Batum.

These were the gains for three Western great powers: Austria-Hungary obtained the right to occupy and administer Bosnia and Herzegovina in the Sultan's name; Great Britain took the Turkish island of Cyprus in return for a promise of aid in the case of another Russian attack; France was authorized to establish a protectorate over the Turkish province of Tunis.

Actually, the Congress did not accomplish anything but an armed truce. Once more the Western chancelleries had tried to divert the ineluctable course of events in the Balkans: the end of the Turkish rule and complete liberation of the native peoples. And to safeguard the European peace they checked the expansion of one power with the expansion of others.

A few months after the Congress of Berlin, another large and futile rebellion flared up in the Kresna region of Macedonia under the leadership of Berovski and Vojvoda Stojan. The rebels took thirty-five villages and the town of Bansko, resisted for six months, and were finally subdued. It was all in vain.

The Congress of Berlin had two fateful consequences: first, the alliance of Germany and Austria-Hungary, and the German push toward the east—*Drang nach Osten*; second, the rapprochement among France, Russia and England. The first alliance was concluded almost immediately, in 1879. Italy joined the Central Powers (in 1882) but switched to the other side in 1915. In 1891 Russia and France signed their own alliance. In 1904 the *Entente cordiale* was established between Great Britain and France, which in 1908 was extended to Russia. In the same year Austria-Hungary annexed Bosnia-Herzegovina under virulent protests from Serbian public opinion, and on the same day Bulgaria proclaimed itself an independent kingdom. The stage was set for the big accounting of 1914–18.

Ever since 1877, Russia, tsarist or communist, has favored Bulgaria, monarchist or communist, as her base in the Balkans and has on occasion looked benevolently on its Macedonian propaganda. The relationship was described long ago by the communists themselves. Karl Marx wrote in the *New York Tribune* of April 21, 1853, that in any country liberated by the Russians a strong anti-Russian movement would follow immediately. True enough, in the small Bulgaria liberated by the Russians in 1878, resistance against the "great liberator" soon took place and a political struggle for independence from Russia began. Lenin himself, in his émigré newspaper *Iskra* (the Spark) of August 1, 1903, described the Bulgarian-Russian relations of the time as follows: "Today Bulgaria looks like a Russian province ... the Prince crawls before the Russian Tsar ... Bulgaria is full of Russian spies who boss the police as if they were in their own country, spy on everything and everybody, withhold the mail. ..."

Macedonian Revolutionaries

HOW did the Macedonians live during the struggle for nationhood? At the turn of the century, in the district of Skopje, out of 150 villages only 70 had their own land. In the whole of Macedonia there were 180,000 peasant households, of which 126,000, or 70 percent, were tenant farmers without their own land. The home of a Macedonian consisted of four walls, of stone or straw, with a few rags on the earthen floor to serve as blankets. He ate mostly bread of rye, barley or oats. It was difficult to find a home with butter, milk and eggs.

Such was the population into which in the 1880s, after the Congress of Berlin, Serbia, too, began to send ever more teachers, priests and books, claiming that the Macedonians were Serbs speaking a Serbian dialect. With the various kinds of propaganda emanating from neighboring countries, there was a danger of thoroughly splitting the Macedonian people into pro-Bulgars, pro-Serbs and pro-Greeks, and also of undermining Macedonian unity against the common enemy, the Turks. This is what the confused situation looked like around the year 1886: the Greeks controlled 846 elementary and high schools in Macedonia, the Bulgars 223, and the Serbs 41, not to mention the Catholic convent schools. There were also Macedonian church-school communes dating back to 1835, firmly resisting the encroachment of the Bulgarian Exarchy and forming the very embryo of the eventual Macedonian republic. The Bulgars, the Greeks and the Serbs fought at first for the control of the Macedonian schools through their churches. Later they fought for the political control of the Macedonians through armed guerrilla bands—Bulgarian and Serbian *komitas* and the Greek *andartes*. Yet it was in the period after the Congress of Berlin that a growing number of Macedonian intellectuals and townspeople began to call themselves "Macedonians," feeling that they were different from both Bulgars and Serbs.

ON October 23, 1893, in the rooms of the Salonika bookseller Ivan Nikolov, a secret meeting of six people was held at the initiative of the Macedonian revolutionary Damjan Gruev. Present were Ivan Nikolov; Damjan Gruev, a schoolteacher; Dr. Hristo Tatarčev, a physician; Peter Arsov; Anton Dimitrov; and Hristo Batandžiev. The group constituted itself as the Internal Macedonian Revolutionary Organization or IMRO, as yet without written rules but setting itself the task of attracting new associates. The first congress was held in the beginning of 1894. It was then decided that 1. the organization would be secret and revolutionary; 2. the territory of activity would encompass Macedonia only; 3. members could be persons born or living in Macedonia regardless of religion or nationality; 4. the political aim was autonomy for Macedonia; 5. the organization should be independent from the neighboring states of Bulgaria, Serbia and Greece. After the adoption of the constitution, the first Central Committee was set up. Dr. Hristo Tatarčev was elected its president, and Damjan Gruev, its secretary and treasurer.

This was the beginning of a powerful revolutionary and later terrorist organization, which did not cease its activities until the Second World War. The IMRO is a most difficult subject to write about. Not only because a good deal has never been recorded but because the rare surviving members will not talk and many have shifted their loyalties or have maintained simultaneously triple loyalties. Taško Naumovski and Gligor Nikolov, for instance, were professional informers for both Bulgaria and Serbia. Boris Sarafov, a Bulgar, had contacts with everybody, including the Austro-Hungarians and the British, and was mowed down by a Macedonian bullet. T. Karajovov asked Austria-Hungary for a protectorate over Macedonia in exchange for a union with the Church of Rome or submission to the Serbian Patriarch in the Habsburg Empire.

A special place in the national liberation movement of Macedonia belongs to Goce Delčev, who is the hero of many folk ballads. He was born in 1872 in Kukuš (in present-day Greek Macedonia). The entire family of four brothers, four sisters and the parents was of revolutionary inclination and took an active part in the struggle against the Turks. One of Goce's brothers fell in a skirmish with the Turks. In his youth, Delčev attended the Salonika high school of St. Cyril and Methodius. There the fashionable word was "revolution," and little "circles" were founded, determined to "fight against tyranny." Many pupils decided it would be a good idea to get some military training. In 1891 Delčev with a few schoolmates entered the military academy in Sofia. There were many young Macedonian émigrés in Sofia. One of them, carpenter Vasil Glavinov from Veles, in 1893 founded the first Macedonian socialist group. One of the members was Nikola Karev, later prominent in the great Ilenden uprising. They all decided to join the IMRO. But Goce Delčev was in 1894 expelled from the military academy for his socialist ideas.

At first the regional groups of which the IMRO consisted acted independently of one another. This changed with the return of Delčev to Macedonia. In the fall of 1894 he found himself a teacher in a village near Štip, where he met Damjan Gruev. Becoming acquainted with the work of the IMRO, he immediately realized its shortcomings. On his initiative, the Second Congress of the organization was held in Salonika in 1896. Goce Delčev and Gjorče Petrov were assigned to work out a new constitution, and Delčev was elected a member of the Central Committee. The new statute extended the area of the IMRO's activities. The first sentence of the constitution read that a member of IMRO could be any person born or living in the territory of European Turkey, regardless of religion or nationality. According to article one of the new constitution the objective of IMRO was to "assemble all the dissatisfied elements in Macedonia and the Adrianople region, regardless of nationality or religion, in order to win through revolution full autonomy for both regions." To accomplish this, the organization vowed "to fight against chauvinist propaganda and nationalistic disputes which split and weaken the forces of the Organization in their struggle against the chief and common enemy."

Macedonia was divided into seven revolutionary regions, and these into districts and communes. Within half a dozen years the IMRO built a dense network of committees in towns and villages. The highest organ of the IMRO was the Congress, which elected a Central Committee of three to six members. The headquarters of the Central Committee were in Salonika. The organization also had representatives in Athens, Sofia and Istanbul. It had its own administration, its secret code, regular secret mail service, and couriers. Each district had one to three armed units which clandestinely roamed the mountains and the villages. In the towns the organization maintained terrorist groups for swift action. According to a statement of T. Karajovov, head of the IMRO, made to Baron Giesl, Austro-Hungarian military attaché in Istanbul, the total strength of these armed bands at no time before the Ilinden uprising of 1903 exceeded 4,000. The IMRO also had its own courts, which often at no cost settled civil law cases among the natives, leaving the Turkish courts without work. Strangely the legitimate Turkish order and the revolutionary order existed antagonistically side by side, with the one taking over when the other declined. For instance, the Central Committee would order the whitewashing of houses—"We have passed through the region of . . . and the houses look like pigsties." It regulated various customs, such as weddings, warning that too much money was being squandered. The IMRO also had its revolutionary tribunals, which sometimes passed death sentences on Turks and traitors. Finally, the IMRO had its underground press. *Na Oružje* (To Arms) was published in Bitola in 1895. Gruev issued *Vostanik* (The Insurgent) in Salonika at the same time. The Skopje organization published *Osvoboždenije* (Liberation) in 1902, while the Serres *Sloboda ili Smrt* (Liberty or Death) appeared in 1903.

The IMRO soon split into two factions. One, with Goce Delčev, Gjorče Petrov, Pere Tošev, Jane Sandanski and others stood for the independence of the Macedonian liberation movement from the governments of the neighboring countries and against the incorporation of Macedonia into Bulgaria or any other Balkan country. The other faction advocated the Greater Bulgaria idea and regarded the liberation movement of Macedonia merely as a step toward unification with Bulgaria. In 1895, in Sofia and in cooperation with Prince Ferdinand's court, this group created the so-called Supreme Committee. The followers of this Committee were named "Supremists," in contrast to the followers of the Salonika Central Committee, who were called "Centralists." Soon the "Supremists" seized the leadership of the Internal Macedonian Revolutionary Organization. When in 1901 the members of the Central Committee were either arrested or absent, they managed to push through as the new president of the Central Committee their man Ivan Garvanov, a high school teacher in Salonika and a Bulgar. Incidentally, there were no Serbs in the IMRO, only Macedonians and Bulgars.

The new Central Committee declared itself in favor of an early uprising, this in spite of the unpreparedness in many districts which doomed it to defeat. Garvanov and his supporters sent letters to individual members of the district committees inviting them to a general congress in Salonika on January 14, 1903. The agenda was an uprising in the spring of the same year. Despite the firm opposition of the Serres and Skopje revolutionary delegations, the congress made a decision in favor of the uprising. It also decided that the uprising should not be general but Partisan, meaning that it should be conducted only by the small armed units of the organization, in hit-and-run guerrilla fashion at a number of points simultaneously, avoiding a mass confrontation and quick defeat by the superior Turkish forces. The authors of the decision believed that a prolonged guerrilla war would prompt the European governments to intervene and force Turkey to grant autonomy to Macedonia.

When they were notified of the decision, Goce Delčev, Gjorče

Petrov, Pere Tošev and Jane Sandanski pointed to the insufficient preparedness of the Macedonian people for an action of such magnitude. However, Dr. H. Tatarčev and others from abroad approved of the uprising and settled their differences with the Supreme Committee. Unable to halt the revolutionary tide among the IMRO leadership, Goce Delčev tried desperately to bring about a postponement of the uprising. On his way to the congress, he was trapped with sixty to seventy armed men in the village of Banica, near Serres in eastern Macedonia, by half a battalion of Turkish troops. The battle lasted one day, from four P.M. on May 4, 1903, till the evening of the following day. The rebels finally escaped, leaving twelve dead, among them Goce Delčev. The Turks, having burned the village of Banica to the ground, severed Delčev's head and sent it to the authorities in Salonika. The headless body lies in a stone sarcophagus under the belfry in the churchyard of the half-underground church of Sv. Spas (Holy Saviour) in Skopje.

TWO terrorist episodes preceded the great Ilinden uprising of August 1903.

Miss Helen Stone, an American Protestant missionary from Boston, came on a visit to Razlog, a village in present-day Bulgarian Macedonia, in the summer of 1901. With her was her pregnant companion Cilka. Jane Sandanski, who had already planned to kidnap another American Protestant missionary, made quick preparations and on August 21, on the road from Bansko to Gornja Djumaja, he captured the two American women for ransom. This was the IMRO's idea of bringing the plight of Macedonia and its struggle for freedom to the attention of the Western world. The affair made world press headlines. The Russian envoy in Sofia, who later was the Tsar's last ambassador to Washington, took part in the ransom negotiations. On January 18, 1902, in the dead of winter, the American delegation, headed by Dr. House, arrived in Bansko with 14,000 Turkish gold pounds, the equivalent of the requested $70,000, securely locked in coffers and escorted by two hundred and fifty Turkish cavalrymen. This was the sum the Turkish government paid to the IMRO for the American captives. Miss Stone and her woman companion with the newborn baby were released. American public opinion became aware of Macedonia as much as it did of China after the kidnapings of its Protestant missionaries by Chinese bandits. Miss Stone became a convert to the Macedonian cause and lectured in its favor. She died after the First World War.

AT the turn of the century there lived in Salonika ten Macedonian students, sons of well-to-do families; they were all imbued with the revolutionary spirit. The leader was a tall, dark, slender young man by the name of Jordan Pop-Jordanov, nicknamed Orceto. Toward the end of 1898, a Macedonian student from Geneva, by the name of Svetoslav Medržanov, arrived in Salonika and made contact with the revolutionary youths. He was in touch with the Russian Social Revolutionaries and distributed anarchistic literature among the Salonika youngsters. Anarchism and nihilism were very much in vogue then. In 1892 alone there were more than a thousand bombs set off in Europe, and in America almost five hundred.

Merdžanov went to Sofia and obtained from Boris Sarafov money for an attempt at the assassination of the Sultan. He let the Salonika youths know that he would give them a share of it if they, too, would do something big in Salonika. It was then that the students conceived the idea of dynamiting the branch of the Ottoman Bank and other objectives in Salonika. Sarafov himself, who had secured ample funds from mysterious British sources, eventually sent the youths 2,000 dollars. He also secured some dynamite in Belgium and managed to pass 220 pounds of it through the Turkish customs in Salonika as copper sulphate stones to be used against vine phylloxers. What with waiting for the money and the dynamite, and digging a tunnel under the Ottoman Bank, it took the dynamiters nearly five years to stage the four days of well planned and executed bombings.

Goce Delčev, who exerted great influence on the Salonika students, asked them to postpone their plan. This was at the time of the IMRO congress which decided on an uprising in Macedonia, and Delčev, who had quantities of guns and ammunition coming in from Bulgaria, was afraid the Turks might take extreme measures after the bombings. Damjan Gruev also asked them to halt their plan. It was all in vain. The students had decided not only to go ahead but to die in the process.

On April 28, 1903, the French liner *Guadalquiver* sailed into the port of Salonika on its way to Istanbul. The students chose this ship because they thought France might persuade Russia to back Macedonia's case. On that spring morning Pavel Šatev walked on board the *Guadalquiver* under the name of Georgi Manasev as a first-class passenger. The policeman investigated the contents of the suitcase and passed it, but had he lifted it he would have found it too heavy to contain shirts and the like. Into the suitcase were sewn 24 pounds of the Belgian dynamite. Šatev went to his cabin and as he explained much later to Stoyan Christowe, an American writer of Macedonian origin who wrote extensively on the Salonika dynamiters, "... I ignited the fuse with my cigarette and ran. The noise was terrific. It tore a hole like half a window through the side of the boat. Soon the engine room caught fire. In five minutes the whole boat began to burn." In the evening, with the *Guadalquiver* still aflame, the Istanbul express ran across a dynamite charge on a small bridge at the outskirts of Salonika.

On the second day Orceto took up a position in the cellar of a house opposite the Ottoman Bank in Salonika to await the explosion. The signal was to be the extinction of all the lights in the town, and the lights were to be extinguished by exploding the gas main just outside the city. One of the students did this at eight o'clock in the evening. Orceto lit the long fuse connected with the dynamite under the Ottoman Bank, then rushed to the second floor of the bank building to warn the director and his family that in five minutes the bank would blow up. A tremendous explosion followed.

Eighteen-year-old Milan Arsov was at the "Casino Alhambra," where in the darkness he put a bomb on a table and lit the fuse. Bombs began to explode in other parts of the city, in theaters, cafés, hotels, on the streets. Troops ran through the town believing the *komitadjie* had invaded it. Vladimir Pingov set fire with a bomb to the Boškov Inn. He threw another at the approaching soldiers and was shot dead. Dimitar Mečev and Ilja Tručkov threw all their bombs into cafés or into the streets. At their home they had some more and, having tossed the last ones through the window, they stood up against the window to receive a hail of bullets from the soldiers below.

On the third day several additional bombs exploded; they were Orceto's. When he had disposed of his last one, he too stood up against the window and was shot. On this day the Turks started a massacre of the local Slavs. Some three hundred corpses were gathered by the city's sanitation department.

By this time foreign correspondents had begun to arrive in Salonika, among them H. H. Munro of the London *Morning Post*, who later became a famed writer under the pseudonym of Saki. He reached Salonika by train from Skopje in the evening of April 30 and sent the following dispatch to his newspaper:

"... Before the train, slightly overdue, drew into the dark and apparently deserted terminal station the news was passed along by obviously demoralized officials that the town was in a state of siege, and that no one would be allowed to leave the station that night.

"In the hope of slipping out by a side exit we therefore picked up our valises and made for an apparent outlet some five hundred yards distant.... As a slight precaution against being mistaken for prowling

Komitadjis we turned down the collars of our overcoats so as to display the white collar. . . .

"About four hundred yards of the distance had been covered when a frantic challenge in Turkish brought us to a standstill. . . . As five triggers had clicked . . . we dropped our valises and up-handed. . . .

"At last two lowered their rifles, and after stalking round us with elaborate caution managed to secure our hands with a rope or sash-cord. . . . The statement that I was *Inglesi effendi* and the demand for our Consuls allayed their suspicions to a certain extent, but nothing would induce them to pick up my valise until the light of day. . . .

"Arrived at the railway waiting-room . . . the terrified officials flocked to release us . . . and two loud explosions in the distance made us feel that we had gained our security none too soon. . . .

"On my asking the members of the picquet why they had not fired, they answered that they had only hesitated on seeing our collars. . . ."

On the fourth and last day, two more Salonika dynamiters met with death. They were Konstantin Kirkov and Trajkov Cvetkov. Kirkov put on a white tie and a silk top hat, and complete with cane and bombs took a stroll toward the telegraph office. The sentry stopped him. Kirkov stepped back, pulled out a bomb, but before he could ignite it, the soldier stuck his bayonet into his chest.

Cvetkov was waiting near the governor's villa to throw a bomb or two into his carriage when he was on his way to his office. The guards became suspicious and wanted to search him. Cvetkov ran back a few steps, ignited a bomb and sat on it until it exploded.

Four of the ten Salonika dynamiters survived by choice or because they were arrested. They were Pavel Šatev, Georgi Bogdanov, Marko Bošnakov and Milan Arsov. They were tried by a special military tribunal and sentenced to death. Sultan Abdul Hamid commuted the sentence to life imprisonment. After three years in the Salonika prison, they were shipped to the Sahara in the province of Tripoli for life. Bošnakov and Arsov soon died. In 1908, after the Young Turk revolution, a general amnesty was proclaimed for political prisoners. But Šatev and Bogdanov did not wish to leave the bodies of their comrades in the sands of the Sahara. One night they dug up the bodies which were in a state of decomposition. They pulled out their knives and cut off the heads. They smeared them with iodine and put them in sealed tin cans. These they carried to Macedonia and delivered to the parents of the dead men. Bogdanov died later. Pavel Šatev survived the Second World War, during which he organized a number of terroristic actions. He became Minister of Justice in the new People's

Republic of Macedonia. But in 1948 he sided with Stalin against Tito, was forced into retirement and died in 1952 at the age of 101.

Three months after the Salonika bombings, the Ilinden uprising flared up in Macedonia and kept the Turkish army busy for almost three months.

The St. Elijah's Day Uprising and After

ON August 2, 1903, the IMRO called a large-scale and ill-fated uprising in Macedonia, known as the "Ilinden (St. Elijah's Day) Uprising." In the liberated mountain town of Kruševo the rebels proclaimed a Socialist Republic, which was to last ten days. The proclamation, addressed to all the Balkan nationalities within Turkey, demanded autonomy for each. This was the first projected Balkan federation; however, the plans were somewhat naive, even for their time.

THE signal for the uprising was given on the eve of August 2. At once the telegraph lines were cut, railroad tracks and bridges on the main roads were destroyed, the towers and the estates of the Beys were burned, and in some villages and towns the surprised garrisons were attacked. At dawn the next day women and children began to leave their villages for the mountains, carrying with them food for the rebels. The peasants set up bakeries in the forests, workshops for repairing arms, and first aid centers. The uprising had been prepared in such secrecy that not one of the proclamations distributed by the couriers fell into the hands of the Turkish authorities. The insurgents sometimes marched under unfurled banners, and the uprising was often announced from the church pulpits, the flags being consecrated by the priests. The emblem of the scythe and the ax was put on the stamps and seals of the rebel General Staff; the design derived from the fact that the peasants often surged into battle with primitive arms like scythes, axes, cleavers, cudgels.

In the regions of Salonika and Skopje the rebellion was rather sporadic, but in the Bitola region it took on a mass character. The rebel force of 26,000 inflicted defeat after defeat upon the surprised Turks, who had only 15,000 soldiers in this region, scattered in small garrisons. The uprising encompassed an area of some 4,000 square miles, with a population of 300,000. The rebels in the first onslaught liberated many villages and a number of towns, such as Kruševo, Kičevo, Neveska, Krisura, Smilevo.

As weeks passed and the Turkish commander, Omer Ruzhdi Pasha, failed to subdue the rebellion, Nazar Pasha was appointed in his place.

He concentrated a large number of *askers* (regular troops), accompanied by the irregular *bashibozuks,* in the Bitola region and ordered scorched earth warfare—burning down villages and massacring the population. According to the report of the Austro-Hungarian consul general in Bitola, August Kral, to his minister, Agenor von Goluchowsky, the Turkish reprisal for one burned estate was the burning of two to three Christian villages. British correspondent R. Wyon, in a letter to the London *Daily Mail,* wrote that burnings, plunderings, massacres occurred every day, that all districts were devastated and that in the countryside one could see nothing but desolate fields and destroyed villages. In a memoire, the IMRO claimed that eighteen towns and 201 villages, including nearly 10,000 houses, had been set afire, that more than 70,000 people were left homeless, that almost 4,000 persons, including children, had been massacred, while 30,000 had fled across the frontiers.

Under such circumstances, it is amazing that 26,000 Ilinden insurgents could resist the fully equipped modern Turkish army of 350,000 for nearly three months.

The Ilinden uprising would have been a senseless undertaking but for the historic significance of the Kruševo Republic, and the fact that the great powers were stirred to action, however ineffective.

ON the very first night of August 2–3, seven hundred and fifty rebels, of whom only three hundred and fifty were properly armed, took up their stations at the approaches to the town of Kruševo, 4,000 feet above sea level and overlooking the plain of Prilep. It had been agreed that when the first shot was fired, a group of insurgents hiding inside the city would start ringing all the church bells. The battle was brief and the small Turkish garrison fled. On August 4 the rebel General Staff, at whose head were Damjan Gruev and Boris Sarafov, entered the town and commandant Nikola Karev made a speech proclaiming the Kruševo Republic.

Nikola Karev was elected president of the new minuscule republic. He was an enthusiastic socialist, and over the city of Kruševo now fluttered a red flag instead of the black-and-white flag with skull and crossbones which was the symbol of the uprising. Kruševo at the time had 15,000 inhabitants—Macedonians, Tsintsars and Albanians. Nikola Karev called a council of sixty prominent citizens, in which each nationality was represented by twenty men. From these he selected six men as the Executive Council, again two from each nationality. The new Council organized bakeries, a hospital for the wounded, and workshops for making clothes and footwear for the rebels.

The Council also published a unique document, known as the Manifesto of the Kruševo Republic. It addressed itself to all the Balkan nationalities: "...We have risen for our rights and freedom, against tyranny and serfdom, against those who suck our blood and exploit our labor. We sympathize with you as our brothers. We realize that you are slaves as we are. Slaves of the emperor and his feudalists, slaves of the rich and mighty, who brought us into the situation where we had to start a fight for our rights and freedom. We call on you to join us in our fight. Moslem brothers! Join us, let us go together against our and your enemies, under the banner of an autonomous Macedonia, so that we can destroy the basis of serfdom and liberate ourselves from pain and suffering. Join us, so we can live in peace and quiet, our Moslem brothers! We understand that you think that the empire is your country and that you are not slaves. You are mistaken, you will soon see...."

The Kruševo Republic was the first socialist republic in the Balkans; it was extinguished after a split second of life.

On August 11, along the steep highway from Prilep moved a large Turkish army. On the following day, the 15,000 infantry, cavalry and artillery of Bakhtiar Pasha, supported by the *bashibozuk* irregulars, another regular column from the south and still another from the west, set out to encircle the free territory of Kruševo. The rebel command wished to withdraw its troops so that the population would not suffer, but one of the commanders, Pitu Gule, dissented, saying, "If there is no liberty, there is death," and refused to abandon his position at the Bear's Rock. Others sided with Pitu Gule, and a hopeless life-and-death struggle followed. Many insurgents, led by experienced commanders, managed to break through the Turkish ring. Among them was Nikola Karev, who escaped to Serbia. But many fell defending the first republic of Macedonia, and the place of honor goes to Pitu Gule and his men.

The Bear's Rock is the highest spot around Kruševo—4,300 feet above sea level. Almost perpendicularly above the Prilep plain, it offers a bird's-eye view of the valley; one can observe from it the Šar mountain in the north and the Pelister peak in the south of Macedonia. There is plenty of deer and bear in the surrounding densely wooded hill country, and lavender flowers bloom in the grass. Great silence reigns here, and of a summer noon there is only the faint rustle of a light breeze. A slab on a heap of stones bears the inscription: "On This Spot on August 12, 1903, Pitu Gule and 40 Rebels Heroically Fought and Fell Defending the Kruševo People's Republic." The monument stands on the edge of the summit plateau. Behind it lies an abyss of woods and rocks. From this last stand there was literally nowhere to retreat. One trench is still visible; in it the cornered rebels defended themselves before gradually retreating toward the abyss, fighting in the end with stones and bare fists.

On August 13 white flags appeared atop the houses in Kruševo. Kruševo had capitulated and the ten days of the Republic were over. The Turks now set fire to everything that would burn.

IN the 1960s one could still visit the Kruševo "cannoneer"—the man who manufactured the cherry-tree cannon for the rebels in the Kruševo battle of 1903. He lived on a very steep street almost at the top of the hill town and could be reached only through winding, narrow, cobble-stoned alleys. He had neatly combed white hair, a long face and a long nose. He incessantly smoked rolled cigarettes and finished a glass of plum brandy while talking. He was a tall, strong man, who had never been sick. He was 86 in 1961. Of mixed Albanian-Macedonian-Vlach blood, Todor Borijar went to Sofia and Belgrade in his youth. He had also been fighting with the *komitadjis*, and he realistically described some of the hand-to-hand combat, such as throttling with bare hands. During the Second World War he joined the Partisans and founded a Partisan organization in Kruševo. By trade he used to be a gunsmith, manufacturing bullets, molds for rifles and the like, but he also made ploughs, stoves, kitchen ranges, and so on.

In the days of the Kruševo Republic, Borijar, his brother and his father thought it might be a good idea to strengthen the spirit of the people by firing cannon. They ordered the peasants to cut and bring in a few cherry-tree trunks, drilled holes in them, and called on the town's blacksmiths to forge the hoops and to collect ammunition. This consisted mainly of bullets and iron weights stuffed into the wooden cannon. On August 5 the first cannon was fired from a hill at the edge of the town. Loaded with gunpowder, it exploded. The mishap was hidden from the simple folk who shouted all over the town, "We will beat the Turks! We have fired our cannon!" The peasants heard it in the marketplace and spread the news through their villages that artillery had been brought to Kruševo. On August 7 another cannon was finished—altogether six cannon were made. Four were fired, and all four exploded with the first shot. Firing was done with a fuse, and everybody had to stand a distance away. The Turks suffered no damage. The two unused wooden cannon they found were later exhibited in Bitola and Istanbul as war trophies.

Cannoneer Todor Borijar also fought in the Kruševo battle, in the end defending his own street. After an all-night battle his father and brother were captured, while he himself went into brief hiding before giving himself up. At his trial he defended himself by saying that he had been forced to make the cannon. Actually he bought himself out with bribes and was released together with some sixty others from his group. The group tried before him had been sentenced to hard labor on the island of Rhodes and in Asia Minor.

Very few people live to see their goals fulfilled. Todor Borijar has lived to see the day of the ultimate victory of his wooden cannon and of a visit by Marshal Tito.

THE Central Committee of the IMRO, through its foreign representatives, on August 10, 1903, delivered to the great powers its "Declaration" regarding the aims of the struggle of the Macedonian people. It said that numerous acts of violence had forced the Christians of Macedonia to resort to an armed uprising. The Declaration asked for a European intervention as the only means to stop the bloodshed. The IMRO suggested that a Christian governor, not connected with the Turkish government, be appointed for Macedonia by the great powers. It also recommended international control of the area, with the right to order sanctions. What the great powers later did was a moderate variation of these proposals.

Conservative newspapers in Great Britain, Germany and elsewhere defended the status quo in Turkey. The liberal press of Europe was at first for moderate reforms and later for a more energetic intervention of the powers in the affairs of Turkey. The social democratic press argued that the only solution was autonomy for Macedonia.

The liberal and socialist intelligentsia in the West responded to the Ilinden uprising by creating "Macedonian Committees," which propagated the Macedonian cause in the press and at meetings and collected money and supplies for the Macedonian people. Particularly well known were the London "Balkan Committee," the Macedonian committees in New York, Philadelphia and Boston, the Paris Comité de Macédoine and the Italian committee Pro Armenia e Macedonia. On October 25, 1903, a big international meeting was held in Paris, at which, among others, Jean Juarès spoke. Anatole France spoke at other meetings. A mass meeting was held in Milan, Italy. More than 200 meetings were held in Great Britain at which resolutions were passed demanding autonomy for Macedonia and a governor responsible to the great powers. Henry Braileford, secretary general of the combined British activities to aid Macedonia, on September 1, 1903, personally left for that country with money, food and clothing. Similar meetings with the purpose of organizing aid also took place in Switzerland, Bohemia, Poland, Russia. The Serbian and the Bulgarian parliaments voted aid for Macedonia, and the two governments supported the numerous Macedonian refugees.

AT the end of September 1903, Tsar Nicholas II visited Emperor Francis Joseph in Schönbrunn, Vienna. During that visit conversations were also held about the situation in the Balkans. They were continued in the small and picturesque Styrian town of Mürzteg and on October 2 led to an agreement on reforms in Macedonia. Basically, the reform program adopted the suggestions that the British Foreign Secretary, the Marquis of Lansdowne, had sent to the British ambassador in Vienna. The main points of the Mürzsteg reform program were: (1) The chief inspector of Macedonia, Halmi Pasha, was to be assisted by two special agents, one from Austria-Hungary and one from Russia; they would direct the Pasha's attention to the needs of the Christian population and to the ill-doings of the local authorities, supervise the execution of the reforms, and report to their governments; (2) a foreign general with foreign officers would be appointed for the gendarmerie; (3) administration and justice must be reformed, and Christians must be allowed in the civil service; (4) a mixed commission consisting of an equal number of Christians and Moslems should investigate all crimes committed during the recent disorders; (5) Turkey should pay indemnity to the Christian refugees and reconstruct the houses, churches and schools destroyed by the Turks; (6) irregular troops (*bashibozuk* and others) should be immediately disbanded.

Austria-Hungary recommended that the head of the Macedonian gendarmerie should be the Italian general Di Giorgis, a suggestion which at length was accepted by Istanbul. Under him were officers from Great Britain, France, Germany, Austria-Hungary, Italy and Russia. They tried to modernize the Turkish gendarmerie by, among other things, opening schools for the gendarmerie in Macedonia.

At first Turkey refused to accept the Mürzsteg reforms. But then Germany joined in the demand that the program be accepted. Finally, on November 24, 1903, the Turkish government accepted the Mürzsteg reform program in principle, reserving the right of negotiating the details. Indeed, Turkey resorted to endless debates about the details. Not until February 1904 was a compromise reached whereby the foreign agents could make inquiries in the presence of Turkish officials, receive complaints from the population, and insist on the execution of the reforms, but they had no right to issue orders. This privilege was reserved for Hamil Pasha alone.

The Macedonians themselves were of not much help. In December 1903 the IMRO denounced the Mürzsteg reform program as being insignificant. The organization's congress at Rila, in 1905, also rejected the program, on the curious ground that it consolidated the Turkish rule by trying to make it more tolerable.

THE catastrophe that befell the Macedonian people through the premature Ilinden uprising led to a new crisis within the IMRO. Gradually the two old antagonistic factions reappeared under the new names of leftist and rightist. The left or the old centralist faction, operating from Macedonia and standing for Macedonian autonomy, was headed by the old IMRO veterans Jane Sandanski, Gjorče Petrov, Pere Tošev and Dimo Hadži-Dimov; the right wing of the "Supremists," operating from Sofia and advocating incorporation of Macedonia into Bulgaria, was led by Hristo Matov, Dr. Hristo Tatarčev, Ivan Garvanov and Boris Sarafov. Damjan Gruev stood somewhere in the middle. From now on the struggle between the two factions often became bloody, resulting in the deaths of not a few Macedonian revolutionaries. For instance, at the end of 1907 the "Supremists" prepared for the assassination of Jane Sandanski and some other leaders of the left wing, whereupon the leftist committee sentenced the instigators, Ivan Garvanov and Boris Sarafov, to death. The sentence was carried out by Todor Panica who shot the two to death just as they were leaving Bulgarian Prince Ferdinand's palace. This terrorist war weakened both organizations and threw the Macedonians into confusion.

Before the Ilinden uprising, it was mainly "Supremist" bands from Bulgaria who roamed through Macedonia. The Greek and the Serbian governments still used cultural-educational methods in gaining adherents. But immediately after the Ilinden uprising both governments began to send their own armed bands into Macedonia. Soon the common guerrilla war against Turkey degenerated into a gangster-type free-for-all among the various bands. This gave the Balkans a bad name and contributed to the Western picture of a Balkanite as a man with a bomb in one hand, a pistol in the other and a knife between his teeth.

According to the Austrian consular reports, a committee was formed in Athens to send armed *andarte* units to Macedonia and direct the Greek activities. The chief organizer of the Greek armed bands in Macedonia at the time (1904) was one Joannis Dragumis, aided by the Kastoria Bishop Karavangelis. Greek bands especially well known were those under "Tole Pasha" and Dedo Kole. According to the Austrian documents, bad blood led to massacres, in which the *andartes* did not spare women and children. Nor did they refrain from open collaboration with the Turks against the Macedonian rebels. Another Greek bishop of Kastoria, Germanos, was renowned for denouncing

Macedonian and Bulgarian insurgents to the Turks. The truth is that the Greeks, too, were victims of the IMRO assaults. In today's Greek Macedonia one can every once in a while see a tombstone where a Greek "captain" had been slain by the "Bulgarian bandits."

Soon after Ilinden, the Serbs, too, appeared in Macedonia with their *komitas* or *četniks*. The first Serbian bands were sent to Macedonia in the beginning of 1904. In 1905 the leadership was centralized in the "Serbian Defense," which took over the systematic dispatching of armed *četas* (companies) into Macedonia. The Glavni Odbor (Chief Committee) was in Belgrade, and a special committee resided in Vranje near the Turkish border. The Serbian government endeavored to promote Serbian influence in Macedonia through an armed struggle against both the Turks and the Bulgarian *komitadjis*. The famous Vojvoda Vuk, for one, who was killed by German bullets during the First World War, had been one of such *četniks* fighting the Bulgars as well as the Turks in Macedonia.

In short, all three governments, the Bulgarian, the Greek and the Serbian, through their bands of irregulars fighting the Turks and one another, were already struggling over the future division of Macedonia.

SUDDENLY, in 1908, the year when Austria-Hungary annexed Bosnia-Herzegovina and Bulgaria proclaimed her full independence from the Sultan, the news was flashed from Istanbul of the Turkish revolution. Sultan Abdul Hamid, the most debauched of them all, had been overthrown by the so-called Young Turks. The victors proclaimed his younger brother Sultan as Mohammed V. Since the new sovereign was a harmless imbecile, the Young Turks, or rather the Committee of Union and Progress, as the party organization of the Young Turks was called, became the undisputed masters of the nation.

The Young Turk movement had started as one of hostility to the fixed ways of the older Turkish generation, derisively called the Old Turks. The Young Turks believed that Turkey could be saved only through Europeanization. They converted many army officers, and in 1906 moved their headquarters from Paris to Salonika. Military uprisings began among the regiments in Macedonia and spread elsewhere, with the Young Turk officers everywhere demanding a constitution. Sultan Abdul Hamid, though it did not help him keep his throne, reimposed the dormant liberal Constitution of 1876 and summoned a parliament. It looked like Western democracy.

The strife ceased in Macedonia. Responsible newspapers in the West spoke of a democratic miracle, while Sir Edward Grey, the British Foreign Secretary, allowed himself to say that "the Macedonian question and others of a similar character will entirely disappear." As a matter of fact, the IMRO's left wing under Jane Sandanski did accept the Young Turks' invitation to cooperate on the basis of agrarian reform in Macedonia, regional self-government and introduction of the Macedonian language in the schools. It also ordered its armed units to descend from the mountains. It even took part in the Young Turks' meetings and celebrations. Finally, the IMRO's left wing decided to abandon its conspiratorial character and become a legal People's Federal Party.

But the Young Turks did not keep their promises. They kept postponing the agrarian reform and the giving of equal rights to all the nationalities in the empire. Soon the name of Macedonia and Macedonians was proscribed, and the name of one common nation, the Turkish, was to cover all the subjects of the empire. As soon as the Macedonians and the other oppressed groups discovered that this was the Young Turk interpretation of the revolution, they fell away from it, and disorders started again. As for the Mürzsteg reforms, they were completely blocked by the Young Turks, who opposed all foreign intervention.

Actually, the Young Turks, though proposing to rejuvenate the moribund empire, were a nationalist movement. The *rayah*, while retaining their religious freedom, were to obtain civil rights only on becoming Turks. The Young Turks, ironically called by a contemporary "the young men in a hurry," tried to denationalize the Balkan Christians and the Albanians in the hope of forging one "Ottoman nation." The results were rebellions and massacres in the Turkish possessions of the Balkans. The Albanians revolted first, and after having put them down several times, the Young Turks in 1912 had to yield and give them home rule.

Young Turk violence continued among other *rayah*. Serbia, Bulgaria, Greece and Montenegro appealed to the great powers to do something about it. As they got nowhere, they decided to take matters into their own hands. In 1912 they formed the Balkan League and made an agreement on the distribution of the Turkish territory in Europe. The war that followed was the result of the bankruptcy of European statesmanship in the Balkans.

THE Macedonian question was—and still is—part of the "Eastern Question." In the 12th and 13th points of his testament Peter the Great (1689–1725) had held that seeking control of the Bosphorus and the Dardanelles was the "historic mission" of Holy Russia. There was another power with a "mission" in the Balkans: since 1683 Austria had waged three offensive wars against Turkey. In the nineteenth century still another power, Great Britain, stepped into the affairs of Turkey, the highway to India. Thus the difficult business of disposing of Turkey and the small Balkan nations became tangled up with many conflicting imperialistic ambitions.

The irresistible Russian push toward the warm sea of the Mediterranean could be completed only by the destruction of European Turkey, and the moral justification of this policy was the liberation of the Balkan Christians. But the Western powers figured that in order to arrest this push Turkey should be preserved as a barrier and that the Balkan nations should not be liberated to become vassals of Russia. Thus power politics brought about the anomaly of autocratic Russia championing self-determination of nations, and democratic Britain supporting infidel oppression. There was only one Balkan nation whose independence Britain favored consistently—Greece, an excellent naval base.

As early as the 1820s, Tsar Nicholas I called the Ottoman Empire "The Sick Man of the Bosphorus." But when he formally proposed an "agreement on the funeral," the Western powers said no. They did not want the sick man to get well, but neither did they want him to die.

The slogans used in this imperialistic contest were "intervention for the Balkan Christians" and "the territorial integrity of the Ottoman empire." Each power tried to intervene for its own benefit. But whenever one of them was about to garner too much, the others invoked the principle of the territorial integrity of the Ottoman Empire. These unceasing conflicts were "justified" by the principle of "the balance of power."

Such were the circumstances under which the Balkan nations had to struggle for their independence. They could not avoid becoming pawns of the great powers, were often incited against one another, and regularly suffered foreign interference in their domestic affairs. But even without interference by the great powers the small Balkan nations intrigued among themselves and through their guerrilla bands fought one another, a situation which Turkey welcomed and which handicapped the West.

The World Wars

The Balkan Wars, the First World War and Yugoslavia

THINGS were coming to a head. In 1912 Serbia and Bulgaria made an agreement on the division of Turkish-owned Macedonia, the agreement to be arbitrated by the Russian Tsar; moreover, Bulgaria promised to support Serbia's demand for an exit to the Adriatic through acquisition of northern Albania.

On February 29, 1912, Serbia and Bulgaria signed a treaty of alliance and, on June 19, a military convention. Article 2 of the Convention said that if autonomy for Macedonia proved impossible, Serbia would recognize its southeastern part as Bulgarian, while the northwestern part, including Skopje, Kumanovo and Tetovo, would be subject to arbitration by the Russian Tsar.

On September 29, 1912, the four small Balkan states—Serbia, Montenegro, Bulgaria and Greece—submitted a collective note to the Turkish government, demanding the establishment of four autonomous regions— Macedonia, Old Serbia, Epirus and Albania—under the protection of the great powers, as provided for by Article 23 of the Treaty of Berlin of 1878, which had never been carried out. Turkey rejected the note, and tiny Montenegro declared war on October 9, followed by Serbia and Bulgaria on October 17 and by Greece on October 18.

Most competent observers in the West predicted an easy Ottoman victory. When the news dispatches of quick, smashing victories over the Turks reached the European capitals, everyone was taken aback. Within six weeks the Osmanli armies, but for the three besieged strongholds of Adrianople, Scutari and Janina, were literally wiped out and the Bulgars appeared before the fortified suburbs of Istanbul. The three fortified towns fell later, and on May 30, 1913, a treaty was signed in London by virtue of which Turkey lost all her European possessions except Istanbul.

Toward the end of November 1912, the Serbian army had occupied the Albanian coast of Alessio and Durazzo, but the European powers, urged on by Austria-Hungary and Italy, placed an interdict on the Serbian exit to the Adriatic. They agreed to create an independent Albania, to be headed by a foreign prince.

Blocked from the Adriatic, Serbia asked Bulgaria for a reapportionment of Macedonia. Tsar Ferdinand of Bulgaria not only would not listen but also made the mistake of attacking the Serbian and the Greek forces. Immediately Rumania and Turkey pounced on him, and the Second Balkan War was over in less than a month. The treaty of Bucharest left by far the largest part of Macedonia divided between Serbia and Greece. Rumania received a strip of Bulgarian Dobrudja, and Turkey regained Adrianople. Bulgaria received a part of Thrace and a tiny part of Macedonia with the town of Strumica.

In the First Balkan War, against the Turks, the left wing of the IMRO under Jane Sandanski also took part. At the time of the Bucharest conference, the population of Macedonia protested against the forcible tripartite division of its land. In the name of some 150,000 Macedonian refugees, a Macedonian delegation addressed itself via a telegram to the peace conferees and the envoys of foreign powers, requesting autonomy for the Macedonian people. The Bucharest peace conference ignored the proposition, and so did the European powers.

FOUR empires fell during or following the First World War: the Russian, the Habsburg, the German and the Ottoman. According to the Wilsonian principle of self-determination of nations, a number of independent small states was created in Central Europe and along the Baltic. In the Balkans, for the first time after settling in the peninsula thirteen centuries ago, the southern Slavs were joined together in their own independent state, the kingdom of Serbs, Croats and Slovenes, in 1931 renamed the Kingdom of Yugoslavia.

In 1915, before Ferdinand of Bulgaria joined Germany and Austria-Hungary, the Entente powers offered Bulgaria Serbian Macedonia east of the Vardar as the price for staying out of the war. But this bid was not high enough. In 1917, the Entente powers tried to make Bulgaria quit the war by renewing the 1915 offer. Bulgaria refused again. The result was that after the war Bulgaria not only did not get Serbian Macedonia but had, in addition to other minor territorial concessions, to yield the Macedonian town of Strumica to Yugoslavia.

Before the Second World War Yugoslavia was not a federal but a centralist state, run mainly by the Serbs under a Serbian dynasty. The Macedonians were not recognized as a nationality. The official language in Macedonia was Serbian, school instruction was in Serbian, all higher officials were Serbs, and the church was Serbian. The Macedonians were considered Serbs, and Macedonia was commonly called South Serbia. This state of affairs prevailed until the Second World War.

IN 1919, after winning a huge majority in the elections, Alexander Stamboliski, son of a peasant and leader of the Bulgarian Peasant Party, became premier of Bulgaria. During the early stages of the First World War, then being in opposition, he advocated Bulgarian neutrality. When Tsar Ferdinand in 1915 decided to join Germany and Austria-Hungary, Stamboliski in a dramatic audience told him, "If you do so, you will lose your throne!" For this a military court sentenced him to prison. Three years later Ferdinand had to flee the country, and Stamboliski came to power. He wanted good relations with Yugoslavia, and in 1923, at Niš, concluded an agreement with that country. This agreement provided for steps being taken to prevent IMRO raids from crossing into Yugoslavia. For 100 yards on each side of the frontier all trees and undergrowth were to be cleared, and suspected sympathizers of the *komitadjis* were to be banned from the frontier zones. Furthermore, the anti-Yugoslav Macedonian organizations in Bulgaria were to be banned. Stamboliski had revolutionaries arrested in the Petrič and Kustendil districts (Pirin Macedonia), the chief IMRO strongholds.

But Todor Aleksandrov and Alexander Protogerov, two redoubtable leaders of the IMRO terrorists, whom Stamboliski had also arrested, escaped abroad and joined a conspiracy with the upper bourgeoisie and the officers of the Military League under Colonel Volkov. During the night of June 9, 1923, a few garrisons in Sofia, followed by others in provincial cities, took over the government buildings and the public services. Stamboliski hurried into the country to organize peasant resistance, but the people were routed by artillery. Stamboliski was captured, tortured, and dismembered, and his remains were thrown on a dunghill. Twenty-five thousand peasants perished at the same time.

The Yugoslav opposition leaders in Belgrade insisted in the parliament that the anti-Stamboliski coup could and should have been prevented by Yugoslav intervention on the ground of Yugoslav security.

The Bulgarian Communist party also remained neutral during the overthrow and murder of Stamboliski. For this it was strongly criticized by Moscow, after the event. As it happened, the same IMRO and Military League helped the Bulgarian government suppress the Communist uprising when it came in September of the same year.

AFTER Stamboliski's death, the IMRO kept up intrusions by small terrorist bands into Yugoslav Macedonia, where it found considerable support because of forcible Serbianization. The IMRO became more and more a terrorist society. Its acts of violence were carried out for the purpose of keeping the world informed of the unrest in Macedonia. The Yugoslavs maintained the Yugoslav-Bulgarian boundary of more than 400 miles lined with barbed wire entanglements and rows of ditches. There were high towers and pillboxes between them. In truth, Bulgaria allowed the IMRO to administer Pirin Macedonia and engage in border warfare with Yugoslavia. To all practical purposes, the IMRO chief, Todor Aleksandrov, appropriated Pirin Macedonia from the Bulgarian government and therein established his own tiny Macedonian state, in which he collected taxes for the support of his organization. Aleksandrov favored Bulgarian annexation of Macedonia.

In addition there was the Federalist group, which genuinely aimed at creating an autonomous Macedonia within a South Slav federation. The Federalists thus represented the more truly "Macedonian" tradition of the earlier IMRO, in contrast to the "Supremist" trend of the Aleksandrov group. The leading members of the Federalists, who formed their own organization in 1921, were Philip Antanasov, Dimitar Vlahov and Dimo Hadži-Dimov. The latter two soon became Communists.

In 1924 came a startling development: a temporary reconciliation among the IMRO, the Federalists and the Communists, and the formation of a short-lived common Macedonian front, called the "Macedonian Revolutionary Organization." The IMRO issued a declaration on its "new orientation," which appeared in the first issue of Dimitar Vlahov's new Vienna publication, *Fédération Balkanique*, on July 15, 1924. Aleksandrov and Protogerov, however, apparently under pressure from home, suddenly repudiated their signatures. Vlahov split with the Federalists and founded a new "United IMRO," advocating an autonomous Macedonia within a Federation of Balkan Socialist Republics; this was in fact the Comintern policy of that period. The Central Committee of the Communist party of Yugoslavia forbade its organizations to support the United IMRO plan. This semi-Communist United IMRO never appeared to have a very large following and was formally dissolved in 1934.

IN the aftermath of the IMRO's Vienna adventure, a long internecine war started among the Bulgarian Macedonian revolutionaries, in which within a decade some 400 persons were assassinated. The first to fall was Todor Aleksandrov. He was murdered in the mountains of Pirin Macedonia on August 31, 1924, on the eve of IMRO's first postwar Congress. One version has it that Communists and/or Federalists did it in revenge for his repudiation of the Vienna Declaration; another, that Bulgarian army officers, fearful of Moscow's influence, collaborated with the chauvinist IMRO elements in the murder; yet another, put out four years later by Ivan Milhailov, that Protogerov was behind it; still another, that Mihailov himself was responsible.

At any rate, Aleksandrov's assassination gave the IMRO an opportunity to assassinate a number of Federalists and Communists. Dimo Hadži-Dimov, Alexander Vasilev, Philip Atanasov, Petar Čaulev, Todor Panica, all were tracked down and shot. Panica, one of Mihailov's bitterest opponents, met his death in a setting perfect for a thriller: a Macedonian woman shot him during a performance of *Peer Gynt* in the Burg Theater in Vienna. Mihailov married her as a reward.

Alexander Protogerov succeeded Aleksandrov as his legitimate heir and leader of the IMRO. But young Ivan Mihailov became a member of the IMRO Central Committee and rapidly came to have more and more power in the organization.

On July 7, 1928, Protogerov was shot dead in a Sofia street. Mihailov issued a communiqué stating that Protogerov's assassination was an "execution" ordered in conformity with the directive of the last IMRO Congress to punish all concerned in the murder of Aleksandrov. Gang warfare broke out between the two groups in the streets of Sofia and elsewhere in Bulgaria. Assassinations in broad daylight were a common sight. The Milhailovist IMRO remained powerful in Bulgaria, protected by the authorities and the king. The Protogerovists, denied such protection, sought allies among the surviving Federalists, Agrarian exiles in Belgrade, and ultimately among the Yugoslavs. Generally, Protogerov and the Protogerovists were more progressive than the other IMRO followers and advocated a separate Macedonia within a Bulgarian-Yugoslav federation.

IN May 1934, a group of reserve officers headed by Colonels Damian Velčev and Kimon Georgiev, together with the Zveno group of progressive intellectuals, carried out a coup which installed the Georgiev government in Bulgaria. This government wanted friendship with Yugoslavia. Almost their first act was to order the disbandment of the IMRO. Ivan Mihailov fled to Turkey, then to Italy, and other prominent Macedonians were arrested.

After the banning of the IMRO in May 1934, little was heard of it. The Macedonian revolutionary movement was quiescent until the Second World War broke out. Even then there was no evidence that the Bulgarian occupation authorities in Yugoslav Macedonia employed former members of the IMRO. As for Ivan (Vančo) Mihailov, he for some time commuted between Western Europe and America and also published a book about a Balkan federation on the model of Switzerland.

Actually, the IMRO between the wars was not a true revolutionary organization. It no longer used propaganda among the Macedonian population it wanted to "liberate," its raids in Yugoslav Macedonia gave way to individual assassinations, and the conflicts with its Macedonian rivals and inside its own ranks degenerated into Chicago-style gang warfare. It became an extortion racket, blackmailing the roughly 100,000 Macedonian emigrants and the inhabitants of Bulgarian Macedonia into buying "protection" from terror and economic boycott through "voluntary" patriotic subscriptions and "taxes." In the early 1930s it engaged in illegal drug traffic. The League of Nations Opium Advisory Committee at one time reported that there were ten factories in Bulgarian Macedonia processing opium. At the IMRO's suppression, its property was estimated at more than four million dollars. For all that, the IMRO had no political, social or economic program, only empty slogans about Macedonian revolution and liberation.

IN September 1934, after the banning of the IMRO, King Alexander and Queen Marie of Yugoslavia paid a ceremonial visit to Sofia. But not many days later, on October 9, he was killed in Marseilles by a Macedonian of the IMRO, who was in league with the Croatian *Ustaši* ("Insurgents," pro-Fascists and later Quislings) and had been preparing for his deed in an *Ustaši* camp in Hungary.

At four o'clock in the afternoon of October 9, 1934, immense crowds thronged a heavily guarded boulevard in Marseilles. When in a long procession of automobiles a certain black car appeared, a young man leaped forward, jumped on the running board shouting "Long live the king!" and emptied a submachine gun into the tonneau. Old Louis Barthou, French minister of foreign affairs, died within a few hours from loss of blood. King Alexander of Yugoslavia expired instantly. The assassin was killed by the mob. Weeks passed before the French discovered that the dead man's name was Vladimir Černozemski and that he belonged to that formidable Macedonian terrorist group, the IMRO.

Actually the assassin's name was Vladimir Georgiev, born in Delčevo, Yugoslav Macedonia. He had many nicknames and aliases. One of them was "the chauffeur." Another was "Černozemski." The word comes from "dark earth" and the nickname, given him by Todor Aleksandrov, meant that the IMRO gunman had put many a man under the dark earth. He had killed, among others, the Communist member of Parliament Dimo Hadži-Dimov and the Agrarian member of Parliament Petko Petkov, both in 1924. In 1930 he killed Naum Tomaleski, Mihailov's right-hand man who had turned against him. Originally King Alexander was to be killed in Sofia during his state visit there in 1934, but on second thought it was decided not to do it on Bulgarian soil. It was Kiril Drangov, a member of the Central Committee of the Mihailovist IMRO, who organized the Marseilles assassination.

The majority of historians believe that it was Mussolini's Italy which stood behind the IMRO and the Croation *Ustaši* conspiracy to kill King Alexander. Some Soviet and other historians believe that Hitler was the instigator. In his book *Operation Teutonic Sword*, published in Moscow in 1966, V. K. Volkov set out to prove that the then German captain and assistant to the German military attaché in Paris, Hans Speidel, organized the Marseilles assassination of 1934. The West German press denied the charge—Speidel was at the time one of the commanders of NATO. But Volkov published two documents confirming that Nazi leaders were the initiators and organizers of the Marseilles assassination, called "Operation Teutonic Sword." Using the diary of Alfred Rosenberg, Volkov argues that the Nazi government considered it indispensable to remove not so much the Yugoslav King Alexander as the French foreign minister Louis Barthou, who in 1934 was working on a French-Soviet rapprochement as the key to European collective security, against Hitlerite Germany. Volkov believes that Hitler and Goering were personally behind the scheme.

THE great weakness of the Communists' Macedonian policy between the wars seems to have been that it was based on abstract theory and lacked means to put it into practice. In theory, the Bulgarian and Moscow Communists believed in an "independent Macedonia" within a socialist Balkan federation. But no attempt was made to create an independent Macedonian Communist party which would fight for independent Macedonia—unless Vlahov's United IMRO is to be regarded as an unsuccessful substitute. In fact, the first and only such party was the Yugoslav Macedonian Communist party, created during the Second World War.

On the nationality question, the Communist party of Yugoslavia passed through the same confusion and policy changes as did some bourgeois parties. Here the story of Svetozar Pribićević is significant. A Serb and a leader of the Independent Democratic party, he was at one time Yugoslav minister of the interior and of education, a devout monarchist and a confirmed centralist. When in 1929 King Alexander abolished the Constitution and the political parties, he among others opposed him, was interned, then released into exile. In 1933, from exile in Paris, he suggested, in his book *La Dictature du Roi Alexandre*, a federation of Yugoslav republics under a multiparty parliamentary system, very similar to the Communist federation of 1945, with Macedonia as a separate republic.

The Communist party of Yugoslavia was founded in 1919, six weeks after the founding of the Third International, which it joined immediately. It took a centralist rather than a federalist position, considering the various Yugoslav peoples to be one nationality. At the Second Party Congress in Vukovar, in 1920, the concept of one nationality and a centralist state again was accepted. This stand remained unchanged for a while despite the warnings from the Comintern, which pressed for an autonomous Macedonia within a Balkan federation. Yet the Communist party, banned in 1921, was very popular in Macedonia in the elections of 1920. It polled 38 percent of the Macedonian vote, becoming the strongest party in Macedonia, and the third strongest in the country.

In early 1923, the entire CPY leadership was called to Moscow. The Comintern recommended that the slogan of "the unity of Yugoslavia" be abandoned and that, for propaganda effects, the CPY adopt a program for the organization of the state along federal lines. The right of independence, not only of the Croatian and Slovenian peoples but also of the Macedonians should be supported. At the Second Party Congress, in May 1923, those who, like Secretary General Sima Marković, continued to favor "the unity of Yugoslavia" were termed "rightists." The conference resolved that each Yugoslav nationality must have the right of self-determination. Nevertheless, Marković continued to argue that the Croatian and Macedonian national movements were bourgeois inspired.

The Third Party Conference (1923), having consulted the Comintern, passed a resolution which stated that "Only the establishment of autonomous Macedonia and Thrace and their union with the other Balkan countries in a federative Balkan republic will establish lasting peace among the Balkan peoples." However, no mention was made of a Macedonian nationality (this was definitely done only twenty years later, during the Second World War).

Actually, the Yugoslav Communist party leadership could not bring itself to follow the Comintern line willingly. In February 1925 fourteen members of the Yugoslav Central Committee were summoned to Moscow once again to hear a proper nationality policy expounded to them. Marković was criticized by several Comintern leaders, including Palmiro Togliatti. Then Stalin made his famous speech in which he said: "It is imperative to include in the national program the right of nations to self-determination, including the right to secession.... The program should include a special point providing for national territorial autonomy for those nationalities in Yugoslavia which do not find it necessary to secede from the country.... To avoid all misunderstanding, I must say that the right to secession must not be understood as an obligation, as a duty to secede."

The Third Congress of the CPY, held in Vienna in 1926, had nothing to add because the policies adopted at the Third Party Conference were considered correct. Sima Marković was ousted, and the Fourth Party Congress, which took place in Dresden in 1928, did not change the new party line. Neither did the Fourth Party Conference, of 1934.

Then, in 1935, a dramatic turnabout took place in the world Communist movement. The Seventh Congress of the Comintern, held that year in Moscow, laid aside insistence on the self-determination of nations and, somewhat belatedly, issued a call for a united front against Nazism-Fascism. In view of the Hitlerite danger, the congress realized that bourgeois democracy was communism's first line of defense and it appealed to the Communist parties all over the world to join with the bourgeois democratic parties against nazism-fascism.

Accordingly, in 1936, the Central Committee of the CPY, meeting in Moscow, resolved to oppose the breakup of Yugoslavia for the time being. The Central Committee confessed: "Until the Seventh Congress [of the Comintern], the CPY understood and propagated the slogan of self-determination, including secession, in a completely sectarian manner. Secession was not considered as a right of the oppressed peoples, but as a basic necessity. About political territorial autonomy, for people who do not desire separation, nothing at all was said." Then it added ambiguously: "The change in the world situation ... impels the CPY to change its tactics on the national question but not, by this, to abandon the principle of the right of all peoples to self-determination, up to secession." The resolution went on to condemn the Mihailov and *Ustaši* organizations, which "are now calling for independent Croatia and Macedonia." The Central Committee admitted that it had been grievously mistaken in ignoring the Croatian Peasant party.

It was not until 1937, when Josip Broz Tito became Secretary General of the Communist party of Yugoslavia, that the first trend toward Yugoslav federalism began. Already in the same year the Croatian and Slovenian subdivisions of the party were created. True, the Fifth CPY Conference, held in Zagreb in October 1940, six months before the German invasion of Yugoslavia, in its resolution called only for "a struggle for the equality and self-determination of the Macedonian people against oppression on the part of the Serbian bourgeoisie ...," leaving in doubt the vital question whether the Yugoslav Communist party really recognized the existence of a Macedonian nation. But there is no doubt that Tito was already working out his solution of the Yugoslav nationality problem on the basis of a federation of six republics, including the Macedonian, a concept adopted during the war at the second session of the Anti-Fascist Council in Jajce (1943) and put into effect in the Constitution of the People's Republic of Yugoslavia in 1945.

The Second World War and Liberation

DURING the two years following the Axis invasion of Macedonia (April 1941), the situation in that region was not within the control of the Yugoslav Communist party. The province was mostly under Bulgarian occupation, with some extreme western areas held by the pro-Italian Albanians. Regular communications with the Macedonian

Communists were very difficult. Even so, the Macedonian Communists did not obey the directives received from the Central Committee of the Yugoslav Communist party; on the contrary, the Macedonians fell under the influence of the Bulgarian Communist party.

At the head of the Macedonian Regional Committee was Secretary Šarlo Šatorov, a Bulgarian Macedonian, who had come to Yugoslav Macedonia just before the war. Less than three weeks after the occupation of Macedonia, he dissolved the existing Regional Committee and went to Sofia where he declared his adherence to the Bulgarian Communist party. He refused to attend a meeting of the Central Committee in Belgrade in May and to carry out the Yugoslav Communist party's directive to conceal arms from the invader. On June 22 Germany attacked the Soviet Union. The Yugoslav party's Central Committee immediately addressed an appeal to the "enslaved peoples of Yugoslavia," saying: "Now the hour has struck for the struggle for your liberation from the Fascist oppressor. . . ." Three days later Tito, in the name of the Central Committee, sent a special letter to the Macedonian Regional Committee, which Šatorov had already dissolved, denouncing Šatorov. The letter condemned the behavior of the "old Bulgar." It said that the Yugoslav party's Central Committee relieved him of his duties as secretary of the Macedonian Regional Committee and expelled him from the party.

Šatorov fought back. On July 2 he issued his own leaflet, declaring, "Full boycott! . . . Long live free Soviet Macedonia!" The leaflet was signed, "the Regional Committee of the Workers' party of Macedonia." Thus Šatorov omitted any reference to the Yugoslav party and adopted the term "Workers' party," which was used by the Bulgarian Communist party. Also, the leaflet did not call for armed struggle, only boycott.

In the meantime the Communist party of Bulgaria had set up a commission to take over the organization in occupied Yugoslav Macedonia, on the principle, "one territory—one party." The Yugoslav Communist party insisted on the territorial integrity of prewar Yugoslavia. In July 1941 Tito sent a letter to the Central Committee of the Bulgarian party, strongly complaining of its attempt to get control of the party organization in Yugoslav Macedonia and of its support of Šatorov. The Bulgarian Central Committee sent a letter back saying that in Bulgaria, and therefore in Macedonia, conditions for an armed uprising did not exist. An appeal was made to the Comintern for a ruling. In August 1941, the Comintern replied, condemning, according to the Yugoslav account, the attempts of the Bulgarian party to bring the party organization in Macedonia under its own leadership. The Comintern decision, furthermore, was that the fundamental task was the armed struggle and that the chief method of the struggle was the Partisan war. Following this Comintern ruling, the Yugoslav party in a letter again called for armed struggle in Macedonia. On August 25, a new Regional Committee was appointed under Lazar Koliševski. Nevertheless, the Bulgarian party rehabilitated Šarlo Šatorov.

LAZAR Koliševski, who became president of the Yugoslav Macedonian parliament after the war, was sent to Skopje to counteract Šatorov. He brought with him the May appeal of the Central Committee, calling on the peoples of Yugoslavia to "prepare for the struggle for freedom." Šatorov refused to disseminate the appeal in Macedonia. Koliševski selected a new Regional Committee under himself. He formed the first Macedonian Partisan detachments at Kumanovo, Prilep and Skopje, under the leadership of his committee. On October 11, 1941, these detachments first clashed with the occupation forces. This date is now regarded by Yugoslav Communists as a "historic turning point" in Macedonian history. The results, however, were disastrous, the detachments were almost all destroyed. This failure was exploited by those who argued that conditions for Partisan warfare in Macedonia did not yet exist and that only passive resistance was possible. The Bulgarian Communist party sent Petar Bogdanov and later Bogdan Balgaranov to counteract the influence of Koliševski. They both maintained the view that conditions were wrong for Partisan warfare in Macedonia and defended Šatorov's "free Soviet Macedonia" slogan. Koliševski was arrested suspiciously soon after the arrival of Balgaranov in Macedonia. He remained in prison until the end of the war.

After Koliševski's arrest Balgaranov moved in and took over what remained of the Regional Committee, which reverted to the Šatorov line. The rump Regional Committee, under Balgaranov's influence, decided in December 1941 to disperse the surviving Prilep Partisan detachment and to cease work on the creation of fresh detachments. In the beginning of 1942 the Bulgarian government decided to carry out mobilization in Macedonia. The Macedonian Regional Committee accepted the Bulgarian Communist party's line that Communists should enter the army, in order to "maintain contact with the masses." Balgaranov continued to use the slogan "Free Macedonia," meaning a Macedonia independent of Yugoslavia. He signed his leaflets merely "The Regional Committee of the Communist party," without any reference to the Yugoslav party.

In early 1942, Tito sent to Macedonia a new representative by the name of Dobrivoje Radosavljević. It took him full six months to arrive. It seems that for a while there were two sections of the Regional Committee, one representing the Communist party of Yugoslavia and the other the Communist party of Bulgaria.

NOT until 1943 did things in Macedonia begin to change in Tito's favor. In February of that year he sent one of his best men, the Montenegrin Svetozar Vukmanović, "Tempo," to Macedonia. This was the real turning point. After his arrival in Skopje, Tempo communicated the decision of the Yugoslav Central Committeee to organize a Communist party of Macedonia within the Yugoslav Communist party. At the same time he disseminated a great deal of propaganda for recognition of the Macedonian nation as one of the member states of a future federal Yugoslavia, rather than an independent or autonomous Balkan state. He tentatively expanded this future Macedonia to include Bulgarian and Greek Macedonians. Then Tempo formed the Central Committee of the Communist party of Macedonia, including Lazar Koliševski, then in prison.

However, the stubborn persistence of anti-Yugoslav feelings in Macedonia led Tempo to caution the Yugoslav Central Committee against the immediate creation of a Macedonian Communist party as "premature." He recognized Ivan Mihailov as one of the obstacles in the path of the Yugoslav Communist party in Macedonia. He reported, "The agents of Vančo Mihailov are working throughout the whole of Macedonia. They are coming out for the unification of the Macedonian people and for their national independence. The Germans are helping and supporting them to keep the Bulgars in check...." It took him several months to dissuade the Macedonian leadership from using the slogans of autonomy. Yet when he went to Albania and Greece to establish contact with the Albanian and Greek Partisans, there was a relapse. In a June 1943 proclamation, future Macedonia was mentioned as a separate Balkan state, nothing being said about Yugoslavia. Finally, by August 2, 1943, the Macedonian party was sufficiently reindoctrinated to publish an Ilinden Manifesto mentioning the "precious sacrifices of the Yugoslav peoples ... and the strength of the National Liberation Army with Supreme Commander Tito at its head" as guarantees of national freedom and equality of the Macedonian people. The manifesto drew up a program for the creation of a "National Liberation Front," such as already existed in the other Yugoslav lands. The newly formed "General Staff of the National Liberation Army and Partisan Detachments of Macedonia" issued its own manifesto to the Macedonian people, in which it said that within the framework of Yugoslav unity, the Macedonian people had "all the conditions for realizing their age-long dream, unification." The era of the Bulgarian party's influence was ended. Balgaranov and Šatorov left the scene. Tito had at last won political control of Yugoslav Macedonia.

Tempo had also ordered the members of the Communist party of Macedonia to fight against Hitler and his Quislings. The first detachments that went into action were those of the Debar, Tikveš and Kumanovo districts, where large areas were liberated in the summer of 1943. On August 2, 1943, it was decided to organize armed units of battalion and brigade strength. Of great practical help was the collapse of Italy in September 1943. A number of Italian units were disarmed in western Macedonia, where the Partisans acquired a large liberated territory. They also seized badly needed arms and ammunition from the Italians. Soon after, demoralization began to set in among the Bulgarian occupation troops; the first deserters came over to the Macedonian Partisans. The Hristo Botev battalion and later other Bulgarian Partisan units were formed in Macedonia and subsequently handed over to Bulgarian command. From the end of 1943 onward the Macedonian Partisans, under Marshal Tito, carried on armed activities of a serious nature. The Bulgarian occupation forces began to take harsh reprisals, including the burning of villages suspected of aiding the Partisans.

Macedonian aversion to Yugoslavia did not disappear at once, not even within the ranks of the Communist party of Macedonia. However, one can generally say that in the Second World War, after the three decades of Serbian domination, the Macedonians received the Bulgarian army with goodwill, only to be disappointed by being treated as an occupied nation. The warm Macedonian feelings extended to the Bulgarian forces gradually cooled off because of the Bulgarian behavior. The Germans did not allow Bulgaria to annex Yugoslav Macedonia, only to occupy it, but the Bulgars took it for granted that the Slavs in Yugoslav Macedonia were Bulgars. Bulgarian officials and a very few Macedonian émigrés were appointed to administrative positions. Eight hundred Bulgarian schools were established. Bulgarian teachers and priests were called upon to serve in Macedonia. A national Bulgarian theater, library and museums were opened in Skopje, and in December 1943 a "King Boris University" was opened there. In July 1942 a law of citizenship was adopted, by which all inhabitants were held to have acquired Bulgarian nationality at the time of the occupation, with the exception of those who opted for their former nationality. If they chose the latter, they had to emigrate. Perhaps as many as 120,000 Serbs were forced to emigrate and resettle in Serbia. Macedonia was incorporated into the Bulgarian war machine, and dissatisfaction deepened with the conscription and the requisitioning of food, transport and buildings. After a while Bulgarian rule in Macedonia began to seem almost as oppressive as the Yugoslav domination had been.

THE very first session of the Yugoslav Anti-Fascist Council, held in Bihać, Bosnia, in November 1942, proclaimed the Macedonians to be one of the five constituent nations of Yugoslavia. But at the second session of the Anti-Fascist Council of National Liberation of Yugoslavia, held at Jajce, Bosnia, in November 1943, where the council proclaimed itself the "Supreme Legislative and Executive organ," it was resolved that "Yugoslavia is being built on a federal principle which will ensure full equality for the nations of Serbia, Croatia, Slovenia, Macedonia, Montenegro, Bosnia and Herzegovina." Thus Macedonia obtained equal status with the five other federal units of the new Yugoslavia.

The theme of unification of all the three Macedonias—the Yugoslav, the Bulgarian and the Greek—within Yugoslavia was not touched upon at the second session of the Anti-Fascist Council. In retrospect, it would seem that Tito had minimum and maximum programs for Macedonia. His minimum objective was to retain Yugoslav Macedonia within Yugoslavia. His maximum objective was to bring about the union of Bulgarian Macedonia and possibly part of Greek Macedonia with Yugoslav Macedonia. On the other hand, the Bulgarian Communist party's maximum objective appears to have been an independent Greater Macedonia closely linked with Bulgaria or quite simply annexation of Yugoslav Macedonia. Its minimum objective was to keep Bulgarian (Pirin) Macedonia out of Tito's hands. It was difficult to tell which was Tito's real policy. Actually it seems to have been a policy of probing the possibilities. He followed the minimum line in pronouncements to the outside world. He followed the maximum line in pronouncements to the Macedonians. On one thing he was clear to both audiences: if there were to be a greater Macedonia, it could only be within Yugoslavia. In December 1943 a Bulgarian Communist document was issued, called "The Fatherland Front on the Macedonian Question." This document provoked the ire of the Yugoslav Communists. By opposing Macedonia's "annexation to any one of the Balkan states" it implied rejection of the Macedonian solution adopted at the second session of the Yugoslav Anti-Fascist Council. In fact, this was a return to the old Vlahov-Comintern line of the mid-twenties about an independent Macedonia within a Balkan federation.

During the first months of 1944, the Partisans enlarged the liberated territory in Macedonia. The Bulgars and the Germans launched their first large-scale offensive against the Macedonian Partisans. Tempo led the bulk of the Partisan forces in retreat to eastern Macedonia, and additional Bulgarian gendarmerie units joined Tito's forces. On April 30 the Germans and the Bulgars started their second and last offensive against the Partisans. The Partisans again managed to retreat without great losses. It was not until mid-1944, when the power of the Axis began to disintegrate and when Allied victory appeared certain, that large-scale Partisan activity developed in Macedonia and the liberated territory was still more enlarged.

On August 2, 1944, the anniversary of the Ilinden uprising, the first session of the Anti-Fascist Council of the National Liberation of Macedonia (ASNOM) took place. One hundred and twenty-two delegates assembled in the monastery of St. Prohor Počinjski. The Macedonian People's Republic was proclaimed to be an equal federal unit in democratic federal Yugoslavia. ASNOM was constituted as the supreme legislative and executive body of the republic. The Macedonian language was decreed the official language. An appeal was made to the population to join the Partisan army under Tito. The Central Committee of the Macedonian Communist party issued another proclamation for the union of all Macedonians within Yugoslavia, on August 4: ". . . you will also achieve the unification of all parts of Macedonia, which were separated by the Balkan imperialists in 1913 and 1919."

In the same month (August 1944), the first Macedonian divisions of the National Liberation Army were formed; and in the following month, the first Macedonian corps. In September 1944, some 66,000 Macedonian Partisans were organized in seven divisions and three corps. By mid-November 1944 the Germans were completely dislodged from Macedonia, and organs of "People's Authority" were established on all levels of administration in Yugoslav Macedonia. Still, 400,000 Germans under Field Marshal Loehr managed to retreat from Greece through Macedonia with a loss of only 30,000 killed, wounded and captured.

The Soviet Union, its armies on the Bulgarian border, declared war on Bulgaria on September 5, 1944. Three days later the Bulgarian government asked for an armistice. When the Communist-dominated Fatherland Front seized power under Kimon Georgiev on September 9, 1944, the Bulgarian army was ordered to change sides and join with the Yugoslav Partisans against the Germans.

THE chief reason for Tito's success in Macedonia was the fact that he left behind him the Greater Serbian position of the erstwhile Communist leader Sima Marković and arrived at the realization that the Macedonian nation did exist and that it had a right to statehood. The exiled Yugoslav government, as well as its representative, Draža Mihailović, was unable to rid itself of rigid Serbianism. The Bulgars dissipated their reservoir of goodwill through narrow-minded Bulgarian chauvinism. The Western powers mostly ignored the Macedonian problem or treated Macedonia as a pawn in great power politics. Thus, those who stood for a Macedonian republic within Yugoslavia won out.

In mid-September 1944, Koliševski, now at liberty, and Tempo attended a meeting of the Central Committee of the Bulgarian party in Sofia to straighten out the Macedonian problem. They agreed to postpone the union of Bulgarian (Pirin) Macedonia with the new Macedonian People's Republic. But the Bulgarian leaders consented to give Pirin Macedonia not only cultural but also administrative autonomy in the meanwhile. The Bulgarian party did not keep its promises. Pirin Macedonia was not granted administrative autonomy, and there was no sign of cultural autonomy until the end of 1947.

The Bulgarian Communist leader Traičo Kostov wrote a letter to Tito in November 1944 in which he spoke hopefully of "the brotherly union" between the Bulgarian and Yugoslav peoples and the union of the Macedonian people on the basis of the People's Republic of Macedonia within the framework of Yugoslavia. In December 1944 Edvard Kardelj, Tito's right-hand man, went to Sofia to win Bulgarian approval for the Yugoslav Communist party's plan for a Yugoslav-Bulgarian federation. The Yugoslav proposal called for Bulgaria to be the seventh republic in the Yugoslav federation. The Bulgars favored a federation between the two countries as equals. In this deadlock an appeal was made to Stalin. At first Stalin inclined to the Bulgarian thesis, considering that Bulgaria had a "tradition as a separate state." But later, according to the Yugoslav account, he accepted the Yugoslav point of view. Britain at that time expressed opposition to any federal arrangement as upsetting the existing balance of power, and Stalin finally declared that the time was not propitious for any change in the status quo. So the federation negotiations came to nothing. By the end of January 1945 the attempt to solve the Macedonian problem through a Yugoslav-Bulgarian federation had broken down.

Yugoslavia had waived reparations claims to the value of 25 million dollars for damage done by the Bulgarian army on Yugoslav territory. The old-time Macedonian irredentist organizations were banned. George Dimitrov indicated an open mind on the question of Pirin Macedonia. Delegates from the Pirin region to the January 1946 plenum of the Bulgarian Communist party claimed that seventy percent of the people there had declared themselves to be Macedonian. The tenth plenum of the Bulgarian party, held on August 6, 1946, passed a resolution on the Macedonian question which said that the Bulgarian party realized that the major part of the Macedonian people was organized as a state, within the framework of Yugoslavia; and that the unification of the remaining parts of the Macedonian people was to be carried out on the basis of the Macedonian People's Republic within the framework of Yugoslavia. However, this resolution was never published and was apparently not communicated even to the ranks of the Bulgarian party.

Then, in August 1947, George Dimitrov and Tito met at Lake Bled in Yugoslavia. The published terms of the Bled agreement provided for abolition of entry and exit visas. There was later to be a customs union. The Yugoslavs again demanded self-determination for the Pirin Macedonians, that is, their union with the Macedonian People's Republic. But the Bulgars again opposed immediate union. This, they said, must be postponed until the Yugoslav-Bulgarian federation had been realized. Tito insisted, however that "the Macedonian people in Pirin Macedonia should have all the rights for full cultural development, as in Vardar Macedonia." The Bulgarian leaders agreed. In implementation of the Bled agreement, the government of the Macedonian People's Republic sent ninety-three teachers to Pirin Macedonia "to assist in the correct teaching of the Macedonian literary language and Macedonian history." They founded a Macedonian National Theater at Gornja Džumaja to present Macedonian plays. They established a publishing concern called the "Macedonian Book," which in a few months issued over 80,000 copies of books, brochures and journals. Macedonian booksellers disseminated the Skopje newspaper *Nova Makedonia*. A special newspaper for Pirin Macedonia, *Pirinski Vesnik*, was founded.

George Dimitrov, although a follower of Stalin's, went his own way. Despite the pressures within his own party, despite the changing and capricious attitudes of Stalin, he patiently, over the years, worked with Tito to realize a Bulgarian-Yugoslav federation and even played with the idea of a Danubian federation of the People's Democracies. For this he was in 1948 castigated by *Pravda*, which said that this was a fantasy and that the Danubian countries "do not need a problematical and fictional federation or confederation or a customs union. . . ."

Within a few weeks after Tito's breach with Stalin and Yugoslavia's expulsion from the Communist Bureau of Information (Cominform) in 1948, the Macedonian teachers and booksellers were evicted from Bulgarian Macedonia. There was no more cultural autonomy for the Pirin Macedonians, let alone talk of a possible federation with Yugoslavia. It is likely that the Bulgarian Communist leaders had not really freed themselves from the Greater Bulgarian nationalism which had obsessed their non-Communist predecessors, and that deep down in their hearts they, like other Bulgars, believed that Macedonians were truly Bulgars. Moscow, on the other hand, never seems to have given a precise ruling on the Macedonian settlement. Thus Bulgarian claims to Yugoslav Macedonia were revived from time to time after 1948.

IN May 1943, Tito's special emissary, Tempo, having reorganized the Partisan movement in Yugoslav Macedonia and made contact with Enver Hoxha's Albanian Partisans, entered Greece and got in touch with the Greek Communists. Hostility between Greeks and the Slav minority in western Greek Macedonia had been brewing since before the war because of the oppression of the Macedonian Slavs in Greece by the dictatorship of General Metaxas. Tempo's aim was to organize the Macedonian Slavs in Greece in Partisan units. The Greek Communists agreed, and SNOF, the Slav National Liberation Front, was formed. A Macedonian by the name of Gočev, or Goci, became the military leader of the SNOF units under Greek command.

But the Greek Communists were not willing to concede to their Macedonians as much as the Yugoslavs had hoped for. In his August 1943 letter to the Central Committee of the Yugoslav Communist party Tempo said: "The Greek Party has the following stand on the question of Macedonia: Macedonia, that is, the Macedonian minority, will receive in Greece freedom and security from all national subjugation. They do not recognize any sort of right of self-determination of these people." Tempo claimed that the fault for the strained relations between the SNOF and the Communist party of Greece lay in the "un-Marxist nationalistic political leadership of the KKE [the Greek Communist Party] on the Macedonian national question."

Still, the Communist party of Yugoslavia soon had its own agents swarming all over northern Greece. In June 1944 the Yugoslav Macedonian Partisan headquarters issued instructions to its agents in Greek Macedonia, warning them not to disturb the fraternal relations with ELAS (The Greek National Liberation Army), but emphasizing that "the national freedom and equality acquired [by the Yugoslav Macedonians] is the ideal of the entire Macedonian people . . . also those in Greece and Bulgaria." Nevertheless, in August 1944 Gočev and his SNOF battalions broke with the Greek Communist party and crossed into Yugoslav Macedonia. They were disbanded and later enrolled in the Yugoslav army.

The Yugoslavs pursued their all-Macedonian line. On October 11, 1945, Tito made this flat statement in a speech in Skopje: "We have not denied the right of the Macedonian people to unite. We shall never deny that right. That is our principle. . . . We shall stand on this aim, that all Macedonians shall be united in their country."

Actually, the Greek Communist party managed during the war to avoid committing itself on the ultimate settlement of the Macedonian question. Even for the first four years after the war it did its best to keep silent on Macedonia. One thing, however, was clear: the Greek Communists were not going to give away any part of Greek territory. In May 1946, the Secretary General of the Greek Communist party, Zachariades, said in an interview to a British correspondent: "Territorial questions between Greece and Yugoslavia do not arise."

BY the end of 1946 a new guerrilla war had started in Greece, this time against the Greek government; the action was led by the former Communist organizer in Macedonia, Markos Vafiades. On December 24, 1947, the formation of the "Provisional Democratic Government," headed by Markos, was proclaimed.

From the start, Markos's army relied for help more heavily on Yugoslavia than on Albania or Bulgaria. He had to revive the Macedonian Slav enthusiasm for the Greek Communist cause. He therefore permitted a fresh influx of military and political organizers from the Yugoslav Macedonian People's Republic. Gočev himself seems to have been among them. Thus in 1947 SNOF reappeared, under the name of NOF (the National Liberation Front), operating nominally under the command of Markos. The NOF professed that its purpose was to secure Macedonian national rights within a Communist Greece.

After the Tito-Cominform break on June 28, 1948, Yugoslav leaders never again raised the question of "unification" of a part of Greek Macedonia with Yugoslav Macedonia. But Yugoslavia continued to support Markos for over six months, and the Greek Partisans continued to use Yugoslav territory for retreat and for taking care of their wounded. However, there was a serious struggle going on inside the Greek Communist party between the pro-Yugoslav and the pro-Cominform factions. The pro-Cominform group finally won out. At the end of January 1949, the Central Committee of the Greek Communist party relieved Markos of "all Party work," allegedly on grounds of ill health, and expelled him from the party. In an "open letter," broadcast by "Free Greece" radio on February 8, Markos on the same grounds laid down his premiership of the "Provisional Democratic Government" and the command of the "Democratic Army." The Moscow-oriented General Secretary Zachariades succeeded to undisputed control of the Greek guerrilla movement.

This was the situation when Tito, in late July 1949, decided to cease supporting the Greek Communist guerrillas and to close the Yugoslav-Greek frontier.

PART II

THE PRESENT

MACEDONIA:
PAST MEETS PRESENT

People and Socialism

Towns and Villages

BEFORE dawn on July 26, 1963, the animals in the zoo of Skopje, capital of Macedonia, became restless. The Australian dingos began to howl, the lions beat their heads against the wall, the monkeys jumped about in panic. At 5:17 A.M., the 228,000 inhabitants of the city were jolted out of their beds by a severe earthquake. No less than 1,070 people died that hot morning and 1,200 were made invalids for life, while 140,000 became homeless. The city remained without water and electric power. Factories and stores were destroyed or damaged, which was a major national calamity, as Skopje represented 38 percent of Macedonia's economy. Altogether three-fourths of Skopje was destroyed or damaged beyond the possibility of habitation.

Within twenty minutes after the first shock, the Macedonian minister of the interior had set up headquarters in a park and had begun to organize rescue and relief. At a meeting of the Macedonian government, held in a park, it was decided to evacuate all women, children and men over fifty-five, and to mobilize the rest. Priority was given to the establishment of field hospitals and canteens, and the setting up of temporary tents and barracks in parks and open spaces for some 30,000 people. The workers were housed in camps around the factories. The erection of prefabricated houses was commenced.

Money, material assistance and medical aid were rushed from all parts of the world in a demonstration of international goodwill seldom to be seen. Soviet and American teams worked in friendly competition. Skopje received altogether more than 300 million dollars in aid from foreign countries and other Yugoslav republics. To state exactly who did how much for Skopje is not possible. At any rate, the United States authorized grants and loans in the amount of fifty million dollars—

actually dinars, money paid to the U.S. for wheat and other surplus commodities under the Food for Peace Program. Furthermore, a few hours after the earthquake, President Kennedy ordered twenty-four Globemasters to carry from Germany a 120-bed Army field hospital, staffed by more than 200 medical personnel. Finally, the United States sent 253 prefabricated houses and an Army unit to erect them.

One of the results of the international aid effort was a vast new city of prefabricated houses, on the west side of the Vardar, covering an area about twelve-and-a-half miles long and five miles wide. Steel structures now arise at intersections. Wide modern streets run through the suburbs, some of which are still composed of neat little prefabricated houses, surrounded by gardens and orchards.

Some of the very solidly built medieval structures, such as the Turkish fortress Kale, the Daut Pasha's bath, the caravanserai or Kuršumli Han, the great stone bridge over the Vardar survived. The minarets of some mosques toppled or were dangling. A few modern reinforced buildings also withstood the shock and stood out among the ruins. The roofed open market as well as the craft and filigree shops of the old town are still there.

Those tourists who knew it will mourn the death of the old-fashioned hotel-restaurant-café "Nova Makedonija" (New Macedonia). In the glum café you could breakfast on a huge portion of ham and eggs with a most excellent roll, while the radio gave forth Chopin's "Ballade et Polonaise," followed by Paganini's "Witches' Dance." Elderly natives sat around with Turkish coffee in front of them, staring into the air or comparing lottery tickets with the numbers in the newspaper. Or you could lunch in the unassuming restaurant listening to a record of Bruch's "Scottish Fantasy," performed by Jascha Heifetz. A sign on the wall said, "We collect ten percent for the service," but tips, considered below the dignity of the waiter, were given even by party members. The hotel with its restaurant and café collapsed, burying more than 200 guests, including Nancy Hamilton Harrison, daughter of the cartographer Richard Edes Harrison, and her fiancé, George Scriabin; they were the only American victims of the Skopje earthquake.

After the earthquake, some experts advised abandoning the old site of Skopje and rebuilding a new Macedonian capital elsewhere. They recalled that Skopje had been destroyed by earthquakes twice before, in 518 and in 1520. The city fathers decided to rebuild on the same site, but with scientific precautions. Some 100,000 holes were drilled under Skopje to determine the safety of foundations for new buildings. Some sites were found safe for twenty-storey buildings to withstand a nine-degree quake on the Richter scale, which was the degree of the

1963 Skopje earthquake. Other sites were declared suitable only for parks. Thus Skopje is today a city of many skyscrapers and many parks.

A modern city of advanced architecture, six-lane boulevards and parks, is rising on the site of the rubble. The modern structures of concrete and glass are silhouetted against the surrounding mountains, towering over the mosques, some with minarets still broken or cracked by the quake. The city does not expect to complete the rebuilding of its center before 1980. But the population has nearly doubled, being at present more than 400,000.

SKOPJE sprawls across a plain surrounded by mountains and it has a big and beautiful forest park along the west bank of the winding river Vardar. The city is divided into the new, modern town on the west bank of the river and the old town on the east bank. Both are connected by several bridges. Skopje is the third-largest city in Yugoslavia, after Belgrade and Zagreb. How much it has grown can be judged by the fact that immediately after the war it had only 70,000 inhabitants. Before the war, there were only two high schools in Skopje, four craft schools, a theater and a faculty of philosophy with 172 students. Today the city has an opera, a ballet, a philharmonic orchestra, the famous "Tanec" dance group, and a university with five faculties and nearly twenty thousand students. Skopje is the nerve center of the Macedonian economy. It has large steel works, built by British capital, and industries producing leather, furniture, paper, knitwear, ready-made clothing, textiles, cosmetics, tobacco, canned fruit, cement, opium alkaloids, electro-chemicals. The steel mill makes steel plates for the Yugoslav shipping industry, for the reconstruction of the city and for export, mainly to the Soviet Union.

Despite the automobiles, bicycles are almost as common in Macedonia as in Holland. Next to the Slovenian capital of Ljubljana, Skopje holds second place in Yugoslavia in the number of bicycles. And you can still listen to *Fidelio* in the Skopje opera house and walk home to the crowing of the roosters. You may still pass by a one-storey house with a door in the middle and the windows reaching down to the ground. Walking through the Skopje streets, you can among the ordinary people spot a Gypsy woman in a multi-colored kerchief, blouse and *šalvare* (wide Turkish trousers). Sometimes Albanian or Turkish women wear *šalvare* over dainty high heels. You will also see young girls with the blown-up pompadour or whatever hairdo is in fashion; or the young *frajeri* ("pretty boys"), with their hair in rolls, or whatever fashion dictates, and dressed in black sweaters. You will pass by an Albanian wearing a white skullcap with a flapping brown or polka-dotted blue kerchief.

You may also, in certain sections, meet a peasant driving a cow and a calf next to a limousine or a motorcycle. You will even, on the main square, observe ungainly, much too dark and hairy women in clumsy dresses, with legs that show they suffered from rickets in their childhood. Yet sometimes you will come across unearthly, Madonnalike peasant beauties. Men also can be impressively handsome, tall, virile.

Every evening before dinner you can mix with the numerous young people promenading in orderly fashion up and down the main Skopje avenue—the Mediterranean *corso*. Women are seldom seen at soccer games or in the cafés and restaurants, though they frequent the movies and the opera. The opera audience interrupts the singer with applause whenever they are stirred, and the singer, often an illustrious foreign guest, must repeat the aria upon request. The artists, presented with bouquets of flowers, toss single flowers at the audience.

EVERY day during the summer several hundred tourists, mostly from Western Europe, call at the Skopje Tourist Bureau for information. They are mostly interested in the oriental *čaršija* shopping section of the old town on the east bank of the Vardar. The lively variety of Skopje life can really best be seen in the old town. Here live Macedonians, Turks, Albanians, Gypsies and Tsintsars. The most sought-after souvenirs in Skopje are the products of goldsmiths, silversmiths and slipper makers.

Most Macedonian towns have old sections with a *čaršija* and cobblestone, narrow, winding streets. Houses here often have balconies and one or two overhanging upper storeys. The Skopje *čaršija* is an exotic bazaar, with rows of small shops and benches along tight and twisty cobblestone streets. Here one can still find a silversmith sitting crosslegged and composing a poem made up of slender silver threads. Or a goldsmith is seen beating his yellow metal with an iron hammer. There are broom makers, and craftsmen who make modern combs from cattle horns. In Turkish times, guns were also cast here. Today nothing is left of that activity but a large number of blacksmiths and the name of one street, Tophana or Gun Street. In the *čaršija* you will see a dismal aspect of the Orient, such as tiny lawyers' offices, dingy one-room affairs in one-storey houses, with a board floor, a few wooden chairs, a table, and shelves with string-bound files. But on your way through the *čaršija* you will also be pleasantly surprised by the sight of small shopkeepers sweeping the cobbles of the pavement in front of the entrances to their shops with small hand brooms. This is an ancient Skopje *esnaf* (guild) tradition. As the saying goes, you judge a woman by the inside of the house and a man by its outside.

162

In the old town of Skopje you will have to visit the Bit Pazar, the roofed market. The sellers are largely Albanians, offering beans, potatoes, vegetables, peppers, apples and sweet chestnuts. The counters have tin tops and stand under tile-roofed colonnades. The whole square is paved with flagstones, and everything is clean. You will want to climb the Turkish fortress Kale, rising almost a thousand feet above the east bank of the Vardar and housing the Museum of History. Here you can among other things see the pistol and the dagger which the new members of the original IMRO kissed and swore on, accepting in advance death by either weapon for betrayal of the organization. You can also have a look at an unexploded cherry-tree cannon from the Ilinden Uprising.

You will also want to pay a visit to Daut Pasha's *amam* (bath). Constructed in the fifteenth century, supposedly for Daut Pasha's harem, it later became a public bath. It consists of two large halls under two cupolas, all majestic stone, the light coming from the openings above. Formerly it was heated by huge wood piles, which caused much deforestation in the Skopje neighborhood. Since 1948 it has served as a gallery of modern Macedonian art. Finally, you will wish to see Kuršumli Han, the Leaden Inn. It was built in the middle of the sixteenth century and has served in its time as a prison, but originally it was a large caravanserai where itinerant merchants could store their goods and find food, forage and accommodation for man and beast. According to Moslem custom, this was free for three days. Kuršumli Han consists of a massive two-storey quadrangle, which on the second storey has barred windows on the outside. Through a strong iron-studded gate one enters the flagged courtyard with a fountain in the middle. All around runs a two-storey arcade. On the ground floor there used to be storerooms, which received light and air only from the courtyard. The upper floor consisted of many rooms under a roof of lead, whence the name of the building. On the columns are inscribed the names of many Dubrovnik and Venetian merchants in black and red. Now the building is the site of the Lapidarium, a division of the Archeological Museum.

The Turks built a considerable number of mosques in the old town, but the number has been reduced by fires and wars. There are still eight mosques left, the most significant being those from the fifteenth century, when the Turks constructed their most beautiful buildings. Yet even in the old town, the minarets are no longer the tallest buildings. They are now exceeded in height by many-storeyed buildings.

OHRID, on the lake of the same name, is the leading tourist attraction of Macedonia. It is most famous for its many old churches and frescoes, but of these we will speak later.

Ohrid's surroundings, approached by boat from the monastery of St. Naum, have been compared with the most beautiful sights in the world. The violet pyramids of the Albanian mountains to the west tower one above the other. A slight breeze stirs the surface of the lake, which reflects the white clouds. Gradually the white hill town emerges from the blue water, with the ruins of Tsar Samuel's fortress at the top. Churches, cupolas, towers appear one after the other. The white walls of the houses, the red and gray roofs, the yellowish rocks, all harmonize with the rich green of the poplars, fruit trees, alders and willows. The lake shore burgeons with oleanders, wisterias, cypresses, rose trees and enormous fig trees. Against this is set off the indigo blue water of the lake, which becomes lighter toward the land until it turns shimmering green near the white beaches.

Ohrid also has an old and a new town, but the old town is not oriental. The ocher-colored houses in the old section of the town climb the hill up to the ruins of Tsar Samuel's fortress and have narrow, steep cobblestone streets. Their upper storeys project over the lower ones and they look like so many inverted pueblos, practically touching at the top. They are all from the eighteenth and nineteenth centuries, and their interior is richly decorated with *bas-reliefs*. A common feature of these houses are built-in closets and windows which open upside-down or sideways into the walls. The entire old section is under the protection of the state, and each year a number of houses are renovated.

The new town's streets below the hill are asphalted. The central square is a park with flower beds and flowering bushes. Gorgeous Turkish gardens used to be here earlier.

The town of Ohrid was mentioned during the second century B.C. as an important station on the Roman commercial road Via Egnatia, which connected the Adriatic with the Aegean Sea and whose milestones you can still see around. Some of them bear the name of Emperor Caracalla, who seems to have liked Lake Ohrid. During the last century Ohrid merchants, who were Slavs but wrote up their accounts in Greek, exported finished leather products to the Sultan's court and to Berlin.

Before the last war there were only two physicians in Ohrid, and one public health station. Today Ohrid is a town of small traders and craftsmen, of fishermen and gardeners. The town has now for some time boasted various factories, producing inter alia canned goods and ready-made clothing. As far back as 1959, the sewer system was partially completed and so was the water main. Not long ago one could still find threshing grounds in villages along Lake Ohrid. In the fishing village of Peštani, between Ohrid and St. Naum, everybody by 1959 had "risen to the bed" instead of sleeping on the floor, and the cooperative had an automobile.

There is a new theater in Ohrid, with a colonnade. There are also some modern architectural barbarities. For instance, one side of the National Bank building is all white, while the side next to it is gray below and red-and-white above with green window shades. There is a handsome big workers' resort on the shore, "Orce Nikolov," with a large marble-pillared hall, drawing rooms, and a spacious park. Various Yugoslav factories also have separate rest homes for their workers in Ohrid. But it is difficult to find a hotel as beautiful as Ohrid's postwar "Palace." It has a park restaurant with arcs and flower beds. Inside, there are massive round marble columns, marble walls and occasional marble floors. The lower part of the pillars and the ceiling on the second floor are in Macedonian "deep wood carving" (high relief) with intricate crevices and convoluted lines. The place abounds in magnificent modern furniture, all of elegant simplicity. The architects were Slovenes.

In the Ohrid National Museum, situated in an ancient theater with a *bas relief* still on the wall, one may see a Turkish dagger from the nineteenth century, with the following inscription on the blade: "What you do not wish your enemy to know, do not tell your friend. Man is plotter and of evil mind. If you do a favor to somebody, beware of him." Such was the code of the masters who for so long ruled the Balkans. It is from these Turks that Serbian Prince Miloš, of the first half of the nineteenth century, must have learned to remark, "He cannot hate me, I have done him no favor."

Lake Ohrid, the southwestern part of which belongs to Albania, is the largest lake in Yugoslavia and the deepest in the Balkans. It lies some 2,300 feet above sea level, and its greatest depth is 940 feet. In the west rises a 5,000-foot-high mountain, and in the east the 7,400-foot-high Galičica separates it from Lake Prespa. Lake Ohrid never freezes over. It is fed by many underground streams, and it is believed, though not proved, that from Lake Prespa, situated at a higher altitude, water filters through the limestone of Galičica into Lake Ohrid. Cormorants dive in the lake, and there are wild ducks as well as herons.

Specialties of Ohrid are silver filigree; "Ohrid pearls," ornaments made of the scales of a small Ohrid fish; and wood carving. But specialty number one is the Ohrid fish. The best liked, praised by all visitors, is the *letnica,* a sort of salmon trout sometimes two feet in length, of splendid coloring, and not found anywhere else. It has been considered a gourmet delicacy since Byzantine times. In Constantine's reign, relays were said to have left Ohrid, then called Lichnidos, each week for Salonika and Constantinople to supply the emperor with his favorite fish. Another Ohrid delicacy is the eel, caught in traps during its yearly migration where the river Black Drim flows out of the lake. This river, which flows from Lake Ohrid to the Adriatic, is used by the Ohrid eels to swim every fall all the way to Bermuda for spawning at depths of more than 20,000 feet in the Sargasso Sea. Upon their return they master the many Black Drim waterfalls by getting on land and wriggling up the side of the precipice, then plunging into the stream again. When a series of dams for a power plant were constructed at the lake's outlet a few years ago, special gates were constructed for the eels.

The fishing village of Kaneo is situated below a steep rock, with houses one above the other, unapproachable by land and often visited by painters. Fuel and other necessities are brought by boat. The boats of the Ohrid fishermen are huge, clumsy, tall affairs with logs along the gunwales, perpetuating a design that has not altered for two thousand years. They are now being replaced by light modern boats.

The big brown bears near Ohrid are normally protected but may be shot if they have attacked livestock or human beings.

BITOLA, on the Yugoslav-Greek border and situated below the imposing Mount Pelister (8,580 feet above sea level), is the second-largest Yugoslav Macedonian town. It is a has-been town, for its glories belong to the Turkish times. This is because the 1913 frontiers dismembered Macedonia, and Bitola, up to then the second-largest Macedonian town (after Salonika), became a provincial border town, away from the main Belgrade-Skopje-Salonika-Athens railroad line and highway. Town life prospered in Turkish times, arts and crafts bloomed, as did culture. At one time there were 1,200 grand pianos in Bitola, and around the year 1900 you could hear Beethoven and Bach being played from behind open windows. There were no fewer than eighteen foreign consulates in the town. There was also a renowned military academy, which Kemal Ataturk attended. Sarah Bernhardt performed in Allied-occupied Bitola during the First World War.

From 80,000 before the First World War, the population of Bitola fell to 35,000 during the interwar years, but it had a comeback after the Second World War. Its population now is 125,000. It is the center of the Macedonian leather industry, which exports to America, and for the production of refrigerators. It also has a well-known National Theater, famous mosques, a splendid museum, and one of the largest Eastern

Orthodox churches in Yugoslavia (St. Demetrius). The *bezistan*, the Turkish covered market, is still well preserved and something to see. The Bitola *corso* is as orderly as the one at Skopje. The visitor ought to take a walk along the charming Crna River running through the middle of the main boulevard. It is actually a rivulet, an integral part of the boulevard, practically its middle lane. One ought also to take a walk through the grand forest park extending toward and beyond the railroad station, preferably at sunset when huge flocks of crows settle in the trees.

French, German, British, Bulgarian and Serbian cemeteries from the First World War are located around Bitola. Some eight miles out, there is an ancient Illyrian cemetery, where gold masks were found after the Second World War. Not far from the town may be seen the remains of the ancient city of Heraclea Lyncestis, dating from the fourth century B.C. Situated on the Roman Via Egnatia, Hereclea was a town with numerous temples, imposing buildings, baths and drainage. It had the largest basilica so far found in Yugoslavia. Eventually the Heraclea site will have 180 square yards of preserved mosaics.

Of all the towns in Macedonia, Prilep is *the* flower and tobacco town. Not only the windows, the balconies, the porches, the yards bloom with flowers, but the flowers grow in pots along the main street. Prilep is now an entirely new town. Driving in the fall from Bitola northward to Prilep through the vast Pelagonia plain, one can observe crows, wild geese, wild ducks and falcons. Motorcycles and sheep will meet you on the road. One will pass through enormous stretches of green pasture and immense fields of grain, corn and tobacco, and will soon glimpse the Golden Peak above Prilep, which looks like a huge fang rising toward the sky. On twin foothills of the Golden Peak rise the ruins of the medieval fortress of Marko Kraljević (Markukule). Just outside Prilep, some rocks will remind one of the strange shapes of certain Arizona formations; one of them resembles an elephant and is a favorite item for camera buffs.

The Tobacco Institute is located below the castle ruins of Marko Kraljević. Individual tobacco growers have contracts with cooperatives, and almost all have built new houses with the money they are making. In the late summer and early fall you will find the whole town covered with drying tobacco leaves; they hang on racks, or from the windows, the eaves, the balconies, the porches, the fences. Much of the Prilep tobacco goes to the United States for blending with Virginia tobacco.

The town of Kruševo is situated almost 4,100 feet above sea level, amidst forests, on a plateau high above the Prilep plain. Some 200 feet above it stands the Bear's Rock, where Pitu Gule and his forty men offered the last resistance to the Turks in the Ilinden Uprising of 1903. Kruševo is a town of low-roofed houses with many tall windows, usually of three storeys; the upper ones are mostly of whitewashed wood and jut out, adorned with loggias and balconies. There are buildings dating back to 1843. On some of the bigger houses you will notice sculptures of dragons and winged horses. On one house there is a sculpture of a big human eye, which indicates the owner is on the lookout for coming friends and visitors. The stately houses along the narrow, winding, steep, cobblestone or flagstoned streets display quantities of flowers, and tobacco leaves in the autumn. You will meet motorcycles with sidecars, see black-and-white folk costumes and observe beautiful children. At dusk you will have to get out of the way of leisurely walking cows, clanging their bells on their way home from pasture.

Kruševo used to be a Tsintsar town, but now the Macedonians predominate. Formerly the people were sheep and cattle breeders, goldsmiths, coppersmiths, tinsmiths. Today there is not one goldsmith left. The inhabitants are now busy with tobacco growing, crafts, handmade Persian rugs, ready-made suits, knitwear and livestock breeding. The town has had a sewer system since the middle of the nineteenth century. Since that time all new houses have been required to be connected with the sewer system.

Up at the cemetery, at the edge of Kruševo, there is a cypress grove with a monument to Nikola Karev, the first president of the first short-lived Macedonian republic. It was from there that the famous cherry-tree cannon was fired.

They say that the Kruševo mountain people easily tire in Skopje or other low-country towns, unnecessarily raise their legs when they walk, and have enlarged hearts but no asthma.

THE town of Kratovo is situated in a mountain gorge, in a beautiful, wild, out-of-the-way region and is known for its flowered balconies, picturesque medieval towers and many high bridges spanning the steep river banks. In the Middle Ages, Saxon miners used to dig coal at Kratovo for the Serbian kings.

Veles is another mountain-gorge town, which, like Kratovo, has a goodly share of natural beauty. Looking from a hill in the distance, you can see the many whitewashed houses with their triangular red-tiled low roofs rise on both sides of a gorge. At its bottom flows the multi-bridged Vardar. The town looks like an amphitheater and dates back to the third century B.C. Veles has a famous porcelain factory, and there is also a big silk factory, producing natural and artificial silk. In Veles, as elsewhere in Macedonia, you will come across asymmetrical faces, caused by generations of malnutrition. But the next moment you might see a dignified old Macedonian with a white beard and black eyebrows, a flat-topped Macedonian sheepskin cap on his head.

The Albanian-inhabited town of Tetovo, on the Albanian border and situated below the second-highest Yugoslav mountain, Šar (9,065 feet above sea level), is known primarily for apples and chrome. It is a nice little town with alleys in which trees have been planted, small gardens and fine examples of the quaint walled-in houses of the former Turkish Beys; garden fountains and high-relief interior decorations beautify these old houses. The famous Colored Mosque (Šarena Džamija), burned down during the last war, is decorated inside and out with elaborate arabesques of birds, flowers and geometrical designs. In the town's big textile factory former Albanian shepherds have become workers and factory officials. With its "Yugo-Chrome," Tetovo is the center of the Yugoslav chrome industry. The famous Tetovo apples cannot be obtained in Tetovo; they are being exported to other parts of Yugoslavia and abroad. Actually, the California apple known as "Delicious" is as widely grown. In Tetovo, as in Veles, Strumica and elsewhere in Macedonia in the summertime one has to fight off clouds of flies in the restaurants and streets. In Tetovo, the war on flies is sometimes announced by sirens, at which time everybody is supposed to start killing them.

From a restaurant in Kumanovo, where you may listen to a radio performance of Brahms's Hungarian Dances, you can watch Gypsy children playing outside and many dirty female dimlije (baggy Moslem female trousers) passing by. There are flowers in a small vase on a table in the corner. Only two tables are occupied, by dice players, on that particular morning. From a third table a character rises, with a dark beard à la Italo Barbo, a gray homburg hat, black leather gloves and a furled umbrella. Hypnotists are to be found in Macedonia, too.

Not long ago, Kavadarci was a dirty backwoods village, but it is now a thrill to come unexpectedly to this handsome little town with numerous new small apartment houses and quite a few big modern apartment buildings. Near Kavadarci we find the great vineyard plantation of "Tikveš," which exports celebrated grapes and wines. A large part of the plantation used to belong to King Alexander before the war. Valandovo, near the Bulgarian frontier, is another appealing little town, whose red roofs are buried in the greenery of many trees. The entire rich plain seems to be bathed in green, with violet and white poppy fields lighting up between the mulberry tree plantations. Gostivar, near the Albanian border, where before the war there was only dust and mud, now boasts modern buildings, factories and macadam roads, though a pig may still stop your car in the street. An equally modernized town is Debar, once the seat of a school of Macedonian wood carving.

If the state of its plumbing is the first thing a house is judged by, it is usually the last thing achieved by a society. There is more electric light and power in Macedonia than there is in France, but city plumbing remains wanting. Macedonian information officers complain that they repeatedly have to apologize to foreign visitors for this state of affairs. However, this too is a passing stage. After all, open sewers ran through the center of some Milan streets as late as the twenties.

BEFORE the Second World War typical Macedonian villages consisted of scattered stone houses on mountain slopes or straw-roofed wattle huts in the plains, with impoverished, wretched-looking inhabitants. In some marsh lands one could come across huts of a prehistoric type: perched on four stilts, constructed of switches woven together and made solid by mud, and covered with straw. After the war, slate roofs were added to more and more peasant houses; and more and more were built of brick, with red-tiled roofs. Only rarely will people now be found living with livestock in the same room. In two-storey village houses the ground floor is made of stone, and the upper floor of wood. The Macedonian village house has no gable, and the roof, instead of being ridged, is in the shape of a low pyramid.

On Macedonian roads may be observed the American influence with which we are familiar in Morocco or other developing countries: a horse cart with discarded Firestone tires. Or you will pass a twisted, burned iron skeleton of a Volkswagen smashed against a tree. You can also, though rarely, observe a woman on horseback with her husband walking beside her, which means that a revolution has really taken place in Yugoslavia. Just before the First World War, camel caravans, led by donkeys, were still passing through Macedonia. Camel tending survived in eastern Macedonia until quite recently; the last camels were sold to a Czech circus in 1937. Along the international Belgrade-Athens highway you will occasionally be slowed down by an old woman leading a donkey loaded with branches for firewood—or by bicyclists who ride in groups instead of single file. There are horses in Macedonia, but they are generally not used for field work, only for riding and pulling carts. Field work, when there is no machinery, is commonly done by oxen, cows and Asian black buffaloes. As mentioned previously, there are no mules in Macedonia, except those belonging to the army. But the donkey is the peasant's friend and beast of burden.

In the irrigated Lipkovo cooperative outside Kumanovo, they can boast tobacco and corn harvests twice a year. You will pass through villages with electric light, radios, electric stoves, and agricultural machinery stacked by the roadside in the evenings. Near the Greek border, in the affluent village of Bogdanci, which has its prosperous "agricultural enterprise," it is interesting to pay a visit to the local restaurant-café in the early evening. It is full of smoke, noise, and mostly young men of the peasant-worker type. There are normally a girl singer, a violinist, an accordion player and a guitarist, performing in front of a microphone. Individual guests come out on the platform and sing. A warning on the wall reads, "Each Deliberately Broken Glass Costs 200 Dinars." A volunteer singer may take out 200 dinars, give them to the waiter, smash his glass against the wall in the middle of his singing, pick up his hat, bow to the public and stroll out.

SOME villages are suspended on steep slopes, as, for instance, in the Radika region along the Albanian frontier. The mountain rivulet Radika cascades at the bottom of a canyon whose slopes, almost perpendicular, rise to 1,000 feet above the torrent. Absolute solitude reigns here, for the villages and the pastures are far below. Mountain villages like Lazaropole and Galičnik are rather difficult of access and so well concealed that they cannot be seen from the valleys below. You will find similarly located villages on the Pindus Mountain in Epirus, Greece. Of course, only sheep owners used to live in these villages, exposed to high winds and extreme cold. Others were seasonal migrant workers, traveling far and wide in the world. Most males, from the age of fifteen on, used to depart for *pečalba*—migrant work.

The *pečalbar*, or itinerant craftsman, is a typical Macedonian phenomenon. Many of these men were masons and would work in Rumania, Greece, Germany, Russia, America, Australia. After some years they would return with a little money, marry and settle down or go abroad again. Sometimes there would be mass weddings, often on St. George's Day. The departure of the *pečalbar* is sometimes cere-monial. In the region of Struga, before the migrant worker leaves, a vessel of water is placed on the threshold, which he kicks over and spills the water to fertilize the soil. Then he eats a piece of bread, wraps up a lump of earth and places it in his bosom.

The village of Galičnik spills over the side of a yawning precipice, 4,620 feet above sea level. The main road is serpentine with no pro-tection against the void. Houses are flung down the side of the abyss. Looking at their roofs below your feet, you may well ask whether people visit here by means of a rope. The view from here sweeps across the Black Drim and Radika Rivers toward the forbidding Albanian mountains. There are trees around Galičnik, and bushes and pastures and cliffs. There are sounds of the sheep bells, the brook below, the carpenter's hammering, the crowing of a rooster, the laughter of children, and the voices of men.

Before the war Galičnik was a village of grass widows. Their husbands and sons over fifteen were scattered over Greece, Rumania, Central and Western Europe, Asia Minor, the north coast of Africa, the Soviet Union, the United States, Australia. In the U.S., the Galičnik men worked at masonry, stonecutting, wood carving, cabinetmaking and the like, earning a living for their families back home. Galičnik masons and stonecutters have worked on the palace of Versailles, the bridges of Budapest, the Cathedral of St. Stephen in Vienna, the Mormon Temple in Utah, the Dnieperstroi in the U.S.S.R., and buildings in New York City. Once a year, in the first half of July, most of the Galičnik men used to return from the great world. Those in America and Australia returned every two or three years.

The Galičnik houses are square, of stone and of more than one floor. Sometimes parts of the upper storeys are made of wooden boards, but the ground floor is always made of stone, often used for livestock. The Galičnik men wear small round black caps without tassels. The women wear black-and-white vests, aprons with horizontal black-and-red stripes, kerchiefs of wild-cherry color, and on the chest buttons of knotted gold thread. The Galičnik people, a dying breed, are ingenious, highly adaptable and very clannish. They will help each other construct houses, will go everywhere and always find jobs, but will never do dirty work. As the saying goes, the Galičnik man "will sell pumpkin seeds and become a hotel manager, but he will not carry coal." With great business acumen and a high artistic sense, as shown in their costumes, these people represent perhaps the quintessence of the Macedonians.

Not far from Galičnik as the crow flies, but much farther along the ground, sprawls the mountain village of Lazaropole. It is reached by narrow hairpin serpentine roads, at an elevation of 4,460 feet above sea level. All around are sheep and their bells. Here you will be treated to the transplanted California apples of the brand "Delicious." And you will be simply forced to gorge yourself on the famous Macedonian *kačkavalj* sheep cheese, which is exported to New York. As does Galičnik, Lazaropole has a rug factory "without a chimney" which helps keep people in the village. It makes Persian rugs for export. Debar, Gostivar and Skopje have factories where rugs are made by machine. But theirs are not Persian rugs, which must not be made by machine. Foreign buyers often demand that each Persian rug have an individual variation in the intricate pattern, and this can only be done by hand.

Thus we have the strange phenomenon of unemployment solved by technological retrogression: while a machine may lead to the firing of people, production by hand may lead to people being hired.

IN 1941, before the enemy occupation of Yugoslavia, the population of Galičnik was roughly 8,000 and the number of houses 1,200. Immediately after the war, 6,000 remained. Soon the number of inhabitants was still further reduced, so much so that in the fifties Julian Bryan felt it necessary to make documentary movies on the disappearing Galičnik people and their customs, especially the weddings. In the early sixties there were 600 people left in 125 houses. Seventy houses had been abandoned. The people had moved mainly to Skopje. The remaining inhabitants still wore their local costumes on Sundays and holidays, and especially at wedding ceremonies, when the wedding flags would flutter from the roofs of the betrothed for a week before the event. There were two cooperatives, with 25,000 and 18,000 sheep each, as well as individual sheepowners. Food for the dying village, whose population kept immigrating to towns and factories, had to be secured beforehand for the six months of winter, during which snow-drifts enveloped the place to a height of three to seven feet. Contrary to the earlier overindustrialization drive, urging peasants to move to the towns, the Macedonian authorities already in the fifties began to devise methods for keeping them in the villages. In Galičnik, for instance, a rug "factory without a chimney" was established for the hand making of Persian and Afghan type rugs for the West, thus keeping the local people busy in the village. Also a small textile plant was erected to keep the women working in the plant or at home. And of course, like Lazaropole, Galičnik continued to export the Macedonian *kačkavalj* cheese. Nevertheless, Galičnik in 1972 was reported to have dwindled to sixteen people. The rest had left for Yugoslav towns or foreign lands, all the way to Australia. Of late, the Galičnik returnees from foreign lands, shocked at what they saw happening, have started a joint action to prevent the village from dying out. Whatever success may crown their efforts, Galičnik will never again be what it was.

IT is not only the mountain villages that are picturesque. In the plains, weeping willows will indicate a rivulet, immobile poplars a road, and clumps of fruit trees a village. At sunset in these plains, south of the canyon of Demir Kapija, one can see fine mists rising from the valleys up to the flaming clouds, which tower like giant mountains over the gently outlined blue mountains below. The sky is painted in glowing yellow, fiery red, deep blue, gray-violet, reddish-brown and greenish colors. The clouds topple over one another until they dissolve in ethereal soft blue. The lights go out in a second when the sun sinks far behind the snowy mountains and rocky masses of Demir Kapija. Only cool blue colors continue to advance toward the eastern mountains.

Between the lake of Doiran and the ancient ruins of Stobi in the Skopje plain, one will pass plantations of vineyards, mulberry trees for silkworms, and white-speckled cotton fields. Also in evidence are many irrigation canals, either at ground level or in sluices raised off the ground. Each local name recalls war to the Macedonians, a battle, invasion, liberation—nothing but war between 1912 and 1945.

Mountain villages are not the only ones that suffer from a rapid decline in population. In the plain of Bitola many villages consist almost exclusively of women, children and old men. Girls sometimes marry young men in Australia who send them photographs and written proposals. A contrast is formed by the plain of Strumica. It is rich and fertile, criss-crossed by irrigation canals, with numerous agricultural machines, where anything seems to grow, from grain to sesame, from opium poppies to rice. The Strumica villages all show a growth in population. The same is true of the villages in the plain of Tetovo, at the opposite end of Macedonia. But there are exceptions.

The fact remains that villages are disappearing from the map of Macedonia. Many will soon be covered with thickets. Where are the inhabitants going? To Macedonian towns mostly, but also to other Yugoslav towns and abroad. The official statistics merely state that between 1961 and 1971 sixty-five villages vanished. In the same period, the population in 234 villages declined by more than one-half. Before the next population census in 1981, another 150 villages are expected to disappear. The rate of disappearing is most rapid in the plain of Skopje.

The peasant population of Macedonia in 1961 was recorded as 61.4 percent of the total, and in 1971 it was given as 51.2 percent. This shows that Macedonia is still a preponderantly peasant country.

Macedonia's Quaint Minorities

OF Macedonia's more than 1.65 million population, only some 1.2 million are Macedonians. The rest is composed of Albanians, Turks, Vlachs, Tsintsars, Gypsies, Jews and others.

SOME 280,000 Albanians, out of Yugoslavia's total of 1.3 million Albanians, live in Macedonia. The majority, some 900,000, live in Kosovo, an autonomous province within the republic of Serbia; the province extends along the northeastern border of Albania. The Albanians are scattered all over Macedonia, though they are concentrated in its north-western corner, around the town of Tetovo under Mount Šar, near the Albanian frontier. "Albanian" is a foreign denomination, connected with the town of Albanopolis or Albaum. Sometimes they are called "Arbanasi," people whose occupation is agriculture: "ar" in Albanian is grainfield, and "banas" is one who does something. But these people still call themselves "Shkypetars," Children of the Eagle.

Albanians are one of the ethnological mysteries of the Balkans. The view is prevalent that they are direct descendants of the Illyrians. Some say that they come from a prehistoric race, the Pelasgians, who are supposed to have occupied the Balkans in a long-forgotten past, a thousand years before the Greeks arrived, which would mean about 3000 B.C. Thus the Basques and the Albanians may have more ancient roots in Europe than any other of today's nationalities or entities. The Albanians' language, mixed with Greek and Latin roots, is a puzzle, too. Those in the rugged northern mountains still occasionally tattoo their chests like the ancient Thracians. Curious social customs, once supposedly common to all Aryan groups, still persist among them, including the vendetta and the sanctity of hospitality.

Yugoslav Albanians are still very largely shepherds and tillers of the soil. But during the winter months many of them go to far-off cities as construction laborers and the like. The traditional occupation of those who come to Belgrade is still to saw firewood in the courtyards of private residences and apartment houses. In homespun white costumes, with folds of colored linen flapping around their ears from under their white skullcaps, they relentlessly wield their saws in rain or snow. A homemade cigarette always dangles from their lips. They spend their nights crowded like sardines on wooden planks in some cellar or attic. Next spring they start for their homes, with a few precious dinar bills concealed under their shirts.

The Albanians do not drink, but they smoke prodigiously, men and women equally. An old man can roll a cigarette in his pocket with one hand in a twinkling. An Albanian will do any work, including street cleaning, which, for instance, a Montenegrin will not do. This is another reason why the Albanians penetrate the towns. Houses in which livestock lives on the ground floor and people on the upper floor are more frequent among the Albanians than among the Macedonians. In a town you may occasionally meet a mountain Albanian, usually a shepherd, having descended from his heights for some business transaction. These are the most conservative, and they are first-rate shots. In tight white trousers with a black stripe up the side of one leg and across the bottom and down the side of the other, in white shirts, with a white headdress enveloping the chin against the cold mountain wind, they remind one of Bedouins.

Some Albanians are Catholic, fewer are Eastern Orthodox, the majority being Moslem. The veil, which the Moslem women—Albanian, Turkish and Bosnian—wore until not long ago, is not ordered by the Koran. It was an Arab custom which the Turks, with other Arab concepts about women, brought to the Balkans. The veil, banned in Turkey by Kemal Ataturk in the twenties, was finally forbidden in Yugoslavia by law in 1950 as an indignity to woman. For a while some Moslem women refused, or were not permitted, to go out; or they covered their faces with their hands. The most backward of the Yugoslav Moslems are among the Albanians. It is still sometimes difficult to bring an Albanian Moslem woman to a male physician or have the physician enter her home. During the brief outbreak of smallpox in the Kosovo province in 1972, many Moslem Albanians refused vaccination on the ground that it was contrary to Allah's will.

Before the war there were no Albanian-language schools in Yugoslavia, nor did the Albanians as a nation know how to read or write. In 1945 illiteracy among the Yugoslav Albanians was 90 percent, and hardly anybody outside the *hodjas*, the priests, could read a paper or write a letter. Today, in the Albanian-inhabited regions, both the Serbo-Croatian and the Albanian languages are obligatory in schools. In Macedonia today there are more than a thousand Albanian school teachers and hundreds of high school teachers with university diplomas, and more than 200 Albanian eight-grade elementary and high schools. In Skopje, the Albanians have a weekly, *Flaka e Vlazismit* (The Flame of Brotherhood); a monthly, "New Life"; a movie house; and a theater called "Brotherhood." Tetovo has an Albanian chorus, orchestra, dramatic section, and a score of Albanian physicians. In contrast to much Albanian primitiveness, there are also Albanian villages with bicycles, radios, TV sets, electric stoves. Let us add that in Priština, the capital of the autonomous province of Kosovo, the Albanians have a university, a film enterprise, a theater, and the daily *Rilindia* (Rebirth).

The common Albanian customs are the blood feud, *besa* (word of peace and protection) and hospitality. The balance of the three establishes elementary security in a primitive society. The blood revenge, vendetta, is as old as mankind. It is a private way of meting out justice where there is no government or no respect for the government. Although forbidden by law, it is still practiced among the Yugoslav Albanians as well as in Albania. The Albanian blood feud is known as Lek's Code, after the Albanian chieftain who in the fifteenth century laid down the rules of the game. For each crime against life or honor the offender "owes blood"; this means that he must be punished by death at the hands of the offended party. Every blood relative of the victim is under obligation to take revenge on the offender or on any of his male blood relatives. A woman's blood is of no account; so is that of an in-law. However, a "blood debt" can be paid in money or goods, if the offended party agrees. Since each killing calls for a new revenge, a vendetta often leads to mutual extermination of families. Sometimes the fields remain untilled because the offender and his male family do not dare to go out. Neither the prewar royal nor the postwar Communist governments of Yugoslavia have been able to eradicate the vendetta among their Albanian minority. Every once in a while blood feud cases appear in courts and in the press. In 1954, for instance, in Cetinje, Montenegro, a trial was held against three Yugoslav Albanians who had killed a truck driver for having accidentally run over their brother.

It is not difficult to make friends with an Albanian. All you have to do is to respect his sense of honor—then he will protect you. There is no greater shame for an Albanian than to break a pledge, the *besa*. Not long ago Albanians were commonly employed as bank messengers or guards in Western countries. Today, in Belgrade, they are often the most reliable superintendents of apartment houses, who consider a tip an offense. As for hospitality, no hungry or thirsty stranger will be turned away. Of all the Balkanites, it is the Albanians who revere hospitality most. Even a murderer, while in the presence of his guest, is safe from blood revenge. Some decades ago, an Albanian guerrilla fighter against the Turks was sentenced to death by the Vizier of Scutari. Just as the executioner was ready to decapitate him, the Vizier shouted, "Halt!" and turning to the manacled, impassive Albanian, he asked slowly, "Before you die, tell me something. Have you ever been in a worse predicament?" "I have," said the man, looking away. "What could that have been?" inquired the astonished Vizier. "Twice," the Albanian replied, "friends came to my house, and I hadn't even bread to offer them. They slept without food." The Vizier lowered his glance for a moment. "Let him go free," he ordered.

As for *besa* and vendetta, there is a Belgrade story of Albanian gratitude. A prewar Belgrade occulist restored the sight of an Albanian. The patient thanked him and said, "Doctor, I have no money to pay you, but if you have an enemy, let me know and he is to be no more."

Here are wartime examples of *besa*. In 1943 a Yugoslav Albanian Communist, a postwar editor of the Skopje Albanian weekly *Flaka e Vlazismit*, Murteza Peza, found himself with his unit encircled by the Albanian Ballista (pro-Italian Quisling) troops. The Ballista commander ordered a mountainside escape route guarded against the nearby Ger-

177

mans so that the Yugoslav Albanians could pass through. And all because the Yugoslav Albanian commander had at some time past been a guest in his house.

On another occasion the same Murteza Pesa with three Partisans was making his way beyond the Albanian frontier to establish contact with some Communist leaders in Albania. In Okštun village they blundered into 400 Ballistas. Retreat was cut off, but instead of surrendering, Peza ordered his companions to march forward and face the fire. Some of the Ballistas raised their rifles, but their commander halted them. "Don't shoot, these men are heroes," he shouted and gave them an escort on the way. A year later the same Ballista commander was captured by the Partisans. Murteza Peza went to see the big Partisan chief, Svetozar Vukmanović-Tempo, who forbade the execution and ordered the release of the Ballista commander.

After the First World War, the royal Yugoslav government decided to colonize the virgin soil of the Kosovo Field, just north of Macedonia and heavily populated by Albanians. It began to give land free to anyone who would work it, and especially to war veterans and landless peasants. The motive was also political: to make the Kosovo Field, the scene of the famous Serbian defeat by the Turks in 1389, a little more Serbian. The local Albanians watched the invasion with growing resentment. Soon they organized raiding bands, called *kačaks* and similar to those of the last century American Indians, which attacked the settlers, plundered, murdered and set their houses and villages afire. Two of this writer's uncles settled there as farmers and began to mix with their Albanian neighbors. One of my uncles, Adam Pribićević, was one day asked to be godfather to a child in a Christian Albanian family. Some time later, because of an injustice done to this family by the Yugoslav authorities, one of them "went into the woods" to join the *kačaks*. From then on, my uncle's life was safe under the *besa*, the promise of peace and protection. The pledge bound not only the members of the Albanian family but any *kačak* band having one of them in its ranks. Conversely, the *besa* of peace and protection covered all the relatives of my uncle. Thus, when my father Svetozar, a prominent political leader and former minister of the interior, was arrested in 1929 for opposing King Alexander's dictatorship and interned on a mountain near the Kosovo Field, a group of *kačaks* offered to kidnap and transfer him to Albania, from where he could reach the West. The project never materialized because my father was stricken by peritonitis and escorted to a security hospital in Belgrade.

ON the Macedonian roads you will often encounter old, eagle-nosed, bearded Turks riding small ponies, their heads in red fezzes swathed in white cloth. Soon after you may pass by a cemetery with crosses of wood or stone, then by a Turkish cemetery with stone turbans on short posts of stone. Nobody takes his hat off to the Turkish cemeteries. That is why the saying goes: "He passed by you as by a Turkish cemetery." The most derelict in Macedonia are certain Turkish villages near the Bulgarian frontier, for instance, around Kočane. They are similar to what you will see among some Moslem Slavs in eastern Bosnia. The change from being the rulers to the ruled brought about self-neglect in many Moslems, just as misfortune can cause apathy in the individual. The Turks are still under the influence of religion, conservative, not given to innovation. Many have "surrendered to misery." But most feel that they have lost their power and their empire because Allah has willed it so. Most are content with what they have and are satisfied that they are not persecuted. Yet regardless of the good relations today, a Turk will not marry a Macedonian or vice versa. The houses of the well-to-do Moslems face away from the road, have walled-in gardens, separate sections for men (selamlik) and women (haremluk), a bath, and a fountain in the flowered courtyard. In the houses of former Beys you will see bathtubs built in the wall with a wood-burning stove attached, all behind sliding doors. The Turks have their weekly newspaper in Skopje, by the name of Birlik (Unity).

There are more than 100,000 Turks in Macedonia. There used to be many more, but after the war there was a mass immigration to Turkey: altogether between 100,000 and 150,000 moved to their ancient homeland. People could take with them their possessions, including a whole shop. The immigrant could also sell his property, especially land or real estate. He could take his livestock with him. The Skopje radio has a regular hour for broadcasting messages and greetings from immigrants in Turkey to their relatives and friends in Macedonia. Many feel nostalgic and order records of Macedonian songs. Not all are content. Too many thought milk and honey awaited them in Turkey, instead of which they found there was no free doctor or hospital, no child allowance, no social security. Some have returned. The freedom of emigration of the Turks from Communist Yugoslavia to their homeland stands in sharp contrast to the lack of freedom of emigration of the Jews from the U.S.S.R. to their homeland.

A special variety of the Macedonian Turks are the Yuruks. "Yuruk" means a "brave man," and this was the name given to Turkish herdsmen expelled from Asia Minor for rebellion. They were settled along the

Strumica-Štip communication line in eastern Macedonia. Some of them are still left, and they live as they did centuries ago.

Then there is a special kind of Macedonian Moslem called Torbesi. They are Macedonian Slavs who, like some Bosnian Slavs, have gone over to Islam and do not speak a word of Turkish. There are a few of them left in the regions of Kavadarci, Debar, Ovče Pole, Štip and Skopje. It can also be said that they are the last Bogumils in Macedonia, for, as in Bosnia, it was particularly the Bogumils who adopted Islam.

On the high plateau of Ovče Pole you find remnants of the Tartar Pechenegs, easily recognizable by their Mongolian features. The Tartar Kumans, after whom the town of Kumanovo was named, have left no trace.

STILL another group is made up of the Vlachs. They are remnants of Romanized Thracians who during the protracted collapse of the Roman Empire gradually retreated into the mountains as livestock breeders and shepherds, which they are mainly today. In earlier centuries they were known to the West as Morlaks, a corruption from Mauro-Vlachs or Black Vlachs. In the fourteenth-century Serbian empire's code of law, the Vlachs—and the Albanians—worked as cowherds and shepherds, privileged occupations exempt from some feudal obligations. Also under the Turks, the Vlachs were exempt from feudal imports and duties in exchange for service as frontier guards, gendarmes, and so on. Today the Vlachs live not only in Macedonia, but in Bosnia, Serbia, Greece and Bulgaria. There are now some 11,000 Vlachs in Macedonia, out of a total population of 22,000 in Yugoslavia (1971).

You will mostly find the Vlachs on the Babuna and Pelister Mountains, leaning on their lance-long crooks, their faces almost lost in the deep hoods of sheepskin capes reaching to the ground, making them look like forbidding medieval monks. They tattoo blue crosses between the eyes of their children, especially in the Kočane and Demir Kapija regions. It is said that the sign of the cross on a Vlach forehead represents the pre-Christian symbol of man. Vlachs are rather primitive people. Some time ago a Belgrade newspaperman ran across such a shepherd who was almost a wild being, did not even know his name, could hardly speak and mostly uttered inarticulate sounds. Such people often had hardly any contact with other beings but sheep, dogs, wolves and bears. But now the migrating Vlach shepherds are hired by big cooperatives or the sheep-owning "social estates," enjoy modern conveniences and thus enter the modern world.

More than one motorist in Macedonia will be stopped on some

asphalt road by thousands of sheep moving in the spring and the fall to and from their mountain pastures. They travel to the Šar, Stogovo, Bistra and Pelister Mountains, and return to the Ovče Pole, Gevgelia and Strumica plains. At such times, fires by the roadside, baby lambs on the spit, shepherds' flutes and sleeping masses of sheep, guarded by enormous dogs, are a common scene in the countryside in the evening. The seasonal migrations of the shepherds, mostly Vlachs, covered the entire Balkan peninsula not long ago. After 1912, they were held within the new frontiers, but inside each country they continued as before.

In order to do away with this nomadic way of life, the Macedonian authorities in the early sixties, using caterpillar tractors, tried to convert high mountain pastures in western Macedonia into fields yielding various kinds of fodder. Sheep flocks could then stay over the winter in new, modern, roofed sheepfolds of stone, living on fodder grown and stored on the spot. The experiment proved overambitious. Some defended the traditional sheep migrations as being more beneficial to lambing. Thus in the wilds of western Macedonia you will still see the *bačila*, the lonely summer villages of the Vlach shepherds, usually built of wattle or stone, with a primitive stockade to shelter the animals from the wolves and the bears. Watch out for their dogs, huge shaggy beasts which take on wolves and bears, and often show hostility toward strangers. This author was once spotted from a distance and had to make a dash for his car. They are called *Šarplaninci*, the Šar mountaineers, for the most vicious come from the Šar mountain. Their height is three feet and they have a head like a bear's. Two such dogs are enough for a flock of 1,500 to 2,000 sheep. The closest European breed is the Pyrenean sheep dog.

Until recently, only the ancient flute was the entertainment of the Vlach and other Macedonian shepherds. Today transistor radios have come to compete with this folk instrument. Virtually all the shepherd settlements, most of them belonging to cooperatives or "social estates," are supplied with battery-powered radio receivers. In addition they now receive mail, newspapers and books. Many shepherds play chess in the woods.

A particular shepherd breed similar to the Vlachs are the Sarakatsans, sometimes called Karakachans. They are nomads with wicker and rush huts in the valleys. You can see them near Lake Doiran, but many more live in Greece and Bulgaria. Their women also have a cross tattooed on the forehead, and sometimes carry wooden cradles slung papooselike on their backs. According to Patrick Leigh Fermor, the Sarakatsans are not related to the Vlachs. George B. Kavadias believes that they descend from Greek peasants who in the fourteenth century sought refuge from the Turks in the mountains and adopted sheep and goat raising as a way of life. He estimated the Sarakatsans in Greece at 90,000 to 110,000 (1965). Half a century ago, the Greek government began to settle them and put them under the obligation of military service—previously they had been either exempt or unreachable. Many stayed in towns, but some are still nomads. The last thirty-five years have probably done more than the previous six hundred years to change the traditional life of the Sarakatsans. It is amazing that they have survived as an ethnic group. The last few decades have changed their ancient ways. Documents, schools, taxes and military service are now imposed on them.

Racially identical with the Vlachs but socially quite different are the Tsintsars. They too are descendants of Romanized Thracians, only urbanized, usually highly educated, often artistic, and mostly merchants by occupation. They spread throughout the northern Balkans and within Yugoslavia are concentrated in Macedonia and Serbia. The Yugoslav population statistics list the Vlachs but not the Tsintsars. However, it is known that in 1890 there were 150,000 of them in the Balkans.

Like the Jews, the Tsintsars are a race rather than a nation, except that they have no religion and no script of their own. Eastern Orthodox by faith, the Tsintsars do not swear or curse and speak among themselves a language derived from the Latin and with a rather limited vocabulary for modern times. Short and broad, with a dark complexion and black curly hair, they can be recognized a long way off by their extraordinarily bushy eyebrows, practically as big as mustaches, and noses so prominent that the Serbian humorist S. Sremac described a Tsintsar youngster as "half child, half nose." Actually, "Tsintsar" is a derogatory appellation coming from "tsints–tsints" (five–five), a mocking description of a haggling merchant. Another derisive nickname for the Tsintsars is "Tsitsifac" ("tsi fac" in Tsintsar means "what are you doing"). The Tsintsars are noted for industriousness and parsimoniousness. You will be told that there is a tombstone in Kruševo with the following inscription in rhyme:

> Here lies Axentius
> That gray old Tsintsar
> Who died in the morning
> To save on his lunch.

The Tsintsars have all the commercial acumen of the old hook-nosed Oriental peoples: Phoenicians, Armenians, Jews. It was they who monopolized much of the Balkan trade and industry in the last century and prevented the Jews from intruding. Hard-working, stingy, and courtly of manner, they were a type completely opposite to the Vlach or the fighting Balkan mountaineer. But they also brought into the Balkan town life the irresistible urge for gain, profiteering and dubious ethics. The Tsintsars are still far from having disappeared through mixture. But the Balkan townspeople have absorbed from them only their vices: greed, and the worship of *podvala*, the technique of cheating. To get the better of the opponent by trickery is still considered the height of ability among most Balkan business executives and politicians. If the native Balkan business people had also adopted the two Tsintsar virtues, industriousness and thrift, they could have competed with any European nation in constructive economic enterprise.

FORMERLY to be called *Ciganin*—a Gypsy—was an insult, an expression of disrespect for a human being. There are still many in Yugoslavia who have not got over this racial prejudice.

In the Strumica region, in the southeastern corner of Yugoslav Macedonia, you drive through whole villages of Gypsies working the land as peasants, something I had never seen or heard of before. To make another acquaintance with sedentary Gypsies, you must go to Skopje. Here, in the Gypsy quarter of the city, on a hillock on the east bank of the Vardar, they live in small mud-and-stone houses and huts, all in blue and yellow or plain blue colors. The women's dresses will assail your eyes with a wild variety of blue, yellow, green, red and other colors; and sometimes Gypsy women wear immense balloon trousers colored bright pink. The Skopje Gypsies are cleaner than the Belgrade Gypsies, and they do not beg quite on the same scale. Unfortunately the begging habit persists among Gypsies more than among other groups and it has increased with the years. The Skopje Gypsies work at crafts, in factories, as domestic help, and so on. They, too, possess radios, TV sets and refrigerators. When Gandhi's private secretary came to Skopje before the last war he could make himself understood to the Gypsies by speaking Tamil, one of the languages of India.

BELOW the Turkish fortress of Kale in Skopje you could, before the 1963 earthquake, see small, old, dilapidated, pink-colored houses—the former Jewish *mala* or ghetto. The houses were abandoned, discolored, with paint and plaster peeling off. No Jew lived there. The city of Skopje had taken over the empty Jewish *mala*, but most of it was destroyed by the 1963 earthquake.

Before the last war there were 75,000 Jews in Yugoslavia. Hardly 15,000 survived. Of these, thousands immigrated to Israel and other countries after the war, so that the Yugoslav population census of 1971 gives the number of Jews as 4,811. The Macedonian Jews are descendants of the Sephardic Jews who were expelled from Spain at the end of the fifteenth century. There were 7,762 of them—3,864 in Bitola, 3,795 in Skopje, 551 in Štip. Some 300 Jews fled to Macedonia from Serbia after the German invasion of April 6, 1941; thus there were roughly 8,000 Jews in Macedonia at the time of the German invasion in April 1941. Of these, more than 7,000 were dragged away to concentration camps, and none of them survived. Today there are only a few hundred Jews in Macedonia.

Let us take the town of Bitola. Of its 3,864 Jews, 3,762 men, women and children were exterminated in concentration camps, while 102 saved their lives temporarily by joining the Partisans or hiding in mountainous Albanian villages. Those who survived the war later found their way to Israel, Pakistan, U.S.A., Argentina, Spain, Italy and other parts of Yugoslavia. In 1963 there was only one Jewish couple in Bitola. He was employed in the city's archives, was old, and had not been to work for three months; he was slowly dying. His wife went to see a Jewish member of the Macedonian government who happened to pass through the town. When told that the cabinet minister could not spare the time to come and see the last Bitola Jew, she shrugged her shoulders, smiled and walked home.

Industries and Workers

IN Macedonia, as in Yugoslavia generally, enterprises employing more than five persons cannot be privately owned. They all come under the rubric of "social ownership"—ownership by society—and are run by workers' councils. These are elected by the workers and, in turn, appoint management boards and directors. "Social ownership" is about as clearly defined in the Yugoslav constitution and laws as is "free enterprise" in the American constitution and laws. In the Soviet Union the owner is the state, there are no workers' councils, and the directors are appointed by the government.

Workers' councils are a sort of industrial democracy, new to the communist countries. To understand them, some American observers have suggested that one ought to think of the workers as stockholders and employees at once. After paying fixed expenses such as taxes, interest, material and supply costs, and the basic wages, the workers' council makes disposition of the net earnings. It can distribute them among the workers as bonuses; spend them on housing, health, recreation, schooling; or it can reinvest them partially or fully. Enterprises can be founded by the federal, the republican or the local government, by other enterprises, or by groups of citizens. Most often they are founded by the local People's Committees. Once established, however, the enterprise is independent of the founder, it only has to repay the capital with interest. Yugoslav enterprises are supposed to compete on the free market and behave like businesses, that is, to make money. Each Yugoslav factory is on its own, much like a private firm in the West. Prices are to be those on the world market, and an enterprise which cannot stand such competition with normal customs protection has to reorganize or close its doors. Actually, hundreds of inefficient enterprises, notably those set up in the past for "political reasons," have gone out of business.

Economic planning in Yugoslavia is done from below, not from above as in the Soviet Union. The Economic Reform of 1965 abolished the yearly plans altogether. It kept five-year plans only as "moral and political commitments" and placed reliance primarily on enterprise plans. In the 1966–70 and 1971–75 plans, for instance, the role of the federal government is mainly advisory. This provides flexible guidelines, which identify high priority sectors without distorting the free market system by mandatory allocation of resources. The five-year plan is updated annually to reflect current performance. Soviet economists call Yugoslav planning "anarchistic."

Yugoslav workers' councils have fascinated economists and given pause to labor leaders and sociologists everywhere. Opinions vary, but most agree at the very least that the Yugoslav experiment is a great laboratory in labor-management relations.

WHETHER the workers' council will function well or not depends primarily on the maturity of the workers. Where there is widespread workers' apathy or ignorance, control may pass to the management board and the director, to a clique of management board members, to a group of the better educated and more skilled within the work force, to the League of Communists, to the labor union or to the local People's Committee.

The workers' councils, especially in Macedonia, have had several difficulties to overcome. There was in the past a tendency toward egalitarianism: against high pay for intellectual or high-skilled work (of directors, engineers, et al.). This populist sentiment ran counter to factory efficiency and counter to the socialist principle of reward according to ability (as opposed to reward according to need in the final communist society). Another difficulty was the occasional efforts of the labor unions to resist the raising of the work norm. This, again, showed a low degree of "socialist consciousness" and rather reflected an attitude of the workers in capitalist enterprises.

Then there was the tendency of distributing the entire net income among the workers instead of reinvesting at least a part of it. This was a result partly of insufficient wages, and partly of undeveloped socialist consciousness; it was not always clear to the worker that the factory was his. Formerly the law specified which portion of the net profit the workers' council could not distribute among the workers. Now it has the right to dispose of the entire net earnings as it sees fit, though the party and the labor union try to persuade the councils to reinvest whatever is considered necessary.

In the past the propositions of the People's Committee or the labor union were not always put on the agenda so far ahead of time that the members of the workers' council could prepare for a discussion. Management representatives used to dominate the discussions. Although the supreme authority in operating the enterprise stays with the workers' council, the complex business of running vast industries has proved too much for occasionally semieducated workers, so that highly educated technical experts have had to take charge.

In Yugoslavia generally, and in Macedonia especially, the majority of the workers still come from the village. This accounts for the psychology and certain inadequacies of the working force in Macedonia. For instance, you will read and hear a lot about the struggle against "primitivism." It is not so much that a Macedonian peasant woman sometimes works in a factory in coarse woolen stockings without shoes as that the Macedonian peasant-worker has not yet quite acquired the factory discipline and the machinelike sense of precision. Once too often it happens that the foreman, after the factory siren has sounded the end of the time set aside for lunch or dinner, must urge the sitting or lounging workers: "Let's go, let's go," and the workers mumble and shamble back to their jobs. The peasant will not be a worker until he begins to look at the clock instead of at the sun and use the micrometer instead of his thumb.

If the peasant-worker is ponderous at work, this partly has to do with his age-long undernourishment. One of the most capable factory directors in Macedonia told me about his workers: "I must drive them to work, and I must drive them to eat; they won't eat." The Macedonian peasant-worker often does not eat enough from a habit of semistarvation through generations. How different this condition is from that in the West can be seen from the fact that in 1973 there were 70 million overweight Americans—one-third of the nation; and from the *New York Times* Washington, D.C. report of September 7,

1960, saying that at the final session of the Fifth International Nutrition Conference "attention was given to solving problems of overeating in the industrialized countries." The problem of developing countries is undereating; the problem of developed countries is overeating.

The peasant also reveals himself by the rough handling of the machine. He has no patience with the machine and particularly ill treats its gears and brakes. In the American machine factory where I once worked I was amazed at the tenderness which the workers showed the inanimate machines. "Oh, she'll be all right again," a worker said about a machine he was repairing, and patted it as though it were a sick person. The machine is a living being to a true worker, and the peasant-worker will not be an industrial worker until he learns to treat the machine like his cow, with love and care, for it nourishes him.

Primitivism from below has its counterpart in primitivism from above. It shows in a proletarian turned bourgeois and imitating the class he has overthrown, such as judging a man by whether he has a villa or an expensive car. But the chief primitivism among management is the superstitious veneration of the machine. As the information officer of a "social farm" gravely explained to a group of Western correspondents: "A cow is a machine for the production of milk."

The task is to create industrial workers out of the men who for thousands of years have been backward peasants. This is what is happening in a major portion of humanity today, and it will take several generations before the industrial worker and mechanized farmer firmly replace the peasant. Despite the handicaps of a new working class, an American survey (by Bankers Trust Company) found that in 1970 Yugoslav workers had a relatively high level of education and training. Forty-five percent of the employees in the social sector were rated skilled to some degree, and 24 percent unskilled. The Macedonian percentages are less favorable. That is why rush training of skilled workers is going on at the engineering, economic and agricultural faculties of the postwar Skopje University; in vocational high schools; at specialization courses in factories at home or abroad; and on the job ("learn while you earn").

However, when the Yugoslav Communists talk of the peasant-worker, they do not have the industrially unadjusted peasant in mind, but a hybrid type of man who is only part worker and mainly peasant by occupation. That is the peasant who with his family works his plot and at the same time takes a job in a nearby factory to supplement his earnings from the land; the peasant to whom factory work is "moonlighting," a part-time job; the peasant who "goes to the factory so he can work the land." This type of peasant-worker, common not only in

Macedonia, has no concept of socialism, but he is not "primitive." He is a small landowner augmenting his income with the aid of socialized industry.

The Yugoslav economy, which is different from that of the Soviet Union, does, in the opinion of some, "converge" with the Western economy. It is indeed something unique, for which there is no model. The political system, however, is much closer to the Soviet than to the Western model. It is based on the ultimate establishment of a class-less and stateless communist society and in the meanwhile allows only one party, the Communist party, to be the supreme and final ruler, or "guide."

IN 1959, in a textile factory near Štip, which has a recreation park, I saw modern lockers and wash basins, but about one-half of the faucets had been left running by the workers, while the floor of the modern next door restaurant was littered with food leftovers and crumpled newspapers. This caused the director to exclaim angrily: "We have modernized the factory, but not the worker!" Technology advances faster than man; this accounts for the loss of contact with reality or a confusion of realities, which is why someone has called it a "schizo-phrenic development." This is an example of schizophrenic development: when in a sleeping car in Macedonia a passenger has pajamas but no soap or neatly deposits his slippers beside his berth in the evening and in the morning leaves the wash basin unused. What is reality to this man? What is the reality about him?

The reality is a wide split between civilization (technological development) and culture (spiritual development). Civilization is far ahead of culture, and that, in a nutshell, is the human condition of the world today. The trouble is that you can build or repair a machine much faster than you can man. Moreover, primitive man can acquire technical knowledge without culture. Modern cleanliness, for one thing, is a matter not only of hygiene but of moral discipline, respect for oneself and for the other fellow. But primitive people do not always understand the uses of sanitary facilities and will sometimes—in Macedonia, or elsewhere in Yugoslavia, or in Morocco, or in other developing countries—use the toilet as a washbasin, a bath tub for slaughtering a pig, a parquet flooring for firewood. It is a passing phase, but it is part of the schizophrenic development.

In 1945 Yugoslav Communists believed that the revolution was about to create the New Man. In the fifties and sixties they thought that electrification was bound to create him. Of course, it will take many more technical innovations and much more time to fashion the New

Man. In the meanwhile, a new house is being built for a basically Old Man. Things will settle down some time after the end of the great peasant migration to towns, and some kind of a new man will emerge. Those who do some thinking about this say it will take at least another fifty years. Man will ultimately win. One must trust the quiet assurance of the director of the Macedonian Information Service who with an undisturbed smile replied to the objection that the factory had been modernized but the man had not: "It will come, it will come!"

FIGURES on industrialization do not tell the story of life. Fifty-six years after the Macedonians had fired their wooden cannon against the Turks in the Ilinden Uprising, I stood in Bitola beside a pole revolving like a barber's and producing letters FF in artificial ice (standing for *Fabrika Frižidera*, the Frigidaire Factory) at the entrance to a modern plant. Inside I watched, fascinated, an eighteen-year-old former shepherd girl make bolts with a Yugoslav-manufactured lathe. All this below the TV antennas recently erected on top of the snowcapped Mount Pelister. Many more are making the same leap from the nomadic into the industrial society in Asia and Africa.

There is much talk in Macedonia about the "big leap." One can speak of a leap only when the jumping-off place is at a low level. Every developing country starts from a low level and makes a big initial leap after which it reaches a more or less mediocre ceiling. You will meet taxi drivers in Skopje whose sons and daughters are judges and doctors. You will see the same in America, though you could not have observed it in Macedonia before the war. It is from this point on that the leap becomes a hard walk. As a Macedonian driver expressed it: "To drive fast is easy, to drive slowly is not."

Before the Second World War there was only one hospital with a few health stations in Macedonia. There were only one main and two local narrow-gauge railroad lines. There were only a few tens of miles of asphalt road. Before the war, the consumption of sugar in Macedonia was five lumps a year per person, and these were kept for special occasions, such as illness or an exceptional guest. Before the war, all that could be called industry in Macedonia consisted of some ninety small plants, producing textiles, dyes, nonmetals, chemical products, and particularly tobacco, the only industry of consequence. Only two of these plants employed more than 250 workers. Before the war there were altogether 8,000 workers in Macedonia, more than half in the tobacco industry. After liberation, Macedonia had only 200 college-educated people. Worst of all, before the war the Macedonians were deprived of nationhood. The Macedonians were supposed to be

Serbs, Bulgars or Greeks. In Bulgaria and Greece they are still regarded as Bulgars and Greeks.

Macedonia is a unique European country in that everything there had to be created at one and the same time—a dictionary, schools, press, literature, arts, factories, power plants, mechanized farms, asphalt roads, "the primer and the university." And all this had to be created out of nothing. Hence the almost childlike enthusiasm of the Macedonians when they talk of themselves and their achievements. "This, too, is ours," they would exclaim about a bridge. Or, looking at the Macedonian inscription on a Yugoslav bank note, a man would say with long-delayed pride, "This is *my* money." All this is part of an unprecedented *blitz* effort to compress a millennium or more into a few scores of years in order to approach the industrial West.

Manufacturing and mining remain the most important sector of the Yugoslav economy, contributing 38 percent of the "social product" (the equivalent of the gross national product) in 1972. But Macedonia's ore wealth is mostly unexplored or unused. There is antimony and sulphur; much chromium, as well as some iron and zinc; and considerable marble. But there is no coal to speak of, and little manganese or copper. Macedonian industrial development is thus oriented toward electric power production; extraction of chromium, iron, zinc; steel production; dyes, nonmetals, chemicals, construction materials and marble; textiles, silk, leather, porcelain, glass, cement, even refrigerators; subtropical plants and, the biggest of all, the tobacco industry. To this must be added tourism and the craft of rug and carpet making. However, except for chromium and tobacco, the Macedonian export list might be misleading, for it has not always meant superabundance. Much has been exported at the expense of domestic needs, either because of the dollar shortage or out of political considerations toward the nonaligned nations. Conversely, Macedonia has to import machinery, foods and consumer goods generally. This again resulted in the fact that between 1953 and 1972 Macedonia contributed only 5.3 percent to the Yugoslav social product.

LET us have a look at four typically Macedonian industries.

The veins of chromium, as previously pointed out, extend from Albania and Greece through Macedonia and the Bulgarian Rhodope Mountains all the way to Turkey, which is the world's biggest chromium producer. The Balkan chromium is the only European chromium. Aside from the Macedonian chromium mines near Tetovo at the Albanian frontier there are still bigger chromium mines in the adjoining province of Kosovo, again at the Albanian frontier. This Eurasian network of chromium veins has not yet been explored in its entirety. The "Yugo-chromium" mined near Tetovo is one of the finest in the world in regard to quality and purity. Much of it is exported to West Germany and the United States.

About four hundred years ago, Hafiz, the Turkish commander in Macedonia, returned from Asia with a caravan carrying gold, silver, silks and a handful of opium poppy seeds. The opium poppy began to blossom around the villages near Kumanovo, Strumica, Gevgelia—all over the sunny plains of eastern Yugoslav Macedonia. The extracted seeds were strewn on cakes and sweetmeats with honey poured over them. Later a fluid began to be extracted from half-ripe poppy heads. The opium poppy grown in Macedonia is of a higher quality than any other. While the Chinese poppy has eight opium units, and the Turkish ten units, the Macedonian has twenty opium units. Machines now do all the backbreaking work in the fields, and modern pharmaceutical factories produce the opium, which is used only for medicinal purposes. It is interesting that in Macedonia, which produces the best opium in the world, the drug has never been used for smoking. Although in the last few years a number of drug pushers have been put in jail, the problem in Yugoslavia has so far been not drugs but alcoholism.

Before the war, the consumption of electricity in Macedonia was seven KWH a year per person. The first postwar Macedonian power plant was built at Mavrovo on an artificial lake above the Radika canyon and facing the Albanian mountain frontier. The plant used to be the third largest in Yugoslavia. It is not any more, but it is still the largest in Macedonia. The plant has large underground passageways lined with marble and with fluorescent lighting and a big marble hall for the generators. All of the plant's equipment was manufactured in Yugo-slavia. The lake, poured into an evacuated village site, is blue and more than 4,300 feet above sea level, lying amidst enchanting mountains and sweet chestnut forests. When told about the capacity of the plant, the two Norwegian newspapermen whom I met on the spot were unimpressed. "We come," they said, "from a country where it wouldn't matter if all the lights were left burning around the clock for a year." There are, they added, other countries which build power plants. The unique thing about Yugoslavia, they thought, was whether it would solve the question of its nationalities. If it did, this might furnish a model for a European federation. The cost of the Mavrovo plant was tremendous, and thereby hangs a tale of international panic. Instead of constructing a short bridge across the canyon for the Mavrovo pipelines, the engineers laid them underground both down and up the slopes. The plans were made in 1948, the year of the Stalin-

Tito break, and executed in 1952. The Yugoslavs were afraid of the Soviet atom bomb, but even so the underground protection was amateurish.

Tobacco used to be Macedonia's "monoculture," to which the region was reduced because of its backwardness. It is still the major single industry of Macedonia. By 1961 about one-third of the Macedonian population was involved in the tobacco industry. Tobacco accounted for 22 percent of the total Macedonian national income. One-half of Macedonia's exports consisted of tobacco. By 1965, seventy percent of the Macedonian exports consisted of products derived from industry and mining, and 30 percent consisted of tobacco and some agricultural products. Bosnia-Herzegovina also exports tobacco, but the chief exporter is Macedonia.

Growing tobacco on socialized farms has proved unprofitable because mechanization produces lower quality; the highest quality, obtainable only through manual labor, is needed for foreign exchange. Consequently, tobacco is planted almost exclusively on privately owned land. The seed is not thrown, as is the practice in America, but for each plant a hole is dug. In harvesting, the crop is not mowed, as in America, but each leaf has to be picked in "storeys" ("hands") from below. The upper "floors" ripen last and are of the best quality. Leaf by leaf is filed on a string for drying. Leaves have to dry for two to three weeks in the fall. Then leaf after leaf is laid in the tonga—a bale of flattened, compressed tobacco. Each tonga has its "type" ("Jaka," "Prilep" or other) and its category A, B, C, and so on. After this the tobacco enterprises, particularly the "Yugo-Tutun," do the buying, then the selling. Macedonian tobacco exports traditionally used to go mostly to the West—to West Germany, the U.S., France, in that order. However, in the early seventies Macedonian tobacco exports veered sharply toward the Soviet Union and the Eastern European countries. But American tobacco representatives still come every fall to Macedonia to buy Macedonian tobacco for blending with their homegrown tobacco. As mentioned earlier, the result is the so-called Turkish blend, so named because Macedonia was Turkish when the trade began.

Tobacco is also exported from eastern Greek Macedonia and Thrace through the tobacco enterprises of the Aegean port of Kavalla. The Greek Tobacco Institute lies just outside the drab little town of Drama in eastern Greek Macedonia. More than one million out of nearly nine million Greeks make a living from tobacco, which accounts for about 40 percent of the value of Greek exports. The U.S.A. and West Germany are the principal buyers. America buys tobacco both from Greece and Turkey; these two tobaccos are also combined with the Virginia tobacco to create a "Turkish" blend. In the opinion of Greek experts, the Yugo-slavs cannot beat the quality of the Greek tobacco.

THE process of industrialization has always had its ugly aspects. We need only recall the description by Karl Marx of British industrialization and that of the French by Émile Zola. In communist countries, too, the burden of the industrial revolution is carried by the workers. The United States helped the Yugoslav growth with 2.8 billion dollars in aid and credits. Despite this, the rural exodus increased more swiftly than the demand for labor in the socialist sector, causing considerable un-employment, reduction in labor productivity, and an increase in housing difficulties and the cost of living. In 1971, unemployment, theoretically impossible in a socialist country, stood at seven percent for Yugoslavia as a whole and a staggering 20 percent for Macedonia, the poorest of the republics. In recent years the problem has been somewhat alleviated by the temporary immigration of Yugoslav workers to Western Europe, primarily Austria, West Germany, Sweden; these workers send hundreds of thousands of dollars back home every year. It is estimated that in 1973 no fewer than 952,000 Yugoslav workers were employed abroad, among them a number of Macedonians.

The situation is also being improved through cooperation with foreign business firms. Yugoslav law permits investment by foreign firms in the form of "joint ventures" with domestic enterprises in order to attract technological know-how and new managerial skills to Yugo-slavia. Investment by a foreign company may not exceed 49 percent of the enterprise's total founder's funds, unless specific approval is given by the Federal Assembly. By mid–1973, there were eighty-two joint ventures, amounting to about 120 million dollars in foreign investment. This investment has come from Italy (25 percent), West Germany (20 percent), the U.S.A. (14 percent) and other countries. Most invest-ments have been in metal goods, electrical engineering and chemicals. The American firm Chemtex, of New York, which manufactures syn-thetic materials and chemicals, has entered into a major joint venture for the expansion of the Macedonian enterprise OHIS—a Skopje chem-ical concern.

How do the workers live? In general, Yugoslav workers are not yet paid enough to enable them to enjoy a really decent standard of living. White-collar workers are better paid. The improvement in the standard of living has generally been slower than the economic growth of the country—the worker always pays for the industrial revolution. Never-theless, the living conditions of the working people are much better than they were before the war; and for some groups, such as textile workers and miners, and in certain regions, such as Macedonia, they are incomparably better.

At the end of the war, in 1945, Macedonian dwellings not destroyed by the war consisted mostly of forty to fifty-year-old one-storey buildings of poor material. The great peasant migration to the towns created an additional housing problem throughout Yugoslavia, not soluble for a long time to come. This happened partly because the government in its early breakneck industrialization drive, encouraged an uncontrolled mass invasion of the cities. Not until the nationalization of buildings in 1959, with rent increases to help finance massive construction work, was the movement into the towns put somewhat under control.

All real wage estimates must take into account that workers, employees and civil servants, receive allowances for each child; free medical, dental and hospital care with generous benefits for childbirth; free transportation for vacations at reduced prices; old age pensions; and other fringe benefits. According to an early 1950 survey, in the nineteen Macedonian towns inspected, 28 percent of the apartments had a kitchen, 15 percent had an indoor toilet, 12 percent had cold tap water and 7 percent had a bathroom with a wood-burning stove. In 1939, before the war, only 21 Macedonian communities had electric light and power. Now most urban households have electric stoves. Water mains have been installed or extended in all Macedonian towns, but the sewer situation still leaves much to be desired (after all, 40 percent of Belgrade had no sewers in 1960).

Many Macedonian enterprises have built their own rest homes and vacation hotels for their workers and employees. Some firms have even erected modern apartment buildings for their people, together with eight-year elementary schools and health stations. As early as 1959 a Macedonian Communist leader declared that socialism must serve not only the future but the present generation by making its life easier, but the fact remains that in Macedonia and in Yugoslavia as a whole industry develops faster than the standard of living. But if one compares the postwar standard of living of the Yugoslav, and Macedonian, worker with his prewar standard, the picture is quite different. According to the prewar Yugoslav official estimate, the minimum income to secure a bare existence for a family of four was 1,620 dinars a month; that of a single person, 640 dinars. The average wage of a prewar Yugoslav worker, however, was 600 dinars a month. The worst off were the miners and the textile workers. There is today a legal minimum wage in Yugoslavia of 1,150 new dinars ($67.50) a month, which, given the Yugoslav cost of living, is enough to enable one to squeeze through.

The Yugoslav standard of living is higher than that of other Eastern European countries, including the Soviet Union.

When all is said and done, it is actually unrealistic to measure the standard of living of the Macedonian or the Yugoslav worker by the standard of living of the prewar Macedonian or Yugoslav worker, of the Soviet worker, or of the American worker. The standard of living of the Yugoslav and the Macedonian worker should be measured by the level of the Yugoslav and Macedonian industrial and other production. By that measurement, it is not adequate.

IN Socialist Yugoslavia, the taste, ambitions and the way of life of the emerging man are often those of the petty bourgeois. A veteran American observer has made a similar comment about the Soviet Union. There are Peorias all over the world. As far back as 1936, Clifford Odets wrote, "Tchitchikovs [the central character in Gogol's *Dead Souls*] of various stripe and shade occupy some of the highest places in the land today." They are now coming to power even in a good many revolutionary lands. There are economists who, like Dr. Kenneth Boulding, of the University of Michigan, believe that "Communism is a ... dogmatic version of the middle-class revolution. . . ."

Until recently, the dominant type in Yugoslav urban life was the restless, rough-and-ready newcomer from the interior who brought, into Belgrade and other cities, an atmosphere of the American frontier towns of a century or more ago, where the rugged man came first and the law afterward. Now the newcomer has begun to settle down in a secure job and to slip into the well-ordered, uneventful life of the conformist Yugoslav Joneses.

In the Veles porcelain factory, in Macedonia, you can see dinner plates, saucers, demitasses, ashtrays displaying a petty-bourgeois taste in design, including little gilded, pink and blue flowers. Another feature of the new petty bourgeois is his quest for respectability, wish for the "finer things" in life, desire to imitate the tastes and ways of the former upper classes. A new Molière might write, not *Le Bourgeois Gentilhomme*, but *Le Prolétaire Bourgeois*. How long the new socialist petty bourgeois will last one cannot say. But apparently all societies have to go through an "aspidistra" stage.

Not all foreign friends of Yugoslavia are happy about the industrialization of the Balkans. Edmund Stillman, for one, believes that it will fatally harm the old Balkan world by the creation of a rootless middle class in search of material things. The industrial civilization, of which we and the Russians are the chief protagonists, proclaims prosperity the sovereign good, but we have seen prosperity incapable of eradicating the demonic in the man of reason. The old Balkans were more than disorder. They were a place of passion and Messianism and of wise unreason, such as vendetta and hospitality. They were also the part of Europe which stubbornly refused to conform. Edmund Stillman could have added that the significant Balkan phrase is not "I will," but "I will not." This is not a mere negative stance, but a contradiction out of which "I will" arises on a higher level. The source of freedom itself is the negative "I will not be a slave," whence the specific Balkan concept of a hero comes: not a man who can master anybody, but a man whom nobody can subdue. The Balkanite said "No" to the Turks. The Serbs said "No" to Austria-Hungary in 1914. The Yugoslavs said "No" to Hitler in 1941 and to Stalin in 1948. The Macedonians said "No" to all who suppressed them. Each "No" seemed unreasonable, but it led to victory.

The Balkan past, Edmund Stillman goes on, denies the facile optimism which is the dominant ideology of our times. The Serbs, in their folk poems, celebrate not victory but defeat, choosing the heavenly kingdom rather than the earthly kingdom involving compromise with the Turks. The Balkans, therefore, are a permanent rebuke to the arrogance of man. For the Balkans have seen more than one empire, victorious and self-assured, go under in blood. Nevertheless, the dominant note in modern culture, as Reinhold Niehbur has written, is the conception of a redemptive history. Even Karl Marx believed that a new life and a new age would rise out of the death of the old one.

Some Macedonian Communists complain that technical progress leads to American-type comfort. But in Macedonia and in all of Yugoslavia technical progress and comfort are still necessary for facilitating work and life; while in America, with comfort having reached its saturation point, there is no excuse for the existence of a single destitute person.

Agricultural Progress

IN prewar Yugoslavia, the peasants made up 75 percent of the population. Sixty-eight percent of them had 12.25 acres, the officially estimated minimum for a family of five, or less. One million, four hundred thousand, out of 11.5 million, had sterile land or none.

In postwar Yugoslavia, the peasants account for more than one-third (37 percent, as of 1971) of the population. They are allowed to own their land. Indeed, 85 percent of Yugoslavia's arable land is in private hands. In Macedonia, the peasants still form a little more than one-half of the population; and more than three-fourths of the land, as of 1968, belongs to individual peasants. Prewar Macedonia was a vastly backward agrarian country. Today it can be described as a developing agrarian-industrial country.

Prewar Yugoslavia had already disposed of the really large estates. The first Communist land reform, of 1946, went further and expropriated all holdings above 50 acres. The major part of the expropriated total went to the poor and landless peasants; the rest to the newly formed state farms and the public domain (forests). In 1953 a new agrarian reform reduced to roughly 25 (24.71) acres the maximum of land a family could own. The local authorities paid a fair price for the surplus land and distributed it among the poor and landless peasants, on the condition that they organize in "peasant work cooperatives." The maximum peasant property allowed today is 37 acres (15 hectares) for a family of five, and 62 acres (25 hectares) for a larger family. But less than one-half of the Yugoslav peasants, as of 1958, owned more than 12.5 acres. Part of a family's income had to come from outside agriculture, mostly from industry, with family members working part or full time in towns.

COOPERATIVES, according to the law of 1946, were of two types. "General agricultural cooperatives" of the Western type: purchase and sales organizations, with neither land nor equipment pooled. More "socialist" were the "peasant work cooperatives." The name is misleading. Not only labor but equipment and land were pooled. The peasant signed a contract for three years, after which time, by law, he could leave with whatever he had brought in. In the meanwhile he retained only the title to his property and a small plot of 2.5 acres, usually for vegetables, with up to two pigs, a cow, some poultry. Work was organized in "labor brigades," and the peasant was paid not according to his share in the pool or production but by his "work days." The "peasant work cooperative" was nothing but a Soviet *kolkhoz* or collective farm.

Different from "peasant work cooperatives" are the "socialist agricultural estates." Former state farms, they are now managed like other social enterprises. They have their workers' councils, management boards and directors elected by the laborers and the employees. The social farms are created or expanded by purchasing land from the public domain or from the peasants abandoning their land in their migrations to towns. Social farms, which in all of Yugoslavia cover 14.7 percent of the arable land, and 22.7 percent in Macedonia, are usually located in the most fertile regions.

In postwar Yugoslavia the peasants were comparatively free until 1949. In that year the government resorted to forcible collectivization of land. Six months after Belgrade's split with Moscow (June 28, 1948), the government, the party and the press launched massive propaganda for the peasants to join the "peasant work cooperatives." So-called administrative measures were applied to enforce compliance: taxes and compulsory deliveries of surplus produce at nominal prices were arbitrarily assessed against those who refused to join. It is believed that Yugoslavia resorted to forcible collectivization partly to show that it could be as socialist as the Soviet Union and partly because of the fear of the Soviet economic blockade and a belief that collectivization would produce more food. It was a miscalculation on both counts. Stalin did not think any better of Yugoslavia for its collectivization of land, and collectivization produced a lag in production in addition to political discontent.

True, the number of "work cooperatives" rose under pressure within two years from some 1,300 to about 7,000. But even though the drive succeeded in forcibly collectivizing 63 percent of the arable land in Macedonia, only 25 percent of the entire arable land in Yugoslavia (including the state farms) found itself "socialized." And this embraced no more than 17 percent of the Yugoslav peasantry.

Forcible collectivization of land encountered sullen peasant resistance, not always passive. At the end of 1951, to the government's consternation, masses of peasants, especially in Macedonia, started handing in notices of quitting the "work cooperatives" the following year. The government forced them to stay on but began to have second thoughts about collectivization. Furthermore, because of the overemphasis on industrial development at the time, investments in agriculture were negligible. What was worse, only 14 percent of these insignificant investments were spent on tools, while 72 percent were used to construct massive stables and grandiose Cooperative and Cultural Homes. Many of these were never used or were left unfinished. Gradually the people tore them down for construction material.

It was in the winter of 1950–51 that the United States sent its first shipment of large quantities of food to Yugoslavia. The combination of peasant resistance, lack of equipment and droughts could not fail to bring about a serious decline in agricultural production. According to Yugoslav sources, agricultural production in 1952 was one-fourth below the prewar level, with a much larger urban population to feed. And in 1953, the acreage farmed was about 1.24 million acres less than had been farmed before the war. In March 1953 the government called a halt. A decree permitted the peasants to leave the "work cooperatives," and there was a stampede. They still exist but are rather few in number, composed mostly of formerly poor and landless peasants, receiving remuneration not according to work days but according to production.

HOWEVER, "general cooperatives" grew in number. Almost every rural community now has a "general agricultural cooperative" with its general store. These cooperatives still mainly deal in buying and selling for the peasants and also in servicing their members with machinery, various kinds of work, food processing, and at times making arrangements with factories. One example might be a fishing cooperative combined with a canning factory, as is the case at Lake Doiran in Macedonia. General cooperatives can also own land, which they acquire through purchase from the public domain or from peasants moving to town. They sometimes grow products on their own farms.

Before the war there were altogether five tractors in Macedonia. By 1960, there were more than there had been in all of prewar Yugoslavia, which means, more than 2,300 tractors and more than 22,000 other agricultural machines. Nevertheless, you will still find places where people thresh grain by walking horses around a pole. Most mechanized, of course, are the former state farms, now self-managing "social agricultural estates." More than 90 percent of their power comes from machines. Social farms and machine-equipped general cooperatives make contracts for "individual cooperation" with peasants who are not properly equipped for the optimum utilization of land. To increase production, the socialist sector lends the individual peasant machinery for ploughing, sowing, threshing, and so on, as well as seed, fertilizer and other materials, in return for cash payment or a share in the produce. The social farm sometimes gives the peasant technical and other assistance, the profit to be divided as per contract. Or the peasant entrusts the entire production to the social farm or the general cooperative and receives a share of the produce. Sometimes the peasant sells his land to the general cooperative or to the social farm and stays on it as an agricultural laborer. It can be said that a majority of the peasants cooperate with the socialist sector in one way or another.

Theoretically, the Yugoslav Communists justify small peasant ownership on the ground that it is a means of living, not a means of exploitation of man by man. The government's ultimate aim is "socialist transformation of the village," meaning socialization of agricultural production. However, this is to be achieved over a long period of time and by persuasion rather than coercion. The 1958 Program of the League of Communists of Yugoslavia, criticized by Moscow and Peiping as "revisionist," has this to say about the peasants:

"... The League of the Communists believes that the process of socialization of land will not consist in a forced nationalization ... but primarily in socialization of agricultural production. . . .

"At the same time, the League of the Communists of Yugoslavia believes that it is indispensable that the peasant should feel secure on his land, that his land be protected by law and that no measures of expropriation—except in cases stated by law, when general social neces- sity so requires—may deprive him of his land as long as he works it ... he himself should decide whether to join in socialist cooperation and large-scale agricultural production, which is the only way to pull him out of backwardness and poverty.

". . . The greater part of the arable land in Yugoslavia is the property of the individual producer. . . .

". . . The peasantry must have equal status with other working people . . . necessary in order to make the peasants . . . interested in exerting the greatest effort to increase the productivity of labor. . . .

"The policy of the League of the Communists of Yugoslavia in agri- culture consists in gradual socialization of agricultural production . . . without forcible interference with the individual ownership of land. . . .

". . . organizers of modern agricultural production . . . today . . . are, first of all, the socially owned farms, peasant work cooperatives, general agricultural cooperatives and supply farms of the agricultural co- operatives."

It is hard to see why the Yugoslav Communists did not think of these things in 1949–53 instead of antagonizing the peasants, their chief supporters during the last war.

IN 1972 Yugoslav agriculture contributed 20 percent to the social product (the Yugoslav equivalent of the gross national product); industry and mining, 38 percent. Social farms account for one-third of the total agri- cultural output but employ only 200,000 workers. The average small holding covers only about eight acres, while the total labor force working on small holdings amounts to nearly five million.

You will often hear in Yugoslavia that the peasants are the best off nowadays. Of course, this is not true of all peasants and of all regions. Rich peasants were a small minority in prewar Yugoslavia, while now- adays there is a substantial percentage of what one might call prosperous peasants in the fertile regions of Vojvodina, Serbia and Slavonia. The prewar peasant indebtedness was officially estimated at $7.50 for every man, woman and child. The prewar peasant went into debt because of the so-called "scissors" between the agricultural and industrial prices. In 1938, for instance, he had to give 44 pounds of barley for two boxes of matches. Three-quarters of the peasants had no beds but slept on straw mats, on rugs, in sacks or on the bare earthen floor. The bed itself was mostly a wooden frame with straw or leaves dumped inside and an old coat thrown over it. There was no linen most of the time. In winter up to twenty persons would crowd into one room. Often livestock slept in the same room. All peasant debts were canceled after the war. There are still places in the mountains or amid arid rocks where people live with livestock and where wooden ploughs are used, but this is on the way out. Also there are fewer landless peasants; also going down is the number of those confined to barren soil. Wattle huts are forbidden by law. Even government health insurance has been extended to embrace the peasants. Electricity, too, has penetrated into the poorer villages. Except for the poorest and most out-of-the-way villages, the peasants have begun to do away with the traditional earth-and-stone hearths; they install wood-burning stoves and use porcelain kitchen-ware instead of the patriarchal wooden and earthen bowls. In many parts, especially in Macedonia, new housing has been constructed of stone, wood and bricks.

THE orientation of Macedonian agriculture has been toward limited grain crops in favor of industrial plants and the so-called plantations. These are vast, single-crop social farms growing only cotton, rice or apples, or consist of vineyards or fields of mulberry trees. The original suggestion for developing "plantations" came from UNESCO (United Nations Educational, Scientific and Cultural Organization). The experts thought that Macedonia might be an ideal site for raising medicinal herbs on large land complexes and furnished financial and technical assistance for such projects. Whereupon the Macedonians got the idea that Macedonia might be equally suited for other kinds of "planta-tion" growing.

This does not mean that grain has been neglected in Macedonia. On the contrary, the American hybrid corn is a favorite high-yield crop, as in the rest of Yugoslavia. So is the Italian wheat. On the other hand, even those who have never visited Macedonia will have heard of the renowned beans of Tetovo. Also much attention is paid, let us say, to apples. Besides the famous native red-yellow-green Tetovo apple, sold "from the tree," that is, before it is picked, there are the American red "Delicious" apple, the red-yellow "Jonathan" apple and the green "New-ton" apple, all gaining ground because of a more reliable yield.

In the Lake Ohrid region you will notice young trees carefully spaced on poor or chalky ground strewn with small rocks. All the way to Bitola along the Greek frontier there is a heroic effort at reforestation of a countryside which once was literally furry with dense woods. Macedonian forests were ravaged by inordinate clearing and neglect, but the most pernicious enemy of the forest was the goat. That is why in 1947 the so-called goat law was passed, compelling, as mentioned previously, the peasants to surrender, for an indemnity, all their goats, which the government then sold for meat and hide and gradually helped the peasants replace the goats with sheep. All around the regions of the Ohrid and Prespa Lakes you will, aside from large tracts of saplings, find yourself among orchards again, as well as vineyards, vegetable and flower gardens, and tobacco fields. Here you will also see the irrigation canals, the Lake Ohrid network being no older than 1958.

North of the town of Bitola stretches the beautiful plain of Pelagonia all the way to Prilep. Unlike some other Macedonian plains, which have to be irrigated, this one has to be drained. It used to be a land of ponds and marshes never tilled, and was until not long ago a hotbed of malaria. In the war of 1912 the Turks made their last stand at Bitola by opening the dams to inundate the Pelagonian fields; in consequence, the Serbian army had to assault the Turkish positions wading chest-deep in water. Today drained Pelagonia can boast social farms. Swerving north from Bitola, away from the Greek border, you will pass through great expanses of grain, corn, vineyards, tobacco, sugar beets and sunflowers, where there used to be only morass and floods.

The entire luscious vastness through which the Vardar makes its way south from the churning Demir Kapija canyon to the Salonika bay abounds in tomatoes and green peppers, and everywhere you behold vineyard plantations. The Gevgelia region on the Greek border is celebrated for its grapes. In this and the nearby Valandovo countryside you drive through long rows of widely spaced trees reminding you of Asian rubber plantations—these are mulberry plantations for raising silkworms. And every once in a while you will spot white-speckled cotton and opium poppy fields on both sides of the road.

Across a mountain range, in the southeastern corner of Macedonia between Greece and Bulgaria, spreads the luxuriant valley of Strumica. Here you will come not only upon vineyards, orchards, fields of tobacco, cotton, opium poppies, but also sesame and peanuts. A social farm is known here for its modern housing development complete with a water-main system. To the north from here, after climbing another mountain chain, you descend into the Kočani basin and its wide rice fields irridescent with rainbow colors in the sun. These fields, also a postwar development, are flooded in the spring to yield excellent rice in the fall. Not far from the nearby town of Štip, at the edge of the bleak and arid Sheep's Field, is another social farm, called "Red Star," created so to speak out of nothing. It was a true pioneering job. Land had to be ploughed up that for centuries had not been worked and on whose mourning face nothing grew. It all began with one horse, two carts and thirteen men on 148 acres, back in 1948, the uneasy year of the Tito-Stalin break.

IN the same southeastern corner of Macedonia, near Lake Doiran, spreads the already mentioned large social agricultural enterprise of Bogdanci. Most of its income is derived from tomatoes, followed by green peppers and grapes. The biggest foreign customer is West Germany. Rice growing, as suggested, is being encouraged in Macedonia, although rice must be imported in large measure. The Bogdanci enterprise was the first to grow rice in this subtropical zone. It also used American hybrid corn. Generally, the peasant in this part of the country does not hold on to the land as stubbornly as he used to. He often sells his plot to the cooperative and works on it for excellent pay. Or else he keeps very little land, for today he can live comfortably on 3.7 acres if he grows, say, green peppers. The Bogdanci social enterprise has built the formerly mentioned coffee-house restaurant-hotel in the village, a movie house, an amateur theater, and a public library. And its streets have electric lights. Earlier, this whole plain was nothing but wild bush country, wasteland and the home of wolves.

The so-called Lipkovo System near the town of Kumanovo in north-central Macedonia represents in some ways perhaps a still greater achievement. It is not only an economical and technological achievement but a human demonstration of what underdeveloped people can do together when set free. Here we have a power plant; electricity and a water main for the countryside and the town of Kumanovo; mechanized and scientific farming; cooperatives with the individual cooperation of the peasants; sanitation and cleanliness; school and road building; a modern standard of living; plus goodwill among neighbors of different backgrounds. The irrigation sprays, consisting of multiple jets, gracefully turn and lilt, each making a separate bow as if in a stately old dance. Work with draft animals is forbidden, only machines till the land. It is a two-crop farm. Italian wheat and American hybrid corn are cultivated in addition to tobacco, grapes and vegetables; there are also cattle and hogs. The peasants here have long done away with hearths and introduced electric stoves; brought in beds; replaced the wooden and earthen kitchenware with porcelain dishes and metal pots and pans; introduced electric lighting and radios.

There is more to Lipkovo. Returning one day before dusk to the town of Kumanovo and passing through one of the once derelict hamlets, now a string of modern villages, I watched a mosque, a school building, many new brick houses under red-tiled roofs, clean children in neatly kept courtyards, tractors and other field machines in repose, Asian buffaloes trudging home, a cow crossing the asphalt road, a man on a donkey crossing a tranquil field. And for a long time I observed people in brown Macedonian wool caps, white Albanian skull caps and an occasional red fez swathed in white cloth smoking and talking peacefully after a day's work. For in the Lipkovo System Macedonians, Albanians and Turks live and work together. It is not difficult to make a peasant use a tractor. It is short of a miracle to make former mortal enemies want to use it together.

Cultural and Spiritual Values

Churches, Frescoes, Wood Carving and the Holy Mountain

IN prewar Yugoslavia there was no Macedonian Eastern Orthodox Church; there was only a Serbian Church. After liberation, in 1945, the first Macedonian ecclesiastical and lay assembly was held. Priests and laymen passed a resolution demanding the reestablishment of the medieval Ohrid archbishopric and the prohibition of Serbian bishops in Macedonia. Procrastination followed until, finally, under the Serbian Patriarch German, the question was solved to Macedonian satisfaction. In 1958 another assembly was held in Ohrid, and His Grace Dositey was elected the first archbishop of the reestablished Macedonian Church. With the Serbian Orthodox Church, the Macedonian Church maintains its ties in purely canonical matters through the person of the Serbian Patriarch. In internal affairs, the Macedonian Church is independent. Reestablishment of the Macedonian Archbishopric of Ohrid was part of the movement for Macedonian national self-determination. It was one of the strangely logical instances where priests and Communists stood together for a great common cause, the cause of national independence.

Subsequently the first national Macedonian Church abroad was founded by immigrants in Melbourne, Australia. It obtained a priest from Macedonia. In the United States, Macedonian immigrants in Gary, Indiana, and in Columbus, Ohio, also had priests sent from Macedonia at their request. In Canada, where Macedonian immigrants are the most numerous, their congregations in Windsor and Toronto also have sent for priests from Macedonia.

THE first Slav churches and monasteries in the Balkans were built in Macedonia. At Lake Ohrid alone, in the seventeenth century, there were around 330 churches, practically one for every day in the year.

Nearly all monasteries are situated on selected spots of extraordinary beauty. Around Lake Ohrid itself there are now some sixty churches, varying in date from the ninth to the seventeenth centuries; some are still in use for divine service. Among them are a number of "cave churches" along the shore, so named because they are built into the rocks. Some can be approached only by boat. Some have frescoes painted on rough stones which serve as walls. The most beautiful cave church is the one at Kalište near Struga.

En route toward the great fortress walls of Samuel's citadel you pass by the oldest church in Macedonia, the ninth-century St. Panteleimon. Here, it is said, in 893 Kliment first preached the Gospel in the Slav tongue and wrote his first treatise in the newly invented Cyrillic alphabet. Here he was buried in 916 in a tomb built by his own hands. The church was later transformed into a mosque, and today only shapeless quadrangular ruins remain. The citizens of Ohrid dug up the relics and transferred them first to a small church and then to the church of the Holy Mother of God Perivleptos. It is this church which today is named St. Kliment's.

You reach this church by scrambling still further to the crest of the hill on which most of Ohrid is clustered. The church, built in 1295, is in the form of a cross. The porch has a low wide flat roof, supported by sturdy columns. Within the porches there is an antechamber. Beyond is a darker antechamber where the not yet baptized and the penitents used to crowd; still beyond is the pitch-dark church for the believers. When cleaned of darkened varnish and oil in 1950, a magnificent collection of art works reappeared. Every inch of the floor, the walls, the ceiling is covered with frescoes which look as if they had been done yesterday. In the "Pietà," the Mother of God laments Christ with her hair flowing down over her shoulders. The faces are alive and each one is different. The men are broad, youthful, fullfleshed, with powerful, athletic bodies; the women too are broadshouldered with muscular arms. Even elderly hermits, or old priests at the altars, are depicted as robust men, full of life and energy. Old age is absent from the St. Kliment's frescoes. The masters, who knew anatomy and how to put action into their paintings, had their names inscribed on them. They were the local Macedonian fresco painters Mihailo and Eurihije. Responsible for frescoes in many other Macedonian as well as Serbian and Greek churches, these two artists are as revered in Byzantine art history as are Cimbue and Giotto in the history of the Italian Renaissance.

On September 10, 1966, a thousand years after St. Kliment's death, a great crowd gathered on the Ohrid hill below the main gate of Samuel's fortress. The Macedonian archbishop in white *kamilavka* (brimless top hat) and veil was there, and other Macedonian prelates, as well as Serbian Orthodox and Moslem religious leaders, and the Roman Catholic bishop of Skopje. The Mayor of Skopje and the Macedonian premier made speeches, a choir sang in the open air, and a priest's powerful Chaliapinlike voice could be heard from a distance thundering above the choir. Watching the crowd and the lake below, one could not escape the feeling that the mountains around were hushed and listened to man. It was a strange Communist-nationalist-religious ceremony celebrating the anniversary of this great churchman, the founder of the Cyrillic schools.

THE glory of Macedonia is the St. Sofia Church at the lower end of the old town of Ohrid. It dates from the first half of the eleventh century and is built on the ruins of a basilica of the fifth century. The Turks plastered over all the frescoes in the fifteenth century and transformed the church into a mosque by tearing down the cupola and erecting a minaret. In 1912 the Serbian army drove out the Turks and tore down the minaret.

Restoration and conservation of Yugoslav, and especially Macedonian, frescoes began in 1950. The whole wall of St. Sofia facing the lake had developed a cant of more than two-and-a-half feet; this was subsequently repaired by experts from UNESCO. First they had to remove the plaster laid on by the Turks, then fix the fresco paintings onto canvas so that they could be peeled off, after which the wall was repaired. In 1955 UNESCO published the book *Yugoslavia, Medieval Frescoes*, with 32 full-page color reproductions, including Macedonian works.

Most of St. Sofia's frescoes date from the eleventh century, the rest are no younger than the fourteenth. Every fresco has been evaluated at more than 20,000 dollars. In these frescoes facial expressions are realistic. Tears and grief are clearly seen on the figures in "The Virgin's Death." It was this fresco that prompted some art historians to claim that the Macedonian painters of the twelfth and thirteenth centuries had made strides toward a new art, which came to bloom in Italy in the fourteenth and fifteenth centuries. The director of the Ohrid Museum said that the Louvre had offered more than 3.5 million dollars for one of the St. Sofia frescoes.

Until recently, the St. Sofia Church in Ohrid was considered a Byzantine creation. But V. N. Lazarev, a member of the Moscow Academy of Science and of Moscow University and an authority on

Byzantine civilization, saw in the frescoes of St. Sofia certain archaic elements which he considered proof of their being the work of Slav masters. Indeed, the St. Sofia frescoes possess the monumentality of the Constantinople frescoes and dignified poses as in the "Immaculate Conception." But in the same church there are also coarse figures depicted in a naturalistic way. Such are the figures on the eastern pilasters where patriarchs are rendered with sharp, severe faces, all alien to Constantinople art.

The St. Sofia angels seem detached from the walls on which they are painted, ready to float into the vault of heaven. On some of the frescoes, such as "The Assumption," you will notice intense human feelings: three figures on the left and two on the right lift the ends of their robes to wipe away their tears; this you would not find in the art of Constantinople. You will also observe elegant, elongated female figures, almost like those of American fashion models. The western wall has on its outside scenes carved from ancient mythology. And you will see a Negro figure in a painting of ascetics.

THIS may be a good place to say something about fresco technique.

First, a reminder. The holes that you so often see in the frescoes do not denote deliberate damage made by the infidels. They were made by the nails the Turks drove through the new plaster to cover the frescoes. They put plaster on the frescoes because human bodies and faces were forbidden in churches converted to mosques. Also the eyes of the saints in many a fresco were poked out, not by the Turks but by superstitious sterile Christian women who drank the scrapings in water to be able to bear children.

The Yugoslavs learned from the Italians the art of taking the frescoes off the walls. But first, how to put them on. The word "fresco" is Italian and means "fresh." In other words, a fresco is a painting on mortar which is still fresh and moist. The old masters would first denude the wall and thoroughly dry it. Then they would flush the wall with water and cover it with several layers of mortar, which consists of lime and sand. The bottom layer is the thickest and consists of coarse sand and lime. The second layer is thinner and is of finer composition. The third layer is of finest dry sand and slaked lime. On this last moist layer of mortar the painter draws the outline and then paints in colors. The colors with which frescoes are painted are earthen dyes, of mineral origin. The dye is diluted in moisture, the lime comes to the surface and calcifies with the dye into a thin solid layer of 1–2 millimeters thickness, firmly attached to the mortar.

The taking off is done as follows. A sheet of linen is pasted onto the surface with a glue that easily dissolves in hot water. Boards are prepared to receive the cut-off sections. When the linen is dry, it is detached from the wall. The linen keeps the fresco in a solid state.

The return of the fresco onto the wall is done in the following manner. The mortar on the back side is taken off with instruments until the fresco is 5 millimeters thick. Then flax linen is put onto the back side and the fresco is mounted onto a wooden or aluminum frame. The linen on the fresco is taken off with hot water and the fresco is put on the wall.

The church and the monastery of St. Naum are named after another pupil of Cyril's who taught Cyrillic letters to the Slavs. The buildings stand a hundred yards from the Albanian frontier at the southern shore of Lake Ohrid. Numerous sources of the Black Drim, a whole network of ice-cold rivulets, spurt right nearby and as a river enter the lake to emerge north at Struga. Actually the latter is a new river, but the people believe that the Black Drim does not mix with the lake and emerges intact. The church and the monastery date from the tenth century and are perched on a rock jutting out in the lake. There are two tombs of St. Naum in the church. One, the original, is underground and the other, artificial one, stands above it. Before the war peasants used to lie down on top of the artificial grave and listen to the "thumps" of St. Naum, who would cure their ills. This is now forbidden, being an act of superstition, but the peasants still believe that St. Naum cures diseases. Contributions are permitted to St. Naum in a special box above the artificial coffin.

The church and the monastery are under government protection as monuments of culture, as is the church of St. Sofia. But there are no monks there any more, only a government custodian. An icon from the eleventh century was taken by the French to Paris during the First World War—the Allied Salonika Front ran through the area.

The church of St. Naum is a dark brown, rather neglected collection of cupolas and roofs, out of which young trees have sprung up. Inside it is very dark, light coming in through little slits in the cupolas. Until recently, the walls were black from a fire which had destroyed most of the frescoes. However, the whiteness of the faces and the hands had survived, and the effect was eerie. The remaining frescoes have now been restored.

ONE of Macedonia's great attractions is the Church of Sv. Spas—the Ascension—in Skopje. It was built at the end of the seventeenth century, after the burning of Skopje by the Austrian general Silvio Piccolomini in 1688. It stands on the east bank of the Vardar, at the foot of the Turkish fortress Kale, half underground, with a high wall concealing it from the street. Stairs lead down into the half-buried church. The Turks did not permit churches to rise above the Moslem buildings, nor did they permit steeples, only minarets. Also, no bells were allowed, only rattles. A wooden belfry, separate from the church, was constructed in 1908, after the Young Turk revolution, with a metal rattle beside it to call the faithful. You will be assured by reliable people that in olden times an underground passage existed to and from the church for the faithful. However that may be, there is an underground passage from the churchyard to the Turkish fortress above. The tomb of the anti-Turk revolutionary Goce Delčev stands in the middle of the stone churchyard surrounded by a ground-floor arcade.

The most beautiful aspect of the church of Sv. Spas is its iconostasis. The screen is more than ten yards long and more than six yards in height. The carving is very deep, several inches, and each figure stands out sharply. The carving displays the same fantastic intricacy we find in Indian ivory carvings. There is scarcely a square inch of flat surface. Everywhere are birds, animals and figures entwined with foliage, with additional carvings in the background. The whole story of the Gospel is enacted here. In the scene depicting Herod and John the Baptist, Salomé, dancing the Dance of the Seven Veils, wears an elaborate Macedonian national costume and holds a handkerchief, as is done in the Slav dance of *oro* or *kolo*; the executioner has an Albanian costume. The Macedonian artists symbolically presented the executioner in the national dress of the perennial enemy. In a scene depicting Abraham, the costumes are again Macedonian. There are also high stalls for dignitaries in Sv. Spas, all embellished with "deep" wood carvings. Here the artists have selected themes from nature: flowers, sheep, deer, hawks, wolves, boars' heads. The iconostasis was made by Peter Filipovski and his brother, and the two brothers Garka and Makarije Frčkovski, all from Galičnik but trained in the Debar school of wood carving. It took them five years to complete the work (1819–24). In a sort of self-portrait, they showed themselves at work at the bench in the lower right-hand corner of the iconostasis. While Peter Filipovski gives instructions, the two brothers hold a hammer and chisel. Peter Filipovski also left behind the equally famous iconostasis of St. Jovan Bigorski in western Macedonia.

Every once in a while swarms of schoolchildren with their teachers invade the church of Sv. Spas. Foreign visitors also come every day, and German women tell their husbands, "*Sehr schön*" (Very beautiful). The church of Sv. Spas was shaken but not seriously damaged in the

1963 earthquake. Incidentally on one wall, where portions of the plaster fell off, traces of frescoes of an earlier date were revealed.

AT this point we might say something about "deep" wood carving. This is neither bas relief nor high relief. A "deep" wood carving consists of hollowed-out spaces and galleries inside the panel, containing fully sculptured figures and objects that are only thinly attached to the main piece of the wood. "Deep" wood carving began in Debar, near the Albanian frontier, in the twelfth century, was later developed in Ohrid and flowered well into the nineteenth century. First used only for iconostasis work, it was gradually extended to serve as embellishments on furniture, walls, ceilings, columns. The tradition was maintained for generations, with Macedonian wood-carvers working for the churches and the Turks alike. In the fourteenth century one pound of "deep" wood carving was worth one pound of gold. There is in Ohrid's National Museum a life-size wooden statue of St. Kliment. Done in the fourteenth century in walnut, and black with patina, it was exhibited at the International Exhibition of Medieval Art in Paris in 1951 and evaluated at about one million dollars.

From the eighteenth century on, Macedonian carvers worked in Serbia, Bulgaria, Greece, Rumania. But in the twentieth century "deep" wood carving has been on the decline, although in 1928 a school was formed in Debar; it was transferred to Ohrid in 1930 and continued for some time after the war. At one time after the war, the "deep" wood carving school in Ohrid had 54 masters and 14 pupils. The cabinets in its workshop look baroque; and the tables look like late Renaissance. You can admire the school's work in some Macedonian government offices and in the Hotel Palace. The Workers' Rest Home in Ohrid also has drawing rooms with "deep-carved" furniture, and a ceiling has been exhibited in the Netherlands. The best material for "deep" wood carving is dried walnut wood because of its hardness and dark color. But oak, cherry, pear and linden may also be used. The composition is usually first drawn on paper to be transferred in indigo onto the wood. Then the wood is cut along the outline. The part outside the outline is planed down to a certain depth, and the area of the outline is modeled. "Deep" wood carving is done with special instruments, the most important being wedges of various sizes and forms. For more intricate work in depth, as many as 200 instruments may be used.

As late as 1959 you could see in the workshop of the Ohrid school a massive walnut bookcase with columns carved in infinite detail—an order from the Netherlands. Not long afterward, the school closed for lack of funds and commercial interest. After all, few people will want a wooden ceiling today. The Skopje School of Arts obtained the inventory of the Ohrid "deep" wood carving school. Today this kind of wood carving is only one of the subjects in the curriculum of the Skopje School of Arts. What remains in Ohrid is a school of carpentry, which occasionally does a piece of "deep" wood carving to order. The carvers themselves have now formed a cooperative where the craft is carried on. Their work now is mostly intricately carved panels and furniture for government offices. Much of it is also exported, and fine examples may be seen in the Ohrid Museum of Modern Art before they are shipped abroad. Still, the masters of the Ohrid "deep" wood carving today earn more with their carpentry than with their art.

WHILE in Skopje one should also pay a visit to at least one of the city's several mosques—the Mustafa Mosque. The big empty round space inside the mosque has niches in the wall. At the center of the eastern wall rise the *mihrab*, from which the *hodja* reads the Koran, and the *mimbar*, decorated with marble carvings, which he ascends to read the prayers on feast days. There are separate enclosures for women on the ground floor and in the decorative circular gallery above. The glass windows are opaque, some broken, some missing, all being part of the original construction. In front of the mosque is a porch standing on six marble columns and topped by three small cupolas. Above it all rises a huge dome made to look like the sky. In the stairwells of the minaret only an occasional tiny slit lets in the light. The top of the minaret is of marble and is ornamented. The climb is an athletic feat. A muezzin—religious public crier—has to climb the minaret five times a day to call the faithful to their prayers. The old muezzin of the Mustafa Mosque climbed it only once a day. There is a magnificent view from the circular gallery below the top of the minaret, from which the muezzin calls to prayer. The old stone work is eroded from many rains and looks like mountain rocks. There are also original stones in the cupola, appearing exactly as when it was first made.

The mosque was constructed by a ruler of Skopje, Mustafa Pasha, in 1492, the year America was discovered and a hundred years after the Turkish conquest of Skopje. Behind the minaret is a vault with the remains of Mustafa and other prominent pashas of Skopje.

IN the environs of Skopje there are many splendid medieval churches and frescoes. South of Skopje, on a once most difficult road, are Kral Marko's church and monastery, with frescoes that rank among the most beautiful in the country. North of Skopje, the tiny church of St. Andreja was built in 1389 by Kral Marko's brother Andreja high above a precipice. But today this church stands only a few feet above the mountain lake with which the recently dammed-up Treska has filled the gorge. The frescoes of St. Andreja, done in the year of the catastrophic defeat of the Serbs by the Turks on the Kosovo field, depict no miracles, no scenes from the Virgin Mary's life, no hermits, but mostly warrior saints. They are rendered three dimensionally, with movements and expressions they would have had in life. The native art historians explain that the frescoes reflect the mood of the time and the struggle against the Turks.

In the village of Nerezi, high up on a mountain slope southwest of Skopje, stand the fascinating church and monastery of St. Panteleimon, built by Alexis Comnenus in 1164. The church has five cupolas, a central one and four collateral ones at its corners, and its walls are alternately of stone and brick. The columns resemble those of ancient Greece. In the monks' quarters the solitary cells have ceilings of wood, with designs using squares and rosettes—a similar design is used in the more affluent Macedonian houses. The Nerezi church is an outstanding example of the Macedonian medieval fresco painting. In 1923–26, a Russian scholar, Professor N. Okunev, succeeded in uncovering the twelfth-century frescoes in one part of the church. After the war, in 1954–57, the rest were uncovered. Two areas of the interior walls of the church have been painted and decorated. The whole of the first area is filled with pictures of hermits, penitents and holy warriors. The second area shows the great feasts. Among the more important frescoes here are "The Lamentation for the Dead Christ" and "The Virgin." The "Pietà" shows the Virgin Mary sitting with the dead body of Christ on her knees, her cheek on his head, contrary to all the canons of the time. In both the "Pietà" and "The Descent from the Cross," Christ is shown as a mortal, suffering man. There is an extraordinary sense of color displayed in all these paintings, and no two faces are alike. Professor F. Mesesnel was so impressed by the realism of the Nerezi frescoes that he gave it as his opinion that the artist must have studied the faces of ordinary people and copied them when he portrayed the faces of the saints. Professor N. Okunov believed the Nerezi frescoes are important for the study of the sources of the Renaissance.

In eastern Macedonia, the church and monastery of St. Gabriel, from 1341, stand 3,000 feet above the town of Zletovo and are reachable only on foot or on horseback. Some frescoes in this church describe lay activities, such as fishing, or the round dance of *oro* or *kolo* with national costumes and instruments in a pictorial presentation of Psalm 148:

"exhorting the celestial, the terrestrial and the rational creatures to praise God."

In western Macedonia, in a rough bear and lynx country facing the Albanian frontier, perching above a river canyon, we find the church and monastery of St. Jovan Bigorski, built in 1017. Again, there are no monks here anymore, only a government custodian. During the Second World War this was the seat of the Regional Committee of the Macedonian Communist party. But St. Jovan Bigorski is well known to the public for a beautiful iconostasis by the famous nineteenth-century master carvers, the brothers Filipovski and Makarije Frčkovski. As in the church of Sv. Spas, here too the masters carved their own likenesses in the iconostasis, showing how they worked at the bench, while Peter Filipovski, with a finger to his forehead, reads the Bible scenes which they are to depict in wood. The iconostasis is indeed comparable to that of Sv. Spas. The walnut panels are hollowed out and contain scenes from the Old and New Testaments, including Salomé's dance and the Last Supper, all done with infinite patience.

ACCORDING to the numerous inscriptions on Macedonian frescoes, the painters were native Slavs. Of course, they had learned from the Byzantine masters, but they were good pupils and developed their own school, as did the equally talented Serbs in the north. The main characteristics of the Macedonian school were rejection of the stylized Byzantine rigidity, strong naturalism, and use of three-dimensional "perspective" or space. These characteristics can, for example, be seen in the frescoes of the St. Kliment church in Ohrid, where the faces seem to be of flesh and blood, and their outlines are indicated by shading. Until the Serbian King Milutin's conquests in the first half of the fourteenth century, Serbia and Macedonia were influenced by both the East and the West, including the Western plastic arts and Italian iconography. There were no ugly faces, no cold Greek figures, no tortured Germanic shapes, no gargoyles. Realism runs like a red thread through the Macedonian school. According to some Yugoslav and foreign experts, Macedonian painters, though grounded in decorative Byzantine art, succeeded in the twelfth and thirteenth centuries in making the first steps toward a new art, which in the fourteenth and fifteenth centuries developed into the Italian Renaissance. This is a bold statement, but there is much to support it.

Macedonian (and Serbian) frescoes belong to the general realm of Byzantine painting. Byzantium was a civilization, and Macedonian art was an individual part of it. The basic principles were Byzantine, but they were worked out separately by the Greeks, the Armenians, the Russians, the Macedonians, and others.

In the sixteenth and seventeenth centuries, under the Turks, fresco art became stereotyped and died out in the eighteenth century.

EVEN a brief survey of Macedonian churches and monasteries would be deficient without a glimpse at Mt. Athos, or the Holy Mountain, in Greek Macedonia.

The Athos peninsula is the easternmost of the three tongues of land projecting from the Greek Macedonian peninsula of Chalcidice into the northern Aegean. The Athos prong, about twenty-five miles long and varying from three to five miles in width, is at its southern end a region of precipitous slopes and romantic gorges. Here surges straight from the sea the 6,860-foot-high pyramidal peak of Mount Athos, often in clouds and snow-capped even in summer.

On Athos there are twenty monasteries. Seventeen are Greek; one is Serbian—Hilandar; one is Bulgarian—Zograph; and one is Russian—St. Panteleimon, famous ever since Rasputin visited it. Great Lavra is the oldest, founded in 963 by St. Athanasius, and it still houses eighty Greek Orthodox monks. The twenty monasteries mostly hang precariously on steep cliffs; they are staggering feats of construction, built on the edges of sheer precipices and equaled perhaps only by the Tibetan monasteries. Tiers of gaily painted balconies decorate the main walls, which are sometimes fifteen feet thick as a precaution against frequent earthquakes and former pirates. The walls often support high towers. In the middle of each courtyard there is a main church and along the walls run monastic cells, sometimes in several storeys.

Athos is an autonomous province. There is a legislative body known as the Holy Synaxis. The executive body, the Epistasis, consists of the representatives of the five leading monasteries: the Greek Great Lavra, Vatopedi, Iviron, Dionysiou and the Serbian Hilandar. The members of both bodies are elected every year. All decisions must be reached unanimously. The highest ecclesiastical authority is the Oecumenical Patriarch in Istanbul. The temporal authority is represented by the governor, appointed by the Greek Ministry of Foreign Affairs. He commands the local police. Permission to visit Athos must be obtained from both the Greek authorities in Salonika and the ecclesiastical authorities in Karyes, the capital of Athos. This is the only Christian monastic republic in the world. In 1963 it celebrated its thousandth anniversary.

Karyes is the seat of the monks' autonomous government and of the Greek civil governor. Its name means "the town of walnuts," for it is surrounded by forests of walnut trees. Karyes consists mainly of residences connected with the monasteries. There are also a post and telegraph office, as well as various shops to supply the monks. Around the square cluster shops with picture postcards, amber beads, incense and various bric-à-brac. There is also a little inn. There is no hotel. Visitors are put up in one of the monastic residences.

The first monks settled on Athos in the middle of the ninth century, before the monasteries were built. In 1933 the Athos population consisted of 7,000 monks. The number has been dwindling. In 1962 fewer than 2,000 monks lived on Athos. In another generation there may be only 1,000 monks left; by the turn of the century, perhaps little more than one hundred. But Athos has carried on for over a thousand years, and it is hard to imagine that it will cease to exist as a religious community.

The Athos monks are permitted to eat meat twice a year. Their diet is simple: fish, octopus, porridge, macaroni, bread, fruit, vegetables, and homemade Turkish delight, downed with ouzo or a beaker of local wine. All monasteries have their own electricity, post offices, hospitals, bakeries. They are linked by telephone to Karyes. Among other activities, the monks make telegraph poles for certain Greek areas, and run quite a profitable export trade in wine and walnuts. You hear church bells only on special occasions. What you regularly hear is the rhythmical beat of the wooden and metal rattles. There are also jackals on Athos.

Until some time ago there were no radios on the Holy Mountain. This has changed. On my way from Karyes to the Serbian monastery of Hilandar, my guide and mule ran into a blizzard and came to the monastery of Docheiariou. This monastery has an impressive set of buildings atop high walls far above the sea, with a high tower surrounding it all. There were the blue galleries, crackling fireplaces, immaculate cleanliness, and a radio in every cell; the favorite programs seemed to be rock music and soccer games.

Precious dusty, crinkled and fragile volumes fill the library shelves. Every church and chapel shimmers with gold and silver—glittering candelabra, chalices encrusted with rubies and emeralds, the hands of statues inlaid with solid gold, mosaic floors inlaid with colored marble, icons encased in scintillating silverwork. The scholarly and historical value of the documents, manuscripts and books in the libraries of various monasteries is unsurpassable. So is the artistic and monetary value of the icons, miniatures, objects of jewelry, gold, ivory, embroidery, brocade and silk to be found here.

On the Holy Mountain you travel on foot or on muleback. It is not always easy to pass through the beauty of the peaceful, thickly wooded and rocky mountain because the paths seldom go anywhere but from monastery to monastery. From the port of Daphne, on the western shore of Athos, you can walk up to Karyes along steep serpentine paths, which in 1963, the year of the millennium, were enlarged to accommodate a bus, the only one on Athos.

No woman can set foot on the Holy Mountain. This prohibition extends to female animals; not even a sheep is allowed. The only exceptions are cats and hens. The reason for the ban is supposedly explained by a legend relating that the Virgin Mary once visited the monks on the Holy Mountain and no female was to set foot on it after that. The rule was first put down in the eleventh century by Athanasius. The founder of Great Lavra said, "Have no animal of the female sex in use, seeing that you have renounced the female sex altogether. . . ."

The Serbian monastery of Hilandar, the northernmost of the group and best known for its splendid library, was founded in 1198 by the Serbian ruler Stefan Nemanja. It is situated by a brook in a valley surrounded by woods. President Tito of Yugoslavia some time ago presented Hilandar with an electric generator and a tractor. At one time the monastery harbored 200 monks. At the last count (1960), the number was twenty-eight. By Greek law, if a non-Greek monastery on Athos falls below a certain number of monks, it automatically becomes Greek. For Hilandar, the minimum number is seven. The Hilandar people complain of Greek "procedural" obstacles to having monks from Communist Yugoslavia join them.

Some Athos monks prefer to live outside the monasteries, in solitary huts and cottages, or in the crevices and caves that dot the grim cliffs of Mt. Athos. These monks live like hermits, the last ones in Europe; sometimes they don't speak to anyone for months. To reach some of them, chains have been fastened above precipices. They say that there are only a dozen of them left, no one knows for sure. They spend their days in meditation and prayer. They eat what they can find in the stony wilderness, maybe a few random figs. You will sometimes see a rope dangling from the vertical crags down toward the sea; a basket is suspended in the rope, and in it fishermen will hopefully leave a fish or two. People will become hermits for all kinds of expiation. When somebody has shown no sign of life for some time, a man will eventually climb up, find a body in a cave, pour wine over it and bury it.

In 1962, a year before the thousand-year jubilee of the Holy Mountain, a Patriarchal Commission visited Athos to investigate the causes of the apparent decline of the monastic ideal. The population of all the monasteries was dwindling and there was difficulty in recruiting novices. Despite this, the Holy Mountain has a message.

In that year I attended a ceremonial all-night service in the cathedral of Karyes. Half-a-dozen bishops of the Patriarchal Commission were in the stalls, and dozens of priests and monks also attended. In tall black brimless hats on bearded heads, with long black veils trailing their flowing black folds, these imposing black figures stood erect along the walls or noiselessly floated about swinging their censers in the darkness dimly lit by hundreds of candles big and small. On all the walls, ceilings and pillars there were paintings. Gold was everywhere—candlesticks, icon frames, candelabra, vestments, utensils—all glittering, blinding, pure gold. I understood why people could be bereft of their senses at the sight of too much gold. And I understood the hypnotizing power of the two predominant colors in Byzantine art: black and gold, the night and the sun.

I had a long talk, in German, with the Athos governor, Dr. C. S. Constantopoulos. The Byzantine Church seeks the Inner Light, he said. He talked about how the painter of an icon "went into the inside, into the archetype," and how praying before an icon meant a transference "into the inside." I thought of trance and self-hypnosis. Present-day science, he said, is superficial, it teaches only technical culture. Personal perfection, he added, means God, science and love. I understood that the modern man must also be a monk. Everything fanatical, including nationalism, must be eradicated.

The governor gave a brief exposition of the spirit of Athos. He spoke of Plato's idea of finding oneself, which came down to finding the first Adam, the Adam before the Fall, who is the archetype of man, hidden in ourselves. For this, it is necessary to hear God's voice. To hear it, there must be silence. Silence gives birth to humility. The governor again quoted Plato as having said that from silence comes the creative word. But we cannot be silent, we talk too much, and always about ourselves, so nobody hears the other fellow. The first stage is silence. The second stage is prayer, preferably before an icon. The third stage is obtaining the form (*Gestalt, morphé*) of the archetype.

If this sounds abstruse, I thought that, of course, one should actively belong to both worlds, the inner and the outer, be both silent and talk, find oneself and others.

Every man is a total personality, not part of a mass. He belongs to groups in a world of variety, but not to the mass. The governor mentioned Nietzsche as having said that New York is a forest of stones. Athos is a place of concentrated spirit, a piece of land which is devoted to the spirit and nothing else. It is an isolated spiritual oasis in the desert of modern materialism.

But the Holy Mountain has of late become a tourist attraction. Is its way of life, as the anticlericals maintain, escapism and a cover for idleness? Or will it reassert itself, making a valid contribution to a world largely starved of spiritual values? Even so, as one clambers over the Holy Mountain, one may feel how the border between reality and unreality, wakefulness and dream, vanishes. It is all too easy for an outsider to view Athos as an anachronistic curiosity, a haven for misfits from a modern world. Sometimes tourists are more concerned with those very material things (food, bathroom, plumbing, women, living accommodations, conveniences) that the monks have rejected. Yet even such a traveler will eventually admit that the feeling of peace and serenity is the greatest single benediction that the Holy Mountain confers.

National Costumes, Dances, Songs, Poems

MORE than any other part of the Balkans, Macedonia abounds in beautiful national costumes. Nowhere in Macedonia will you see a woman in an all-black garb with a black kerchief, so common in Serbia, Dalmatia, Greece, Italy, Spain. On the contrary, Macedonian female costumes are a delight to the eye. Macedonian roads, streets and marketplaces still display an inexhaustible wealth of colorful female peasant dresses, tempered by good taste and sometimes of elegant cut.

On the weekly market day in Ohrid you will not see two women wear the same costume or the same colors. The female costumes here are mainly of various shades of green and light blue. Around the nearby Lake Prespa the costumes are black and white and red and white. Elsewhere the costumes are red of different shades and light yellow. Generally, they are almost tropically multicolored. Women often wear heavy aprons in front or in the back or both, sometimes consisting of fringes, more often of solid rugs. They are red or red and white, sometimes with vertical green stripes, or just multicolored like Oriental rugs. Near Gevgelia on the Greek frontier women wear flowers in their hair, which is also a Greek custom. Women's vests are red, green, blue, cherry-colored, often with gold filigree buttons and with yellow, white, orange and gold embroidery. Kerchiefs are brown, light yellow, light blue or white, with a leather strap under the chin. Sometimes the chin is wrapped in the kerchief like a bandaged jaw. Around the town of Bitola on the Greek frontier you will see white kerchiefs framing the face like triangles.

The Byzantine gold-and-black colors are worn by some females around Skopje. In the region of the Skopje Crna Gora women wrap their heads in a tower of white haberdashery, covering their hair and part of their faces. In the northwestern Macedonian region of Polog women wear a long white shirt with black ornaments and over it a sleeveless vest and a multicolored apron, all adorned with gold and silver coins. In the Lake Mavrovo region of western Macedonia women wear corselets of wild-cherry, blue or green color with many ornaments of gold or silver threadings. The vests of the women of the Radika canyon in the same region are strewn with gold filigree buttons. There are kerchiefs and scarves in Debar in southwestern Macedonia with embroidered designs that have come down from Egypt through Greek priests. In the regions of Štip and Kočani in eastern Macedonia women wear multicolored trousers. The Tsintsars in that area still wear black, and the women are distinguished by wide pleated skirts with narrow waists as well as heavy caps.

The headgear of a bride sometimes consists of a plume of cock feathers resembling some Mexican Indian or an African magician's headdress. In the region of Radoviš in southeastern Macedonia you will come across fantastically beautiful costumes of white-embroidered pink trousers showing from under the aprons, with red kerchiefs, sported by women riding horses covered with vivid oriental rugs. Such women riders might also wear red aprons and black kerchiefs, sometimes with a bridal-like white veil.

In Strumica you ought to sit in a cafe and watch the costumes pass by. You would see many dirty Gypsies. Also a woman with a hind apron with gorgeous multicolored designs. Then you would notice red white-speckled women's trousers. Then a beautiful black-white-pink dress with an embroidered red belt. Then you would observe a vest and apron all black with horizontal red lines. Or an Albanian with charcoal eyebrows and mustache in a brown skullcap, black cloth wound around it with the flap hanging in the back in the fashion of the Foreign Legion, brown trousers tight at the ankles and with a slanting black stripe down the side of each leg plus a red sash. Then three pretty rustic girls in multicolored kerchiefs and dresses and trousers, with green being the predominating color. All this among myriads of flies.

On the road from Skopje to the Greek border you may meet a woman in a horsecart in a red-rimmed white cape and a hood with two vertical black stripes, or another woman in a black cape with pink seams, or still another woman in a white cape with red embroidery and a red hood.

In contrast to the female costumes, the male attire in Macedonia is distinguished by moderation and simplicity. Macedonian men usually wear multicolored socks, white trousers, knee-long white shirts above the trousers, white sashes, black or brown flat-topped sheepskin caps. In roughly one-third of Macedonia, men wear aprons, and with pride. Moslems and Vlachs do not wear aprons. All those without aprons taunt the male apron-wearers by asking, "Are you women?" Male aprons are simpler and less flamboyant than the women's: their patterns mostly consist of vertical or horizontal black and white stripes. Men in modern dress may also be seen wearing an apron.

MARICA Antonova introduced me to the mysteries of Macedonian embroidery. We can only guess what the symbols in ornamentation mean. We have positive information about only a few; for instance, that a stylized jug on a bride's sleeve means that plum brandy is being drunk in her honor. As a rule, only those who worked the symbols knew their meaning, and they are no more. Macedonian embroideries, especially those from the Bitola region, are very similar to the embroideries of such non-Slav tribes as the Mordovians and the Cheremiss on the Volga. Why this should be so, no one knows.

The Skopje embroideries are very different from those of nearby Kumanovo. The latter favor black and red. The Skopje ones are black and white, with much srma (cotton thread around which a gold or silver thread is wound). The Skopje embroideries often have a gryphon for motif, the fabulous animal with the head and wings of an eagle and the body and hind quarters of a lion; it was believed by ancient Greeks to inhabit Scythia and guard its gold. Throughout Macedonia almost anything can be an embroidery motif: candles, leaves, flowers, especially the carnation; Poseidon's trident and Mercury's wand with two serpents wound around it; stylized men in an oro dance; the Byzantine emperor's head or the things he wore; a stylized townswoman, a bear's paw or simply the letter "C." Other motifs are stellar constellations, eyeglasses, vases, stylized butterflies, insects; symbols of X for Christ; a fish as an amulet against the evil eye. You will also encounter motifs such as arrows and even of airplanes in some of the latest embroideries. The greatest number of embroideries consist, of course, of undecipherable hieroglyphics. All kinds of geometrical figures, starting with concentric circles, also serve as motifs. Among the many cross symbols, meaning man, there is especially in the Bitola region the motif of the hooked cross, an inverted swastika with the hooks rounded and turned leftward, as a symbol of good luck (the word coming from Sanskrit svasti, meaning well-being, luck).

Embroideries are usually made according to set patterns—a village normally has two to five models stored away. First a drawing is made of the design with needlework. To embroider one shirt might take one year. In the villages all winter is spent on embroidery.

AS Havelock Ellis has said, dancing and building are the two primary arts. All other arts derive from them. Rhythm is at the root of the universe, and all human work is a kind of dance, since both are essentially rhythmic. It is impossible to imagine the ancient costumes of the people of Macedonia other than in the setting of their national dances and songs. And thus dance, song and costume combine to make a beautiful whole.

Most often folk dances are performed on Sundays and holidays. Traditionally, dancing and singing also accompany collective field work, especially following the completion of a harvest. The most festive occasions, however, when people indulge in folk dances with the greatest zest and skill and in the finest national costumes, are the main holidays (Christmas and Easter, St. George's Day, St. John's Eve), country fairs and church festivals. Such occasions resemble improvised, enthusiastic and resplendent folk art and fashion shows, at which one can revel in dances and dresses which make up a colorful aspect of our largely gray modern life.

The Macedonian dances are the earliest recorded dances in Yugoslavia and belong among the oldest recorded dances in the world. The prevalent ancient Thracian dance was a round dance, preserved today as the Macedonian *oro*, also known as *kolo* among other Yugoslav peoples, *horos* in Greece, *horo* in Bulgaria, *hora* in Rumania. *Oro*, according to the Thracian expert Tomaschek, is a Thracian word and means "jumping around in a circle." It was a wild, ecstatic Dionysian dance; today it is a gay dance with intricate, fast steps. A characteristic of the Macedonian *oro* is that it remains measured. Each step is calculated. Gradually the dance gains in tempo and becomes more rhythmical. The *Bridal Oro* is a specifically Macedonian dance, deriving from a ritual dance of the Thracian priestesses, which is depicted in a *bas-relief* on a stele recently excavated by an American archeological mission on the Greek island of Samothrace.

Sword dances have been associated with the Christmas-New Year-Winter Solstice season in many European countries since the Middle Ages. These dances date back to prehistoric times. But *Russalia* is a specifically Macedonian conversion dance. Xenophon described this originally Thracian dance in his *Anabasis* some 2,380 years ago. Much later, Macedonian Slavs adopted it in a pagan-Christian ritual symbolizing conversion. It is done as follows.

Teams of 20 to 60 young men, in pairs, form a loose circle with two leaders in charge. All are dressed in white, with short white skirts and fur caps, a red ornamented scarf across the chest. The dancers carry wooden swords; the leaders carry axes. Drummers and flutists provide the music. Sufficiently spaced, the dancers execute measured sword movements and slow-motion steps and figures, meant to bring about healing of the sick and a good harvest. Beginning with the first day of Christmas and for twelve days *Russalia* was performed like a dramatic road show in various villages. To the sound of the music, with unsheathed swords pointed upward, the dancing team left its native village. Except for the two leaders, the dancers were committed to absolute silence for twelve days. No one was permitted to cross himself during these twelve days or to pray, for all were supposed to be pagan. The dancers were greatly honored in each village and invited to the bedside of sick persons, over whose heads they crossed their swords for "good health."

When two teams of traveling *Russalia* dancers met on the road, one team had to declare its submission by pointing its swords downward and passing under the crossed swords of the other team. Such surrender being considered most shameful, the *Russalia* parties in the past used to wage regular wars resulting in casualties. The dead were buried without ceremonies in the *Russalia* cemeteries.

On the twelfth day the *Russalia* group, having visited many places, returned to its native village. The dancers entered the church with their fur caps on and, their unsheathed wooden swords pointed upward, they walked up the women's side of the aisle to the altar and stood still. The priest said a separate prayer before each man. The dancers then moved to the other end of the altar, pointed their swords downward as a sign that they revered the new faith, and their foreheads and swords were sprinkled with holy water. They then left the church, surrendered their swords, reentered the church bareheaded and with candles in their hands, crossed themselves and kissed the cross. Upon their return to their homes, they got new clothes, and a long celebration began with the slaughter of a lamb.

The *Russalia* dancers do not travel any more, and the whole ceremony is performed in the native village itself.

WEST Macedonian dances are similar to the Albanian: slow-motion dances, danced only by men, with long, measured steps. The only accompaniment is the drum and a high-pitched wind instrument. One of these dances is *Teškoto* (the word means "difficult," "hard"). Now it is called a shepherd's dance, of nimble leaps from rock to rock, watching for the possible beast or bandit. Actually, it is an archaic Macedonian dance from pre-Slav times, dramatizing the difficult life of the Macedonians, recalling border warfare and raids, the unending battle to defend the flocks, the land, the tribe.

In the beginning, says Dr. Mane Čučkov, Macedonian musicologist and economic geographer, people had nothing but body movements to show how they lived. An example of this is the *Aramijska Igra* (bandit's dance), during which men attack from ambush. The *Kaladžijska Igra* (tinsmith's dance) depicts how twice a year tinsmiths went around to put a new coat of tin on the peasants' brass vessels by rubbing them with their feet and wet sand, and the same movements are reproduced in the dance.

Another dance similar to some Albanian dances is *Čamče*. It is danced by men or women. The dance is serious, dignified, almost solemn, slow and stately, one might say like a classical sarabande.

There are also ancient Macedonian dances performed to the beat of drums only. And there are silent dances with no instruments or singing or hand-clapping at all. They are the eeriest, sometimes interspersed with weird cries. In "silent" dances rhythm and beat are supplied either by a measured repetition of an accented dance step or by the jingling of the coins and trinkets with which the women's dresses are adorned, or by periodic shouts. It is these strange and haunting "dumb" dances, where the feet thud in precise unison without a sound of song or music and men every once in a while leap high into the air, which more than any other stir the spectator in a profound way.

The instruments accompanying the Macedonian dances are usually the drum and various wind instruments. Among the latter is the *kaval*, an ordinary pipe. The longer the pipe, the more sonorous its sound. The *kaval* has no "tongue" or whistle-head. You blow it as you do a pencil cap, across the edge of the opening. The *zurla*, a wood instrument similar to the oboe, has a double mouthpiece and two whistle-heads and is a double-reed instrument. In London the *zurla* player of the dance group of *Tanec*, Slave Taševski, created a furor. You could ask him to play this song or that or "just nothing," that is, to improvise. He could not read music. The *zurla* and the drum are not Turkish, as often believed. You find them in frescoes preceding the Turks. They arrived in the Balkans before the Slavs. The Macedonian bagpipe has a seventh little hole with a straw, not for producing a tone but for ornamenting it: it does the murmuring. It is therefore called *mrmorec*—the "murmurer"—and is only one-and-a-half millimeters wide.

On January 27, 1956, the Macedonian folk dance group *Tanec* triumphantly appeared in Carnegie Hall, New York. The problem with *Tanec* was this: it was necessary to create a dance ensemble, but also to prevent it from turning into a ballet. When Dr. Mane Čučkov and

Živko Firfov agreed to form the folk dance ensemble of *Tanec*, Firfov accepted the task on the condition that he only trim and prune the original folk dances, edit them for stage performances. He wanted a folk dance group, not a ballet group, a folk dance group that would do the dances in their pure original form, not adapted for the ballet. In 1950 *Tanec* received its first international award, in Llangollen, Wales.

MACEDONIAN melodies are admittedly the softest and the most beautiful in the Balkans, the least affected by Oriental and church chanting. But their rhythm is highly irregular. Melodies often have polyrhythmic combinations, where 4/8 is followed by 5/8, 7/8 by 4/8, 9/8 by 11/8—variations of time and beat frequently unnoticeable to the Western ear. No one can say where the Macedonian rhythm came from. The typical *sedmorka* (the seventh) 7/16, for instance, is a three-beat measure. The Macedonian beat is 3–2–2, while the Bulgars make it 2–2–3, which, I was told by a musicologist, sets the Macedonian nation off against the Bulgarian. There is also the Macedonian 13/16 measure. To understand all this, I was advised, one must live there and "smell the peasant shirt and dirt." Macedonian music also knows quarter tones and even smaller interval fractions.

According to some musicologists, there is so much archaism in Macedonian music, as well as in costumes, dances and customs, for the reason that this region has lived so long in a servitude which precluded foreign influences. Nevertheless, Macedonian music has some similarities with Indonesian music. Orientalism, well expressed in Turkish songs, penetrated only the church chanting in Macedonia. It did not make any headway among the peasants, though it did invade the town love songs. To folk singing it brought only the augmented second. In the second half of the last century, as contact with the West grew and the sons of the well-to-do families began to be sent abroad, the thirds and the sixths and harmonization were gradually introduced into folk singing.

The Macedonian woman must be given most of the credit for preserving the purity of the Macedonian folk songs, especially those which contain the folk legends and traditions of the Macedonian people. Among the many songs for females only we must mention the songs of St. Lazarus (*lazarice*), sung in combination with dances performed by girls only on St. Lazarus Day, eight days before Easter, on the eve of Palm Sunday. They are actually the songs and dances of rebirth, a Christian adaptation of the pagan spring songs and dances. The girls would hold rehearsals every evening for a while before St. Lazarus

Day. The first evening of rehearsal was held at the house of the oldest girl. From then on, all further rehearsals were held at the other girls' houses in order of age. Related to the *lazarice* are the *kraljice* (Queens) on St. George's Day or at Whitsuntide. The tall miterlike headdresses, often adorned with a sacred picture, help to make it a wonderful show. The singer-dancers used to carry swords, later replaced by handkerchiefs and fluttering bannerets of red silk or roughly woven cloth, decorated with apples, bells and magic plants. The aim of the *kraljice*, like that of the *lazarice*, is to bring health and happiness.

In the last ten years of the nineteenth century, around 400 Macedonian folk songs and melodies were collected and published in Sofia. From the First World War onward, a large number of Macedonian folk songs were published by Serbian, Bulgarian and Macedonian musicologists. Up to now more than 2,500 have been published. The first collectors of the Macedonian folk songs were under the influence of Western European musical traditions and could not easily analyze the Macedonian meter and rhythm. Ivan Klinkov was an exception. The first person who attempted a systematization of the meter and rhythm of Macedonian folk music was Athanas Badev.

WE have mentioned Macedonian folk poems in connection with the brothers Miladinov in the chapter "Rebirth of the Written Language." The first collectors of Macedonian folk poems were three non-Macedonians. The first was the famous Serbian folklorist Vuk S. Karadžić, who published 27 folk poems and called them "Bulgarian," probably because they came from Pirin or Bulgarian Macedonia. After Karadžić, the Russian professor Viktor Grigorovich collected some Macedonian folk poems and had them published in *Vjedomosti*, Kazan, Russia, and in *Kolo*, Zagreb, Croatia. Then there was the well-known collection by the Croatian Catholic monk Verković, published in 1860, one year before the Miladinovs' collection, again under the title, "Folk Poems of the Macedonian Bulgars." The best collector was Marko Cepenkov, who was self-educated, like Vuk S. Karadžić. In 1959–60 Cyril Penušliski published three volumes of Cepenkov's folktales, many of which, especially those dealing with bishops and judges, could not be published in Cepenkov's time. So far more than 1,800 Macedonian folktales and more than 15,000 proverbs have been published. Interestingly, the common Serbian and Macedonian folk-poem hero Marko Kraljevic or Kral Marko, idealized in the Serbian version, is reduced to realistic proportions in the Macedonian folk poems—for instance, he is capable of losing a fight and then resorting to trickery.

IN the thirty years following the creation of the Socialist Republic of Macedonia, some 16,000 titles have appeared from the pens of more than 160 poets, short story writers, novelists, playwrights, critics, essayists and scholars. The four Skopje publishing houses have put out a total of 48 million copies for a population of 1.6 million, not all literate.

The following foreign writers have been published in translation in Macedonia so far: Pushkin, Lermontov, Gogol, Tolstoy, Dostoevski, Turgenev, Chekhov, Gorki, Shakespeare, Dickens, Corneille, Molière, Balzac, Hugo, Flaubert, Zola, Maupassant, Goethe, Heine and others.

Among the translated modern writers will be found the names of Henri Barbusse, Albert Camus, Tennessee Williams, Arthur Miller, William Faulkner, André Malraux, Ernest Hemingway, Robert Frost, Franz Kafka, James Joyce, Karel Čapek, Leonid Leonov, Mikhail Sholokhov, Alberto Moravia, Pablo Neruda and others.

Among the 49 magazines appearing in Macedonia, one should point out the monthlies *Sovremenost* and *Razgledi*, of Skopje. There are also *Jehanna*, a literary monthly in Albanian, and *Sesler*, a literary monthly in Turkish. Upon liberation, the Turkish minority weekly newspaper *Birlik* began to appear, while the Albanian minority has its weekly newspaper *Flaka e Vlaznimit*. There is also a press for children in the Turkish and Albanian languages.

Today eight theaters are active in Macedonia, of which two are in Skopje. There is also in Skopje an Albanian-Turkish theater. The Macedonian stage has so far presented theatrical works by the following international playwrights: A. Kataev, K. Simonov, T. Williams, C. Odets, J. B. Priestley, Lorca, B. Brecht, W. Saroyan, J. Anouilh and others.

In 1947 opera singing and staging emerged within the Macedonian National Theater as a separate activity. The beginning was made with *Cavalleria Rusticana*. The first appearance of the young ballet ensemble was in 1948, in *La Traviata*. The famous folklore dance group *Tanec* has performed with huge success in Great Britain, Albania, Bulgaria, Greece, Italy, Israel, Canada, both Germanies, the Soviet Union, the United States, Ghana, Guinea, Switzerland, Sweden, Belgium, the Netherlands, Mali, Senegal, Nigeria, Zaire, Rumania, Luxembourg, and other countries.

A philharmonic orchestra was unknown to Macedonia before the Second World War. The first one was created in Skopje in November 1944, immediately upon the liberation of the city. After the war it performed in Poland, Czechoslovakia, Hungary, Bulgaria, East Germany, Denmark, Switzerland, Italy, France, Spain and Mexico. It accompanied such international violinists as Oistrakh, Kogan and Schering, pianists like Ciccolini, and others.

The society of painters and sculptors of Macedonia has more than a hundred artists as members. In an atmosphere of absolute creative freedom, all kinds of painting have developed, from figurative to abstract, from the traditional to the most daring modern schools. Typical representatives of the old generation of painters were Lazar Ličenoski and Nikola Martinoski, and in sculpture, Dimo Teodorovski. Representatives of the young generation of painters, such as Gligor Čemerski and others, belong to the schools of surrealism, cubism and geometric abstraction. Here also belong sculptors like Tomislav Andreevski and others.

Before the Second World War there were only two museums in Macedonia. In 1945 the National Museum of Skopje was founded. Today there are eighteen museums in the Socialist Republic of Macedonia, among them the new Museum of Contemporary Art.

As pointed out previously, before the Second World War there was only a section of the Belgrade Philosophical Faculty in Skopje, with instruction in Serbian and with 163 students. Today there is a university with nine faculties and nearly thirty thousand students. In 1945 the main job was the struggle against illiteracy (75 percent of the population) and raising the skill of the workers, which was on a very low level. In 1967 the Macedonian Academy of Sciences and Arts was established. Today the Macedonian language is being studied at the universities of Moscow, Warsaw, Bradford, Utrecht, Leyden, Paris, Cologne, Naples, Craiova, Kansas and Chicago. There is a Macedonian grammar in English by the American Professor H. Lunt, of Harvard. There are two bilingual dictionaries, a Macedonian-Russian and an Italian-Macedonian.

The number of radio sets in Macedonia in 1973 was 232,255. Today almost one-third of the population of Macedonia have radios and TV sets. In 1939 there were 23 movie houses in Macedonia. In 1973 there were 86. Of the nearly 1,300 churches and monasteries in Macedonia, only six are under government protection: St. Sofia, St. Panteleimon, St. Naum, St. Jovan Kaneo (all at Lake Ohrid), Sv. Spas (in Skopje) and St. Jovan Bigorski (in the mountains of western Macedonia).

In 1961 a group of art enthusiasts arranged a concert in Ohrid's church of St. Sofia. Since then the "Ohrid Summer" festivals have been held every year between July 10 and August 20. The following international artists have so far appeared in the "Ohrid Summer" presentations: the Soviet violinists Leonid Kogan and Igor Oistrakh, the Soviet pianist Sviatislav Richter, the Soviet cellist M. Rostropovich, the French pianist Aldo Ciccolini, the U.S. violinist Ruggiero Ricci, and others, as well as foreign chamber music ensembles. By the end of 1973, 32 plays had been staged at the "Ohrid Summer." Since 1971, the "Ohrid Summer" concerts have been relayed via radio to 17 countries.

Since 1962, the "Struga Evenings of Poetry" have been held at the end of August every year in Struga, on the shores of Lake Ohrid. This is an international literary gathering. Every year some 200 poets and critics from Yugoslavia and other countries gather in Struga and deliver their poetic messages and speak of their experiences. So far poets and essayists from the following countries have taken part in the "Struga Evenings of Poetry": Australia, Austria, Algeria, Belgium, Great Britain, Greece, East Germany, India, Ireland, Italy, Canada, Colombia, Morocco, Norway, United Arab Republic, Poland, Rumania, the Soviet Union, West Germany, Tunisia, Turkey, Hungary, Finland, France, the Netherlands, Chile, Czechoslovakia, Sweden, Yugoslavia, and others.

Ancient Customs and Beliefs

ON Lake Doiran people still catch fish not only with trained birds but, since time immemorial, with the aid of migratory birds. Every fall and spring flocks of various water birds from Russia, Poland, Germany on their way south and north stop to feed and rest at Lake Doiran, which is not more than 33 feet deep and is possibly the European lake with the greatest abundance of fish. The birds scare off the fish which then make for the reedy shallows which in the fall also serve as their refuge from the deeper, colder waters. Nearly all the fishing is done at or near the village of New Doiran, where several miles of reeds, sometimes ten feet or more in height, grow along the shore. The fish traps, called *mandras*, are made of reeds, their openings facing the lake. The *mandras* are subdivided into several underwater compartments or pens, each smaller as they approach the shore. Out in the lake, in front of the *mandras*, huts on stilts are constructed of boards and reeds and mud, three to five feet above the surface, for the fishermen to control the bird fishing. Herodotus, who in the fifth century B.C. visited Lake Doiran, then called Prasias, and described the bird fishing, gave the following picture of the pile dwellings. You reached them by a bridge from the shore. In each pile dwelling there was a trapdoor opening onto the water. Small children were roped by the leg so as not to tumble down. There was so much fish that when you lowered a creel on a rope through the trapdoor you could soon pull it out full of fish.

As the fish crowd into the first compartment of the *mandras*, the fishermen from the top of the pile dwellings frighten off the birds by waving their arms, shouting, throwing stones, rattling various objects. They pull a network of strings with old tins attached which stretches over the water. Men in canoes also patrol the reeds and prevent the birds from invading by shouting, banging, swinging their oars. The birds are allowed to fly only over the "white waters"—the open lake.

Now it is the turn for other birds to help the fishermen catch red perch, carp and pike. These are the so-called "working birds"—wild birds, especially cormorants and certain ducks, caught in nets by the fishermen who clip their wings so they cannot fly. When the first compartment of the *mandra* is full, these birds are placed on a perch above it, from which they dive after the fish. Frightened, the fish scamper through the opening into the second pen. The process is repeated until the fish find themselves in the last and smallest compart-ment of the *mandra* at the shore, from which they can be scooped out with a net. By April the wings of the "working birds" have grown again and they are released. Each season between four and six hundred "working birds" are used.

The Doiran fishing boats are also of a type that is centuries old; they have a flat stern and sides narrowing toward the gunwales so that the bottom is broader than the top; this creates stability. The fishing season takes place between October and March, during the bird migra-tions. Of the yearly fish kill, it is estimated that one-half is devoured by birds. Of the rest, one-half is caught by nylon nets. Fishing with migratory birds also survives in Japan. Bird fishing in China is different. There it is done with cormorants; rings have been slipped around their throats so they cannot swallow the fish and they have been trained to bring the fish back to their masters.

Of late, new methods have been introduced in Doiran fishing. Boats with dynamos glide swiftly over the waters. Two metal rods are con-nected with the dynamo. The electrodes are placed in the water and the current is switched on. The electrocuted fish float up to the surface immediately. Although the state of shock lasts only a few minutes, this is long enough for the fish to be scooped up into the boats. This has greatly increased the annual catch.

OF the numerous extinct and current customs and beliefs let us mention just a few.

Until not long ago, in the Katlanovo marshes near Skopje, people lived in houses on stilts and fished with spears. Katlanovo is now being drained and a spa has been built there. Dervishes' dances could still be watched in Skopje between the wars. Now you can witness these dances in Prizren, in the nearby Kosovo province, with people in a trance or self-hypnosis piercing themselves with knives without feeling pain or drawing blood. The people still believe that thunder is caused by St. Elijah driving his chariot over cloud-cobbled skies. This is a derivation from the thundering car of Zeus as it rolled across the vault of heaven, which again was a reminiscence of the still older solar cult which had it that the sun drove in a chariot across the sky. At one time the wedding customs of the Gypsy quarter began to be accepted throughout Skopje and created quite a traffic and privacy problem: people sang and danced in the streets and the squares and invaded private apartments to have everyone join in the jolliness. In the environs of Radoviš, previously mentioned for its costumes, women carry their babies papoose fashion on their backs. We have already mentioned the practice of *couvade*. In the wild Mariovo region in southern Macedonia matriarchy still reigns, costumes and customs are still archaic, and civilization has only begun to arrive with a road built recently. In the region between Debar and Struga on the Albanian frontier, the first *čarapče* (little sock) that the mother has knit and embroidered for her baby goes to the church as an offering. Or the first embroidery goes to the Mother of God. Like the Serbs, the Macedonians celebrate the *krsna slava*, the patron saint of the house whose icon hangs on the wall. The Patron, if revered conscientiously, is supposed to help in all misfortunes. The scientific interpretation is that the Patron Saint's Day was the one on which the family, or the clan, was baptized into Christianity centuries ago. But the origin of the cult is really the pagan belief in house gods.

The Macedonian fertility rites, some of them savage, were witnessed by foreigners and recorded in the native press just before the Second World War. One of them was the slaughter of roosters and lambs to induce fertility in sterile women, performed on Sheep's Field near Štip and described by Rebecca West in her *Black Lamb and Grey Falcon*. The other ritual was the yearly charming of the *poskok* vipers on a "snake hill" near Skopje, making them slither over female garments spread out on the ground, thus bringing fertility to the winners. These rituals are now prohibited by law.

The six-foot-high Cowherd's Rock on Sheep's Field used to be all reddish brown from the blood of the animals that had been sacrificed on it. You had to pick your way among the bleeding cocks' heads. A man who had placed a small child on a rug would walk three times around the rock with a black lamb in his arms, bend, kiss the rock, and hand the lamb over to a man standing on the rock. Then the father would fetch the child and climb with it onto the rock. Now the man holding the lamb drew a knife across its throat. With the lamb's blood the father made a circle on the child's forehead. He was doing this, it was explained, because his wife had gotten this child by coming here and giving a lamb.

About ten miles from the city of Skopje there is a village called Orman. Outside the village rises a jumble of bare rocks, Snake Hill, believed to be the capital of the Snake Tsar of the world. Actually, thousands of *poskoks* ("jumpers") live in its fissured slopes. This is the deadliest of European vipers. March 14 and 22 used to be the days of the sacred Orman snakes. Men, women and children from all around, dressed in their best costumes, gathered at the foot of Snake Hill arranging shirts, skirts, belts and caps on the ground. A chorus of girls took up the chant to the melancholy notes of the Macedonian flutes:

> Jump out, O Snake, and see
> How beautifully I am dressed!

Joyous shouts greeted the first "jumper"; then another slithered out of a crevice, tens, hundreds of them, hissing softly and swaying their uplifted heads. The rule was that no snake should be injured on such a day, and the belief was that none would strike. For nine days afterward a sterile wife washed the "trampled" garment in hot water in which her husband then bathed his face. The next year they would expect a male baby.

PEASANTS generally have elaborate rituals for all occasions. Let us try to simplify some of the Macedonian rituals.

Up to thirty years ago, Christmas was considered the biggest holiday of the year in Macedonia. The Christmas customs covered a span of nearly two months; they were rooted in old pre-Christian winter cele- brations, dedicated to the birth of the sun, the solstice, and were later grafted onto the Roman festival of Saturnalia. Christianity adopted the pagan celebrations and transformed them into the festival of the birth of Christ—Christmas.

According to popular belief in the Skopje plain, Christmas and Easter are two brothers. While the younger brother, Easter, is neat and well dressed, Grandfather Christmas rides a lame donkey, does not care much about his appearance and is good-natured, but he wants every- thing in the house and in the field to be in order. Children especially wait for his arrival. One buys all sorts of things for Christmas, including the sweet chestnuts, which one throws into the sheepfold for fertility. A number of other customs are adhered to in order to increase fertility of man and livestock and fields and to create abundance in general. Pigs are slaughtered and all kinds of dishes prepared, especially the many sacred cakes and breads. The day before Christmas Eve, the children of the village go to the woods to cut sticks, which they decorate and with which they tap at the doors of the villagers while singing the *Kolede*, the songs wishing for a fruitful year. On Christmas Eve a great fire is made with the sacred Yule log on the hearth to commemorate the dead and to promote fertility and happiness. The master of the house brings in the Yule log and spills wine and grain over it. This symbolizes the entry of Grandfather Christmas, who is supposed to bring happiness and well-being. Then candles are lit. Straw is spread where dinner will take place, and handfuls of grain are thrown about. Then people sit on the floor for a very plain dinner, for Christmas Eve is a feast of poverty. People sleep in the same place where they have dined. But the first day of Christmas is a feast of abundance. Again there is a big fire, and after the rich meal, accompanied by ritualistic practices, people go to a big gathering where they sing and dance. On the second day of Christmas the young people continue to sing and dance, while the elderly visit each other. On the third day the song and dance still go on. Then the mood changes.

The twelve days following Christmas, until Epiphany, are devoted to reverence of the dead. During this period, the souls of the dead are supposed to walk the earth and take part in all our doings and joys. But evil spirits also have a new lease of life on earth, and certain precautions are taken against them, such as not going out after dark. There is also a ritual magic dance with songs and music performed during those twelve days to drive away the evil spirits. It is called *Džamala* and is very ancient. The word *džama*, according to Indian mythology, means the god of the dead in the underworld. To deprive the evil spirits of the power to cause harm, in this dance two old men, "sorcerers," represent the two worlds, the underground and the terrestrial, and fight until the good spirit defeats the evil spirit, or summer conquers winter. This magic dance is known throughout Macedonia.

The *Džamala* dancers most often perform on New Year's Eve, thus welcoming the New Year. The dance is performed in the following manner. A group of forty to fifty people, middle-aged and young, gather in a house in the evening. From the crowd four persons with the best sense of humor are selected. They must be two "old men" and two young women. Other players represent the "children" or the armies. The old men are bedecked with bells to make noise and frighten away the evil spirits. The old men, to appear more terrifying and ridiculous, smear their faces with soot and make themselves into hunchbacks by putting straw under their coats. They wear mustaches, a beard and a wig of hemp. They carry a piece of wood stuck in their belts as a pistol, and they hold in their hands a spindle for knocking at the house doors. The *Džamala* players mostly play the drum and a wind instrument. At the end of the *Džamala* dialogue with the head of the house, the two "old men" make peace and offer the host a *Little Oro*.

AMONG other festivals, the most important and attractive are the Easter rites of rebirth and renewal of nature. In order to get an idea of Macedonian Easter customs, let us look at the Poreč region. It is a very inaccessible area of Yugoslav Macedonia, where customs have been preserved from pre-Christian times. Many Easter customs go back to the ancient festivities of Dionysus. In his honor and to celebrate the spring awakening of nature, tragic, satiric, comic and other plays and dances are arranged. In Macedonia, the Easter holidays are purely spring festivals whose alleged aim is to ensure the fertility of man, beast and field. The plays and the dances, sometimes masked, remind us of the old Dionysus festivals.

According to popular tradition in Poreč, Easter and Christmas are two brothers. Christmas is the older brother, who does not care how well he is dressed as long as he is well fed. Thus "there must be a whole pig on the table even if there are bare feet under the table." Easter is a handsome young man, well dressed and decked out. Thus one of the Easter customs is for everyone to get a new suit or dress.

The custom of coloring and ornamenting eggs for Easter originated in pagan times. In Macedonia, this custom has been particularly practiced by women. The ancient pagans believed that red was the color of life and colored the eggs accordingly. Christianity adopted this custom. There is a legend that blood from the nailed feet of the crucified Christ trickled onto the white stones around the cross. Thus the red on white eggs became the symbol of Christ's blood shed for humanity. Ornaments in white are often put on the red eggs, such as flowers, leaves, birds, geometric figures, the cross.

On Tuesday before Easter eggs are collected to be painted. It is believed that since the earliest times among almost all peoples the egg was regarded as the source of life; so also in Macedonia. On Wednesday dyes are prepared to color the eggs. They are mostly red but can be blue, yellow or other colors. On Holy Thursday the eggs are colored, with various designs, such as stars, chicken heads, and so on. The first egg cooked and painted in the early hours of Holy Thursday is kept before the icon for the whole year to protect the well-being and the health of the family. On Good Friday no work is done, no food prepared and no liquids consumed. This severe fast is ordained by the Church. On Saturday the specially ornamented un-leavened Easter bread is baked and various Easter cakes are made. On Easter Sunday, after the church service, the family heads of the entire village throw Easter eggs at each other in the churchyard as an Easter greeting. No one visits anyone else on Easter Sunday, but after lunch all people gather in the churchyard or in the village square for singing and dancing. On the second day of Easter people gather again in the village square for singing and dancing. Before the Second World War, a satirical play *The Camel* was also performed. On the third day of Easter, "Little Easter," the holiday is "escorted out" with singing and dancing. The festivities are closed with a play devoted to the fairies who are supposed to protect the people, their livestock and their fields from any harm throughout the year.

St. George's Day is an important spring holiday. Girls dance by the fountain in festive costumes, watch their own faces in the water, dance to beautiful folk songs, throw twigs and flowers at each other, adorn the houses with them, perform various kinds of friendly "magic," including *milogled*—the "good eye" as opposed to the evil eye. The milking of sheep begins on St. George's Day. A dance festival is also held, and swings are hung up. Girls swing from dogwood trees and wash their faces in the dew. Eggs are painted, and extraordinary cos-tumes like Oriental rugs are worn. The St. George's Day customs are still part of village life in many areas.

A number of superstitious cults and practices are disappearing. Among them are the belief in spirits, and various kinds of magic to combat them, and exorcism—a sort of shamanism. People would dance over a sick child or woman; or around a sheep or a house to thwart evil spirits or ill fate. The drumming sounded often like the tom-tom of the jungle. Also, the symbol of the cross would be put on a child, woman, house, sheep. Gifts used to be deposited at fountains, in churches, on paths, bridges, to propitiate God or nature or fate. In the magic war against the "evil eye," pearls were often worn, especially by the Moslems. Also, shepherds would often hang a horse's skull from the roof of the milking stall or impale it on a fence against the "evil eye."

VERA Kličkova, the chief ethnologist of Macedonia, who is of the opinion that Sir James George Frazer's *The Golden Bough* is still the most important work in her field, complained to me that the folk customs are dying out. Whole villages are being erased from the map through the movement to towns, and all the old customs must be recorded and filmed before it is too late. Where tape recordings and movies were made some years ago no one lives now. In one village the only inhabitants were two old men, but they were waiting to sell their sheep and then leave.

Industry pulls people down from the mountains. "Tremendous changes have occurred in our country," said Vera Kličkova. "Neither the nineteenth century nor the wars have done so much damage. Now not only great industrial migrations are going on but whole villages, entire economies, whole cultures and ways of life are being wiped out. Is this really to the good?"

Vera Kličkova maintains that invisible public pressure is the strongest force in society. Custom is stronger than the law. You can cheat the law, you cannot cheat custom. You break the law more frequently than you break custom. Only custom changes the man, not the law—law must become custom to change the people. It is no help merely making a new law. It is the custom that must be changed. New habits have to be created.

It is still common, says Vera Kličkova, to see flower gardens next to Macedonian houses or at least flower pots in the window sills. Foreign travelers still write that every house is like a park and that there are gardens even in front of shops.

All Balkan peoples are known for their hospitality, but along with the Albanians, the Macedonians are probably the most hospitable of all. A guest is a sacred person to the common folk. In Western countries he is welcomed but is expected to conform to the rules of the house; in the Balkans, especially in Macedonia, the rules of the house are suspended to accommodate every wish of the guest. Hospitality requires that an old woman, whether you know her or not, be respected. You will always be asked to stay for lunch. Hospitality has its counterpart: it is an offense not to accept hospitality (or to look at your watch while being a guest). When you meet somebody older than yourself, you must help him, you must get up, you must accord him the privilege of beginning the conversation, you must listen to what he has to say— such is the unwritten code of good behavior. It is the older ones who are supposed to begin eating at meals—children eat separately. Never must a child raise his voice at his mother or at an older person. This is not being "patriarchal"; this again is based on age-long experience in human relations. Very often people understand each other silently— they "read the eyes." You must not be hasty, you must think things over, then you will not make an error.

The more cultured a man is the more of the folk customs he will retain, for he knows that they represent the culture of the heart. "If we preserve everything that our ancestors had, we can create perfect relationships in our socialist community," said Vera Kličkova. All the ancient conceptions and customs have not yet been written about, she added. Someone ought to do it. "Our socialism should adopt them all. We have among ourselves all the precepts for perfect human relations."

EPILOGUE

The Macedonians in Greece

IN 1961 the president of the Macedonian government held an international press conference in Skopje. I asked about the situation of the Macedonian Slavs in Greece; he replied that they were exposed to "extermination," because they were being forced to renounce their language and to emigrate. The Yugoslav press did not publish this statement, but the French press did. An exchange of recriminations between Athens and Belgrade ensued, and I decided to see for myself. The Greek ambassador in Belgrade advised me to go to Athens. There the Greek foreign minister, Evangelos Averoff-Tossizza, organized a trip for me in the border region of northern Greece (Greek Macedonia).

Greek Macedonia, or Northern Greece, as it is officially called, with the second-largest Greek city of Salonika on the Aegean coast, extends south of the Yugoslav republic of Macedonia, from which it is separated by a range of snowcapped mountains. The great majority of the population are Greeks. There are also a few Albanians, some Vlachs, and a sizeable contingent of Slavs, claimed by both the Yugoslav Macedonians and the Bulgars as their conationals.

Nobody really knows how many Slavs, called "Aegean Macedonians" by the Yugoslavs, there are now in Greece because of the long-standing Greek policy of repression of the Macedonian-Slav nationality. The Yugoslavs claimed that there were 250,000 of them after the Balkan wars (1912–13), and the Greeks, as of 1961, conceded that their number was 41,000. The best estimate is around 100,000. There is no doubt that they have been decreasing in number since 1912.

The Slavophones

THE official and generally adopted Greek position is that the Slav-speaking inhabitants of Greek Macedonia are not a nationality or a national minority but Greeks who also, or solely, speak a Slav dialect.

So the name for them is "Slavophones." In reality, "Slavophones" are Slavs who also, though not always, speak Greek.

The Greek foreign minister, in his office in January 1962, explained the "Macedonian question" to me as follows. International recognition of a national minority implies the admission of a foreign territorial claim, and Greece will never sign a treaty regarding the protection of a Macedonian-Slav minority. Such a treaty would imply the right of foreign supervision and intervention on Greek territory. Besides, Macedonian Slavs are not a nationality. In Yugoslavia, in twenty years or so, there may be created a Macedonian nation in the fullest sense of the word. "That is their affair," he said. In Greece it is different. There are in Greece ethnic groups who speak non-Greek languages, but they are not national minorities. The exception are the Turks, 100,000 of them, in Greek Thrace. They are a national minority recognized by treaties and conventions with Turkey.

The treaties and conventions about the Turkish national minority were signed by Greece after her defeat by Kemal Ataturk in 1923. Thus we have a situation where the Greeks do not of their own free will give the Slavs the rights they have been forced to give to their former common oppressors, the Turks.

The Greek Civil War and Yugoslavia

YUGOSLAV Communists' involvement in Greek Macedonia goes back to the Greek guerrilla war against Hitler. In 1943, one of Tito's chief lieutenants, the Montenegrin Svetozar Vukmanovic–"Tempo"–had Yugoslav Macedonian Partisans cross into Greek Macedonia. The Greek Communist-led ELAS (National Liberation Army) refused to have Tito lead the Slavs of Greece but agreed to the formation of a Slav national liberation front under Greek command. In a report back home "Tempo" complained that "there was no mention [by ELAS] of any right of the Macedonian people ... to a claim of self-determination ... by reason of its participation in the people's liberation struggle."

In the Greek civil war of 1945–49, the Aegean Macedonians took part on the side of the Communist-led guerrillas, and this left a trauma in the Greek mind.

Tito was the chief supporter and supplier of Markos Vafiades's rebellion to the very end. According to Yugoslav sources, more than half of Markos's forces were Slavs of Greek Macedonia, and Markos's government contained representatives of these Slavs. Markos was a pro-Yugoslav–not a pro-Soviet–Greek Communist guerrilla leader. Yugoslav organizers, including "Tempo," were permitted to enter Greek

Macedonia, and Macedonian Slav national rights were promised in future Greece. No wonder Yugoslavia, after the split with the Cominform in 1948, continued to support Markos, despite Stalin's opinion that the Greek Communist rebellion was unrealistic, as the West would never permit it to succeed.

A struggle arose within the KKE (the Greek Communist party) between the Markos and the Zachariades (pro-Stalin) factions, and in January 1949 Markos was expelled from the Party. Within a few months, Yugoslavia stopped all support and accepted the refugees.

Greek Feelings

GREEK feelings about Greek Macedonia run high. The most extreme position is that of the scholars of the "Society for Macedonian Studies" (a department of the "Institute of Balkan Studies") in Salonika: the Slav Macedonian nationality and language have been invented. Greek diplomats in Yugoslavia will sometimes say that it was Tito who invented them. Many feel that these Slavs, on both sides of the frontier, have no right to call themselves "Macedonians." For this was the name of the nation of Alexander the Great which, they say, was Hellenic. Prominent members of the Greek parliament expressed nostalgia for the simple old times when E. Venizelos of Greece and N. Pašić of Serbia, after the Balkan wars, in 1913, agreed on the Greek-Serbian (later Yugoslav) frontier so that to the north there would be only Serbs and to the south only Greeks, and no "Macedonians" on either side. At the height of the polemics with the Yugoslavs in 1962, an Athens newspaper set forth the Greek position in a front-page editorial: "The basic fact is that there is no [Macedonian] minority in Greece.... There live today in the border areas under discussion only people who are purely Greek. Nobody denies the fact that in Greece...there are Greeks who speak a second language in addition to Greek. But they are pure Greeks with a Greek national consciousness."

The Greeks cannot help seeing behind the "Slavophones" their Slav Communist neighbors, Yugoslavia and Bulgaria, and the Slav Communist colossus between the Aegean and the Pacific waters. Despite Yugoslav denials, they suspect Yugoslav territorial ambitions to be behind the Yugoslav concern for the "Slavophones" in Greece.

Yet not all Greeks feel quite the same way about the Slavs in their country. While hardly anyone recognizes the "Slavophones" as a national minority, responsible Greeks admit there are different "ethnic" or at least linguistic groups in Greece. And while everybody thinks the Macedonian language is no more than a nondescript dialect, if not a manufactured language, most agree that it should be freely spoken.

The Greek Communist party itself has always opposed Macedonian-Slav political self-government in Greece. But in 1962, in the midst of the Greek-Yugoslav polemics, the Central Committee of the party, in a broadcast from Bucharest, agreed implicitly with the Yugoslav stand that there existed a Macedonian-Slav minority in Greece. In January of that year it passed a resolution, saying that rights should be recognized for minorities living in Greece. Slav-speaking people were not explicitly mentioned, although it is clear that it was they whom the resolution referred to.

As for EDA (*Enomenon Demokratiki Aristori*—United Democratic Left), its spokesmen have been anything but talkative. It refrained from making any statement on the "Macedonian question" in the parliament or otherwise. Its newspaper *Avghi* only published the above-mentioned *KKE* Central Committee's resolution. The *EDA* people have recognized the existence of a Slav minority in Greece, without specifying whether this was a "national" or merely a "linguistic" minority. One of the reasons is that many Greek leftists, too, are touchy on the subject of the "Macedonians" in Greece.

Yugoslav-Greek Relations

THE foreign editor of the former Athens publication *Ethnos* once said that the only good thing America had done in the Balkans was to bring General Plastiras and Tito together in 1952. This was after a secret meeting of Yugoslav leaders with Averell Harriman in Slovenia, in 1951, at which Tito asked for U.S. military protection against the U.S.S.R. and Harriman replied that the protection lay in joining NATO. In 1954, Communist Yugoslavia signed the Balkan Pact of military and cultural cooperation with Greece and Turkey, indirectly involving the NATO forces in case Yugoslavia was attacked by the Soviet Union or its satellites. After the reconciliation with the Soviets under Khrushchev, Yugoslavia began to deemphasize the military part of the pact until it became a dead letter.

In 1958, on the Greek island of Corfu, a gentleman's agreement was made between the king of Greece and Tito to the effect that the issue should be deferred and neither side should raise it in public. By a convention of 1959 transit points for "small border traffic" were established along the frontier for Yugoslavs and Greeks to cross daily on business or personal affairs. In 1962, after the outburst between Yugoslavia and Greece over the "Aegean Macedonians," Greece banned the small border traffic. It was resumed in 1964 and ended again by the Colonels, who in 1967 proclaimed a dictatorship in Greece.

After the military seized control of the Greek government in April 1967, relations between Yugoslavia and Greece reached a new low point. The friction over the Macedonian question was revived. The military government not only refused to acknowledge the existence of a Macedonian minority in Greece, which all former Greek governments had declined to do, but it made claims against Yugoslav Macedonia. In 1968 General Patakos sent a message to a meeting in Salonika declaring: "The territory of Macedonia, the entire geographic area of Macedonia, has been and remains Greek. All others are conquerors or oppressors, old or potential."

Americans and the Macedonians in Greece

AMERICAN diplomats in Athens and Salonika are, on the whole, well acquainted with the facts of Greek Macedonia. Skeptical about Yugoslav intentions, they are also apprehensive of some Greek extremism. Some think that the UN Declaration of Human Rights might be a feasible foundation for the freedom of the Slavs in Greek Macedonia. The Americans generally agree that one's nationality depends on how one feels. But, some argue, perhaps the Slavs of Greek Macedonia are not fully conscious of what they really are; and that they may not like to join the Yugoslav Communist dictatorship. The counterargument, of course, is that historically nationalism overrides ideological considerations, so much so that, for instance, the Sudeten Germans chose even Hitler over Czechoslovak democracy.

The crucial question for the American diplomats in Greece, from the NATO security point of view, is: do the Slavs in the NATO border zone of northern Greece prefer Tito or Bulgaria (Moscow). Naturally, the Aegean Macedonians conceal their feelings. Although some well-informed Greek journalists believe that the "Slavophones" are for Bulgaria (Russia) rather than Yugoslavia, some high Greek government officials do not think so. Actually it is hard to see that the Aegean Macedonians would make any ideological choice between the two: whoever helps is welcome.

Some American political officers and some Greek newspaper editors were surprised at how few Greeks realized that the creation of Yugoslav Macedonia kept Bulgaria out of Yugoslavia.

Greek Macedonia

THE districts of Kastoria (Kostur, in Slav), Florina (Lerin, in Slav) and Edessa (Voden, in Slav), in Greek Macedonia west of Salonika, are the areas in which most of the Aegean Macedonians are concentrated. This region has less industry than Yugoslav Macedonia. The roads are mostly good, the towns picturesque, and the villages similar to those of Yugoslav Macedonia. The countryside presents the same landscape of wooded hills, barren brushland, mountain lakes and lush plains.

In this land, devastated by the Second World War and the subsequent civil war, you can still come across abandoned pillboxes or blackened remains of burned down houses. Elsewhere you may pass by desolate-looking stone houses or through a village with dark brown roofs and large dark brown window frames on white-washed walls, as frequently seen in Yugoslav Macedonia. And you will be surprised by the many new houses, often painted pale blue, mostly of one storey. On the road you will encounter buses, trucks, three-wheeled motor vehicles, donkeys carrying firewood or branches—a sight common, except for the three wheels, in Yugoslav Macedonia. But you will notice many roadside crucifixes and chapels, many priests and many airfields and soldiers. The NATO frontier runs here.

In 1962 I took off in a government jeeplike station wagon for Kastoria, near the Albanian frontier. Kastoria is a stunning little town on top of a promontory; its beauty is reflected in the tranquil waters of a mountain lake. It has some 11,000 inhabitants and some seventy old churches. Several thousand Kastorians live in the United States and Canada, most of them in New York City. About 80 percent of the population of Kastoria make furs out of fur factory leftovers sent them from the U.S. by Kastorian immigrants. Kastoria reexports finished fur coats, mostly to New York.

You can read Hellenized Slav names above some shops, but there are more Slavs in outlying villages. There is a bust of General James A. Van Fleet in Kastoria. He used to visit Greek Macedonia during the civil war and local officials say that, as head of the U.S. Military Mission, he did much to bring that war to a successful conclusion. Markos Vafiades's guerrillas never took the town of Kastoria.

My official driver said he was a Bulgar, and we conversed in Bulgarian and Serbian (the two languages and the Macedonian being similar) in restaurants and with policemen on our way to Kastoria. He took me to a restaurant in Kastoria whose owner told me in Macedonian Slav that he was a *Makedonec*. He spoke to me freely and repeatedly in his Macedonian Slav before his Greek customers. He refused to do so on the following day in front of tax collectors who had come to inspect his books and he protested in Greek against being addressed by me in Serbian. Later he spoke in Macedonian again. On the mountain road from Kastoria to Florina, a monument to the

Greek soldier stands between two villages with mostly Slav-type houses.

Florina lies in an immense lush valley below the forbidding, snow-capped Yugoslav frontier mountains. Markos's guerrillas never conquered this town either, but they controlled all the surrounding hills, where as late as 1962 shepherds were maimed or blown to pieces in the still uncleared minefields. On Sunday mornings you could hear songs of soldiers marching outside Florina to the sound of drum beats and bugle calls, while the town square still displays two cannon pieces captured from the guerrillas. No one in Greek Macedonia is allowed to forget who won the guerrilla war.

On market day, which is Saturday, you can see many Macedonian Slav costumes and hear much Macedonian Slav talk in the Florina marketplace. And you can see and hear Macedonian Slav peasant women discussing the various items for sale and their prices in the Florina shops. Unlike the Yugoslav Macedonian female costumes, the costumes of the Slav women in Greek Macedonia are rather on the somber side and show little diversity. In front, women regularly wear heavy, ruglike aprons, black or of another dark color, with vertical red stripes. White kerchiefs cover their heads and chins. Occasionally you will notice elegant sleeveless coats with tight waists and embroidered borders.

In the Florina district prefect's office I talked to two Aegean Macedonian returnees from Yugoslavia, who had come to receive a Greek government loan to develop their land. They had been led away at the age of six and said, in Macedonian Slav in the presence of the prefect, that they had been treated well in Yugoslavia and given good food and good schooling. Some local Greek officials told me that the "bandits" had taken some 30,000 children to various Communist countries as "hostages" (actually many were taken out of the country for fear of reprisals or forcible Hellenization). The officials added, however, that Yugoslavia had returned all the children who had been staying on her territory.

Greek and American sources agree that at least 30,000 adult guerrillas fled to Yugoslavia at the end of the civil war. From other sources one learns that another 30,000 Aegean Macedonians fled to Albania, Bulgaria, Czechoslovakia, Poland, even Kazakhstan in the U.S.S.R. None returned.

Edessa has been built on a breathtaking site; it is something like Venice, located on top of a Niagara Falls in miniature. It lies on the edge of a plateau above a sheer drop. A delta of waterfalls squeezes in between the houses and plunges down to a vast plain between two mountain ranges. Edessa itself is rather dreary. It has some 16,000 several textile factories and the headquarters of an army division. At the head of the water chutes perch a beautiful old church and a one-time Turkish pasha's exquisite verandah. The ancient city, the seat of the kings of ancient Macedon before they moved to Pella, was situated at the foot of the waterfalls. The acropolis was at the head of the waterfalls. Ancient coins can still be picked up along the goat path leading down from the plateau.

Occasionally you can read a Slav name with a Greek ending above a shop and now and then hear the Slav language in the streets. Many Macedonian Slavs, however, live in the countryside outside Edessa. On market day (Saturday) they stream into town in their costumes and you can overhear much Slav. As in Florina, I saw Slav "repatriates" in Edessa, this time not former children but former Slav guerrillas returned from abroad and receiving agricultural loans. Also in Edessa I found confirmation of the fact that urbanization aided Hellenization: a physician, born Slav, spoke Slav and Greek but felt himself to be a Greek; his peasant mother who lived with him spoke only Slav and felt herself to be a Slav.

Below the Yugoslav frontier mountains north of Edessa, as well as in the big plain to the south, you pass through villages and little towns populated mainly by Greeks from Asia Minor and their descendants. The original settlers were refugees who by the hundreds of thousands left Asia Minor after Kemal Ataturk defeated Greece in 1923. Under the Lausanne agreement between Greece and Turkey, 638,000 Greeks from Asia Minor were settled in Greek Macedonia in the twenties; while 348,000 Turks left the region. The newly arrived Greeks came from the culturally and economically advanced environments of Smyrna and Trebizond. They were in general an energetic and hard-working lot and more militant than the local Greeks. They raised the productivity of Greek Macedonia and made it the chief grain-producing area in Greece. Originally many of them showed leanings toward communism, but this changed with the gradual rise in their standard of living. Ethnographically, they made the population of Greek Macedonia 88.1 percent Greek, according to the 1928 census. Many of their villages are strategically located among the Slav inhabitants along the frontier. Some villages defended themselves successfully against the guerrillas, and sometimes the clusters of their tall stone houses look like fortifications. Yet even here, on market days, you will see people in Slav costumes coming in from the countryside.

Eastern Greek Macedonia embraces Salonika and the districts of Kavalla, Drama and Serrai to the east. Beyond the river Strimon, Greek Thrace extends farther east to the frontier of European Turkey. The northern neighbor is Bulgaria or, rather, Bulgarian (Pirin) Macedonia.

There are not many Slavs in eastern Greek Macedonia. Most of them left for Bulgaria in the twenties, after a Greek-Bulgarian agreement on an exchange of populations. Those who remained will tell you that they are Bulgars or Macedonians. The Greeks will tell you that they are Greeks who speak two languages.

In the excavated city of Philippi, beyond the hills of Kavalla, they will show you the ruins of the stone cell where St. Paul was presumably first incarcerated in Europe. Long ago Slav invaders also conquered this city. Inside Philippi's excavated basilica, you can read a wall inscription in Greek from the tenth century saying that God has punished the enemies of the Bulgars. You will occasionally come across Slavs in Salonika itself, running, for instance, news stands next door to the big seashore hotels; or at the bus terminal, coming from or going to their villages and speaking their Slav language freely even before Greek army officers.

Slav Villages under Greek Language Oaths

THE fact that there has been forcible Hellenization of Slavs in Greece since before the Second World War was recently confirmed by American diplomatic and intelligence experts (S. E. Palmer, Jr. and R. R. King, *Yugoslav Communism and the Macedonian Question*, Archon Books, 1971). It is not only from the Yugoslav Macedonian leaders that you will hear that under the prewar dictatorial regime of Greek General Metaxas the Aegean Macedonians were given castor oil when caught speaking Slav. After the civil war of 1945–49, many Slavs in Greek Macedonia had to immigrate, especially to Australia, because of discrimination, the Slav side claims; to which Greek officials reply that they immigrated voluntarily. Official commissions, headed by scholars, Hellenized the names of Slav settlements, and every Slav can use his first and last name only in the Hellenized version.

It was the U.S. consul general in Salonika who, in 1961, gave me the names of three "Slavophone" villages in Greek Macedonia where a public collective oath had been extracted from the inhabitants who swore that they never again, not even at home, would speak Slav, only Greek. He added that the Greek government had forbidden the practice. These villages were Kria Nera (Kastoria district), Atrapos (Florina district) and Karidia (Edessa district).

I subsequently secured back issues of Athens and Salonika newspapers which confirmed imposition of the Greek language oaths on the three villages. The oaths were taken in the summer of 1959, collectively and in public, before representatives of the Church, the government, the police and the army. The "Slavophones" swore *en masse* that from then on they would never again speak Slav among themselves, only Greek. For instance, the Athens *Vima* of July 8, 1959, said in part, "The Macedonian Slav language should have been abolished earlier. But it is still not too late, and this should be emphasized and used as an example for other Greeks inhabiting Macedonia and still using that language." According to the Salonika *Hellenikos Vorras* of July 8, 1959, the collective public oath ran as follows: "Before God and man, as faithful successors of the ancient Greeks, we swear that in the future, voluntarily, at no place and at no time shall we use the Slav language dialect."

According to the U.S. officials in Athens, the last such oaths were imposed in some places in 1960. The official Greek explanation to me was that the language oaths were the work of "overzealous" local officials who thought they would get a decoration for patriotism.

I had no opportunity to visit Kria Nera, but I did go to Atrapos and Karidia, accompanied by a local Greek official who spoke English.

Atrapos is a village of stone houses tightly packed along a steep cattle track. The Slav inhabitants, mostly raising sheep and growing strawberries, have many relatives working in Germany and Australia. During the civil war, the guerrillas had held the ridge above the village. The Greek authorities took to Florina all the young men for the duration of the civil war.

It was Sunday. Everybody was out, and I heard men, women and children speak their Slav language.

Among the forests of walnut trees near Edessa, the Slav village of Karidia straddles a rushing brook. It had 640 inhabitants when I visited it. They cultivated land, grew strawberries and picked wild fruits (walnut, sweet chestnut, wild pear, wild apple). One-half of Karidia was burned down during the civil war. Many young men had joined the Communist guerrillas, whereupon the government removed the entire village population to Edessa for the duration of the civil war. My Greek escort told me that populations of a number of villages, Slav and Greek, in the Edessa district had been herded into towns during the civil war—altogether some 70,000 people. In all Greece, he said, around 750,000 people had been evacuated from villages to towns during the civil war.

A crowd of elderly men stood under a tree in the middle of the Karidia square waiting for a Greek judge to come and read from his list the names of those who had been selected for old-age pensions. Nearly all spoke English, having worked in Ohio (Dayton, Springfield, etc.) on railroads, in restaurants, shops, and so on. I overheard a few

Slav phrases. I spoke to them in English, then in Serbian. In the presence of my Greek escort and awaiting the pension judge, they smiled but did not answer in Slav. In one of Karidia's storerooms I saw flour received from an American church organization—22 pounds per person.

Conclusion

MY observations and conclusions concerning Greek Macedonia were as follows:

Most "Slavophones" proclaimed themselves "Macedonians" to me. Some said they were Bulgars. One emphasized that he was a Greek in front of government tax officials. Almost all spoke Slav before Greek officials. A few in towns were Hellenized. Some "Slavophone" villages had voted for rightist Premier Karamanlis rather than for the leftist EDA—out of conviction or under pressure or for protection. I was officially assured that if an old Slav woman could not speak Greek in court she was allowed to use Slav through a court interpreter.

A visit to Greek Macedonia will show that the Slavs there have no intelligentsia; no organized labor of their own; no bourgeois middle class of businessmen, lawyers, physicians, engineers, teachers; no press of their own; not even priests, for Eastern Orthodox services for them are performed in Greek. The Slavs of Greek Macedonia are almost entirely a backward peasant class. The few members of the intelligentsia that did exist went largely into exile after the civil war.

Yugoslavia lost the civil war in Greece. She can now realistically demand only elementary human rights for the Aegean Macedonians: free use of their language and freedom from racial and economic discrimination. Despite certain pressures and incidents, the general toleration of the Macedonian Slav language and the apparently fair distribution of social security benefits and agricultural loans which I observed could provide the basis for a lasting Yugoslav-Greek understanding on the "Macedonian" question. After all, it is not normal that the Aegean Macedonians should have the right to publish newspapers in their own language and have their cultural and economic organizations in the U.S. and not in their native country.

All Yugoslavs agreed, after my return to that country, that the free use of the Macedonian Slav language and nondiscrimination should be the absolute minimum, after which it would be up to the Aegean Macedonians to carry on from there. All Yugoslavs were afraid that the Aegean Macedonians were lost in the long run.

Obstinacy, however, persists. In February 1965 Greek centrist Pre-

mier Papandreou paid an official visit to Belgrade. A Yugoslav spokes-
man said, "Greece thinks the [Macedonian] problem does not exist,
but she cannot solve it by ignoring it. However, we will bypass this
now because we agree on so many other things and will wait until
the Greeks have another point of view." When newsmen queried
Papandreou about this statement, he told them testily, "For Greece
the problem does not exist, therefore it was not discussed."

It is too bad that high Greek and Yugoslav officials do not say in
public what they told me in private: that there would be no ban on
the free use of the Slav language in Greek Macedonia and no discrimination against the Slavs; and that this should be enough as a basis
for an understanding between Yugoslavia and Greece. But both sides
were afraid of the extremist nationalist backlash in their own countries.
Yet the mere fact that I was a guest of both the Yugoslav Macedonian and the Greek governments shows that there is a basis for
understanding.

Bulgars, Macedonians and Russians

A South Slav Federation?

A FEDERATION of the Yugoslav peoples and the Bulgars in a South
Slav state "between the Adriatic and the Black Seas" has long been
a dream of patriotic southern Slavs, including many Communists. My
late father, a Serbian bourgeois leader, proposed it publicly in 1933.
But a federation of all the Balkan peoples also was a long-term, though
less realistic, program of the Balkan Communist parties and it enjoyed
the support of the Soviet Union.

After the establishment of the Popular Front government in Bulgaria on September 9, 1944, the Bulgarian party, upon Soviet suggestion,
embarked upon a policy of friendship and cooperation with Tito.
Bulgaria recognized the Macedonian as a separate nationality and
came out for a unified Macedonia within a South Slav federation. In
December 1944, six months before the end of the Second World War
in Europe, Tito's chief lieutenant, Edvard Kardelj, went to Sofia with
the proposal of a federation in which Bulgaria would be the seventh
South Slav republic, in addition to Serbia, Croatia, Slovenia, Bosnia-
Herzegovina, Macedonia and Montenegro. The Bulgars wanted a federation in which they would be one unit and the whole of Yugoslavia
the other. According to Yugoslav sources, Stalin favored first the Bulgarian version, then the Yugoslav, only to declare in the end that the

time was not ripe for a South Slav federation. Great Britain was also reported to oppose any such federation.

In July-August 1947 Tito and Georgi Dimitrov, premier of Bulgaria, held a conference at Lake Bled in Slovenia. The communiqué announced close economic cooperation, an eventual customs union, common action against the "frontier provocations" by the Greek "monarcho-fascists," and Yugoslav renunciation of the war damage claim of 25 million dollars. The communiqué said nothing about a federation and afterward Dimitrov declared that "a federation of the South Slavs or a Balkan federation . . . was not the subject of talks at the conference." However, after the Yugoslav-Soviet split of 1948 a resolution of the Bulgarian Communist party's Central Committee stated that the two governments "had agreed on a series of measures regarding the forthcoming establishment of a federation." Within it the parts of Macedonia would be united to form a separate unit. According to S. E. Palmer, Jr. and R. R. King, Bulgaria was supposed to be compensated for the loss of Pirin Macedonia by return to her of the Serbian western border region acquired by Yugoslavia after the First World War and of Greek Thrace taken from her in 1913. According to the same authors, it was suggested that Yugoslavia receive also Aegean Macedonia, and in exchange for the loss of Greek territories the Greek Communists would receive extensive Yugoslav and Bulgarian aid in their war against the Royal Greek government. No documentary evidence has been revealed to shed light on any of this, but the Greek Communist party in public statements before the Bled agreement strongly opposed any such transfer of territory. So the question must remain open.

The Soviets came out against a South Slav federation as considered at Bled. In response to a statement by Dimitrov in Bucharest suggesting customs-union arrangements among all the countries of the Soviet bloc, *Pravda* editorially denounced federations: "What these countries need is not a problematical and artificial federation, confederation or customs union, but the consolidation and defense of their independence and sovereignty." Then Stalin reversed himself and in February 1948 urged federation on the two partners, but then the Yugoslavs balked.

Nevertheless, after the Bled agreement the Yugoslavs were allowed to publish a newspaper (*Pirinski Vesnik*—the Pirin Messenger) for the Bulgarian Macedonians. The teaching of Macedonian language and history was also allowed in Bulgarian Macedonian schools and teachers from Yugoslav Macedonia were allowed to enter the country. Relations between Yugoslavia and Bulgaria were probably happier in 1947 than at any other time in their history.

A New Dispute over Macedonia

AFTER the Cominform Bureau, in June 1948, read Yugoslavia out of the Soviet bloc, Bulgaria forbade the teaching of Macedonian language and history in Pirin Macedonia, expelled the Yugoslav Macedonian teachers, and banned the Yugoslav Macedonian newspapers. But she continued for a while to recognize the Macedonian nationality. It is true that Dimitrov in December 1948 (he died in July 1949 in Moscow) still claimed that Macedonia was Macedonian and could be unified only within a South Slav federation. But Sofia and Moscow had now taken the prewar Comintern line that Macedonia should be an autonomous unit within a general Balkan federation. Apparently in February 1949 the Cominform came out for a separate and independent Macedonia composed of all three parts. The same resolution supposedly called Markos a "nationalist."

According to the Bulgarian population statistics of 1956, there were 189,000 Macedonians in Bulgaria, of whom 179,000 lived in southwestern Bulgaria known as Pirin Macedonia. In other words, 63.6 percent of the population of Pirin Macedonia was listed as Macedonians. After 1956, Bulgarian population statistics no longer mentioned the Macedonians, and Bulgarian historians began to explain why their country had the right to all of Macedonia. Even in periods when Bulgarian-Yugoslav relations were good, academic historical controversies continued, frequently causing political repercussions. But it was not until 1958 that Bulgaria publicly denied the existence of the Macedonians.

Although following Stalin's death in 1953 the Soviet Union effected a reconciliation with Yugoslavia—witness Khrushchev's apologetic visit to Belgrade in 1955—relations worsened in the winter of 1957–58. In 1958, the Yugoslav Communist party (League) held its Seventh Congress, at which a program was adopted denouncing both the Western "neo-colonialism" and the Soviet "hegemony." The Soviet Communist party boycotted the Congress. In the same year Bulgaria celebrated the 80th anniversary of the Treaty of San Stefano concluded by Tsarist Russia and the Ottoman empire after the 1877–78 war and creating a Greater Bulgaria which included all of Macedonia. This celebration was followed by energetic Bulgarian propaganda denying the existence of the Macedonian language, culture and nationality and reaffirming Bulgarian rights to Macedonia. The Bulgarian Academy of Sciences, in its *Historical Review,* instructed the Bulgarian historians to defend the "Bulgarian" history of Macedonia against "falsifications" by the Skopje historians.

Yugoslav Macedonian party leader Lazar Koliševski replied to the Bulgarian Communist propaganda that the Bulgars had developed imperialist appetites, which the Serbs had abandoned. In a spirited booklet of 1958, titled *Macedonian Reality and Foreign Aspirations*, he charged that "the leaders of the Bulgarian Communist party have reactivated the old thesis of the Greater Bulgarian bourgeoisie that Macedonians are not Macedonians but Bulgars." Koliševski quoted Karl Marx as saying in the *New York Tribune* of April 21, 1853, that in any country liberated by the Russians a strong anti-Russian movement would follow. He added that Lenin himself, in his émigré newspaper *Iskra* (the Spark) of August 1, 1903, described the then Bulgarian-Russian relations as follows, "Today Bulgaria looks like a Russian province... the Prince crawls before the Russian Tsar... Bulgaria is full of Russian spies who boss the police as if they were in their own country, spy on everything and everybody, and withhold the mail...."

In 1960 Bulgaria again celebrated the Treaty of San Stefano for having drawn the "natural" frontiers of Bulgaria. And again L. Koliševski struck out at a meeting in Skopje saying, "Macedonia has through its entire history been in a permanent, all-out conflict with Greater Bulgarian designs...." Although annulled by the Berlin Congress of the great powers in 1878, the Treaty of San Stefano became a blueprint for Bulgarian national rights, royal or Communist. Ever since, with the exception of 1915 and 1941 when she joined the enemy, Bulgaria, royal or Communist, has remained a protégé of Russia, Tsarist or Communist.

Yugoslav-Soviet relations improved again in 1962, when Gromyko and Brezhnev visited Yugoslavia. At the time the Soviet Union seemed to have dropped the idea of a Balkan federation and Soviet diplomats gave assurances that the Balkan frontiers ought to be left as they were. But the Bulgars were slow to follow suit. Attacks against Macedonian nationality continued in the Bulgarian press. Bulgarian chargé d'affaires in Athens voiced support of the Greek position in regard to the Greek-Yugoslav differences over Macedonia. While Moscow radio in its Macedonian hour used the Skopje dialect, the Sofia radio used a dialect close to the Bulgarian language. And so on. Finally, to make its position clear Moscow sent Patriarch Alexis, head of the Russian Orthodox Church, to Yugoslavia and Bulgaria. His last stop before going to Sofia was in Skopje, to visit the Archbishop of the Macedonian Church.

Finally, at a meeting in 1963 Bulgarian premier Todor Zhivkov told Tito and the other Yugoslav leaders that "the Bulgarian leadership and party will pursue and develop Dimitrov's course with respect to the Macedonian national question." But the polemics did not quite stop.

In 1965 Tito made a state visit to Sofia, taking the highest Macedonian officials with him. Again Zhivkov declared a return to Dimitrov's ideas on Pirin Macedonia and on Macedonia in general. He also vowed that the Macedonian question would not be treated polemically in the press but left to scholars for discussion. This despite the fact that the Bulgarian population census of the same year found fewer than 10,000 Macedonians in Bulgaria.

The polemics on Macedonia, however, continued. Krste Crvenkovski, a leading Yugoslav Macedonian, visited Sofia in 1967 and discovered that the stands of the two sides were irreconcilable. In June 1967 came the six-day Israeli-Arab war. Yugoslavia, overcommitted to Nasser, found herself momentarily in the Soviet bloc and forgot about Macedonia. In the beginning of 1968, in celebration of the 90th anniversary of the Treaty of San Stefano, the Bulgarian press again spoke up strongly about Macedonia, causing a new outburst of Bulgarian-Yugoslav polemics. When the armies of the Soviet Union, Poland, East Germany, Hungary and Bulgaria invaded Czechoslovakia in August 1968, and the Yugoslav party denounced the invasion and undertook measures to defend its own country against the Soviet Union, the polemics over Macedonia became more bitter than ever. Relations plummeted to the point where, on September 28, 1968, the Bulgarian news agency had to release an officially authorized statement that the Bulgarian government "did not and does not have territorial claims toward any other country" and that Bulgaria accepted the "inviolability of the frontiers established after World War II." In 1972, after Nixon's visit to Peking, Bucharest and Moscow, the Bulgars again, prompted by Moscow, initiated amity talks with Belgrade, and Yugoslavia again discouraged public polemics against Bulgaria. Kosygin visited Skopje in 1973; nevertheless, polemics flared up in 1974 over the Bulgarian omission of the Pirin Macedonians in a report on national minorities in Bulgaria.

A Visit to Sofia

IN 1961, in Belgrade, I applied to the Bulgarian Embassy for a visa to do research for a book, in English, on Macedonia. At the same time I applied to the Greek Embassy in Belgrade for a visa to visit the restricted frontier zone of Greek Macedonia. I obtained the Greek visa and facilities. Upon return from Greece to Belgrade in February 1962, there was still no answer from Sofia to my visa request. The explanation was that Macedonia was a sensitive question. In May 1962 I left for the U.S. without having received a reply.

Back in Belgrade in 1966, I obtained the Bulgarian visa immediately.

The Bulgarian Embassy had advised me not to give Macedonia as the reason for my trip, just tourism. In Sofia I tried in vain to reach Velichkov, whom I had known as chargé d'affaires in Belgrade in 1961–62 and who now was a member of the Bulgarian Central Committee. I decided to see only literary and scholarly people and not to try to enter the restricted zone of Bulgarian Macedonia.

Sofia has so many parks, gardens, flowerbeds that it has been called "the most beautiful peasant city in the world." It has many fine Byzantine churches, especially the Alexander Nevski with its light green roofs and green-golden cupolas which look sunlit even in rain. Sofia's "corso" is not flooded in the evening with huge masses as in Belgrade and there were far fewer automobiles. But pigeons can be heard cooing everywhere all day, and at dusk the sound is disturbingly loud. Sofia is one of the cleanest cities I have seen in my life—you hesitate to drop a cigarette butt on the pavement. Women in kerchiefs and with brooms help keep the streets clean.

Changing into fatigues, I mixed with the people without an escort—the Serbo-Croatian and Bulgarian languages are similar. In streets and in restaurants people displayed warm and friendly feelings each time I mentioned I was a Yugoslav or a Serb and asked for directions or help. A Bulgarian artist remarked that the Bulgarian people had always felt that way and that it was the "politicians" who tried to "poison" them. The people are not very fashionably dressed. Generally the Bulgarian is the most healthy and handsome race. The men impress you as being virile, and both men and women seem to possess a special kind of beauty: strong lines and jet-black hair, brows and eyes. Neatly uniformed women sometimes drive Sofia's taxicabs. People in the street, like the Yugoslavs, chew gum quite a lot, but, unlike the Yugoslavs, they do not swear in public. They do not litter like the New Yorkers, they do not drink, and they spit in the street much less than do the Greeks and the Yugoslavs. They are industrious, more even-tempered than the Greeks and less irascible than the Yugoslavs. They stand in lines like Londoners, and men do not molest women in the street. They are the most self-disciplined nation in the Balkans.

There were very few Western visitors, but endless groups of drab Eastern bus tourists invaded the hotels. The newspapers still could afford only four pages. I could obtain a notebook for my work in only one store and had to stand in line. In what shops had to offer, Sofia in 1966 was hardly above Belgrade in 1945, although Bulgaria had suffered no devastation during the Second World War, only Soviet domination afterward. In the people's self-service restaurants there were no peaches or green salad in July, although Bulgaria is a fruit-and-vegetable country. A few years before there was only rye bread. But now there was plenty of bread and pastry of all kinds, hard-boiled eggs, sour milk, small shishkebabs with fried potatoes, tomatoes, cabbage, cucumber salad. And you could always get vanilla or milk ice cream. My breakfast in the people's self-service restaurant consisted of three grilled meatballs, coleslaw, two pieces of bread, baklava and black coffee, all for 41 cents.

I found three incongruities in Sofia.

There is a "Home of Atheists" in that city (the Yugoslav Marxists have none), but you will bump into black-robed Eastern Orthodox priests in Sofia's streets every day.

There is a mausoleum in Sofia, where the embalmed body of Georgi Dimitrov is exhibited inside a big glass case. Dimitrov, the hero of the Reichstag fire trial, was born in Yugoslav Macedonia and though feeling himself to be a Bulgarian was always a friend of Yugoslavia. He intervened for the Serbian prisoners in the First World War, just as the Bulgarian peasant leader Alexander Stamboliski opposed Bulgaria's entry into war against Serbia. In 1937, as secretary general of the Comintern, he sponsored Tito for the post of secretary general of the Yugoslav Communist party. He even, after the 1948 U.S.S.R.-Yugoslav breach, advocated a united Macedonia within a federation with Bulgaria. Every day people shuffle in reverent silence past the body of Georgi Dimitrov, but their government does not adhere to his policies.

Sofia has many monuments to foreign liberators of Bulgaria—Tsar Alexander II and Stalin. No statue of a Bulgarian liberator stands beside them. No other country expresses so much gratitude to foreign potentates for its liberation.

Director of the National Library in Sofia Mme. Kalaidžieva said she was from eastern Greek Macedonia and felt herself to be a Bulgarian. She asked what purpose I had in mind with my book on Macedonia. She thought an all-round book on Macedonia was impossible for one man to do or would at least take many years. It would have to include, she said, all of the Balkans and the great powers. She said that the only solution was a South Slav federation from the Adriatic to the Black Sea, with a united Macedonia as a separate and equal unit.

The president of the Bulgarian Union of Writers, Georgi Džagarov, with seven members of the union, received me in the conference room of the organization. He walked up to a platform and from behind a desk read from a manuscript for a full three hours. This was my first experience of "brain washing" (called "brain massage" in Yugoslavia). The manuscript was a young Bulgarian historian's essay on

Macedonia, allegedly based on the writings of the Soviet academician Smirnov. The thesis was that Macedonia is the cradle of Bulgaria. The manuscript began with the five Tartar brothers who spread culture through Europe and one of whom founded Bulgaria. It led via the medieval Bulgarian Tsar Simeon all the way to the Macedonian Revolutionary Committee of the end of the nineteenth century. Džagarov insisted he was only against falsifications and for facts: Macedonian Tsar Samuel of the tenth and eleventh centuries was a Bulgar according to Byzantine texts; Yugoslav Verhovic in the nineteenth century recognized that there were Bulgars in Macedonia; Bulgarian and Macedonian nouns have only one case (so also has the English, I thought to myself). In short, the Macedonian language and nationality, said Džagarov, are Bulgarian, and Yugoslav Macedonia is an artificial creation of anti-Bulgarian Serbs. However, it is only realistic to leave the frontier alone, he concluded, else there might be war, and humanitarianism is against war. It would be enough, he proposed, if Belgrade recognized Yugoslav Macedonians as Bulgars.

Orlin Vasilev, a former director of the National Library, said I would hear no other opinion than that the Macedonians were Bulgars. He comes from Yugoslav Macedonia and looks upon himself as Bulgarian. He had just visited Yugoslav Macedonia and found that things had changed there: "Everybody thinks he speaks Macedonian." However, a Macedonian state did exist, history had rendered its verdict, there was no use starting a fight all over again from the positions of the past. Unnecessary polemics should also be avoided, else we would all appear ridiculous in the eyes of others. Vasilev saw no solution in either a South Slav or an all-Balkan federation. "You are not a Marxist," he explained, "but our view is that nationalism will slowly be overcome and give place to a large integration of nationalities where they will not be confined to frontiers and where it will not matter who is of what nationality." Vasilev thought my book on Macedonia would be difficult to write. "Don't try to please anybody," he advised.

Cartoonist Boris Angelushev was born in Greek Macedonia of a Macedonian mother and a Bulgarian father; he thought of himself as a Bulgarian. But his brother felt himself to be Macedonian. This demonstrates that whether one is Macedonian or not is something one must determine in his own mind. Boris Angelushev was the only Bulgarian intellectual who refused to sign the anti-Tito declaration on the occasion of the Stalin-Tito split in 1948. He disagreed with Džagarov and said that Sofia-Belgrade-Skopje should be like an isosceles triangle, geographically and politically. He added nostalgically, "Once there was an idea of a community from Trieste to Varna, but no more."

A Yugoslav economist, visiting Bulgaria, said that in that country Communist intellectuals were more rigid, less tolerant, and more inclined to complicate the issues than did men of other classes.

SUMMARY

THE Macedonian case shows that small nations, too, can act imperialistically and oppress each other, using the great powers to their advantage. The Macedonian question of the nineteenth and twentieth centuries was made worse by the memories of past grandeur—of the medieval Bulgarian and Serbian empires. Each empire included Macedonia in its realm, but neither lasted more than a few decades. The truth is that in the nineteenth and twentieth centuries, the great powers converged on the Balkans, including Macedonia—the power vacuum of the moribund Ottoman Empire. Tsarist Russia pushed toward the Mediterranean in the two-pronged Istanbul-Salonika drive via Bulgaria (1877–78); Austria-Hungary occupied the westernmost Slav-inhabited Turkish province of Bosnia-Herzegovina (1878); Great Britain buttressed its control of the Suez by taking over Turkish Cyprus and stopping the Russian march on Istanbul. It all came down to a Western defense of Turkey against Russia and her Balkan friend Bulgaria, but not quite. Western Europe did not want the "Sick Man on the Bosporus" to get well, but neither did it want him to die, especially not in Russian arms. In this big power tug-of-war the Bulgars, the Serbs and the Greeks tried to promote their own claims against Turkey and designs on Macedonia.

The Coburg dynasty organized the Bulgarian nationalist state and it pushed the Russian San Stefano plan of Bulgarian annexation of all Macedonia even after Russia had abandoned the plan during the First World War. It is interesting that the Soviet Union should have inherited from Tsarist Russia the two-pronged drive toward the Mediterranean via Istanbul and Macedonia, though it has exerted it only sporadically. Which goes to show that nations follow what they believe is their vital interest regardless of ideology. The expansion of Bulgaria has mostly meant the expansion of Russia.

Soviet policy toward Yugoslavia was erratic even before the Stalin-Tito split of 1948. Before the Second World War the Soviets advocated a Balkan federation with a united Macedonia as an equal partner. At the same time they favored a possible dissolution of Yugoslavia, according to the formula of self-determination of nations, including secession. In 1935, in view of the growing menace of Hitler, the Fifth Congress of the Comintern adopted the policy of the united front with the social democrats, peasant parties and bourgeois liberals against Nazi-fascism. Bourgeois democracy was accepted as the Communists' first line of defense. Secessionist movements, such as the Macedonian and Croatian, were branded as Nazi-fascist causes. In 1936 the Yugoslav Communist party's Central Committee, from Moscow, passed a resolution condemning the breakup of Yugoslavia. The three Balkan Communist parties— the Greek, the Bulgarian and the Yugoslav—interpreted the 1935 Comintern line each to its own advantage. The Greek party never felt it should hand over Greek Macedonia to anyone. The Bulgarian party almost always thought that all of Macedonia was its province. The Yugoslav party, after protracted confusion, ended up under Tito with a program of federation of Yugoslav nationalities, including Macedonia as a separate nationality and constituent republic. Deep in their hearts, the Yugoslav Communists began to believe that both Bulgarian and Greek Macedonia ought to join Yugoslav Macedonia.

Macedonia is an example of how the Russians perennially play a game with the territories and nationalities of small countries. History is constantly being rewritten, small nations do exist or do not exist by the will of the Tsar or the Central Committee. The Soviet Union can be understood only if one keeps in mind that it is a nationalistic big power in the first place and a union of socialist republics in the second. Bulgaria must subordinate its Macedonian stand to the Soviets' changing relations with Yugoslavia, but Bulgaria does not always oblige. Generally, when Moscow-Belgrade relations are good, Sofia grudgingly restrains its Macedonian ambitions to a point; when Moscow-Belgrade relations are bad, Sofia lets fly with a virulent campaign about Macedonia.

THE Macedonian question still smolders and gives rise to international tension. Aside from the three local powers—Yugoslavia, Bulgaria and Greece—being at loggerheads over Macedonia, the Balkans are still a point of convergence of the two great power blocs. The situation is as follows. The Greeks claim neither Yugoslav nor Bulgarian Macedonia but will give no autonomy to the Slavs of Aegean Macedonia. The Bulgars claim all of Yugoslav Macedonia as theirs. The Yugoslavs believe that all Macedonians should be united in one Macedonian republic within a Yugoslav or a South Slav federation or that the Bulgarian and Greek Macedonians should at least enjoy political autonomy. These feelings are deeply rooted in the hearts of the three local antagonists. In the meanwhile we have a cold war or a cold peace about Macedonia, depending on the changing Soviet line toward Yugoslavia, or toward the United States, in matters of Central Europe and the Middle East. However, in the present balance of power, Bulgaria is allied with the Soviet Union and the Warsaw Pact nations. Greece, although relations became strained after the Turkish invasion of Cyprus in 1974, is allied with the United States and NATO. Yugoslavia is a no-man's-land allied with neither.

Officially, neither the Soviet Union nor Bulgaria advocates a change in the frontiers in the Balkans. As for the Yugoslav leaders, they have privately written off Aegean Macedonia and believe that nothing can be done about Pirin Macedonia in the present situation. In fact, ever since the break with the Moscow bloc in 1948 and the Communist defeat in the Greek civil war in 1949, it has been clear that the Macedonians of both Bulgaria and Greece are lost to Yugoslavia. Realistically, the Yugoslavs could expect Pirin Macedonia and the Greek Macedonian enclaves to join Yugoslav Macedonia only in a vast change of power relations in Europe. But the existing balance of world forces permits no change in the Balkan status quo. The Macedonian question has not yet been solved among the governments or ruling parties of Bulgaria, Greece, Yugoslavia and the Soviet Union, and thus Macedonia will continue to be a source of friction. A convenient solution would be a united Macedonia within a Yugoslav-Bulgarian federation. But such a federation is unthinkable as long as Bulgaria remains a member of the Eastern bloc or as long as the world is divided into two blocs.

BIBLIOGRAPHY

Books and Monographs

Abadžiev, Gjorgji. *Balkanskite Vojni i Makedonija.* Skopje, 1958.

Adamic, Louis. *The Native's Return.* New York: Harper & Brothers, 1934.

Apostolski, K. i Matvejev S. *Lov Riba u Ogradama Pomoću Ptica na Dojranskom Jezeru.* Skopje, 1955.

Apostolski, Mihailo. *Osloboditelnata Vojna na Makedonskiot Narod.* Skopje, 1965.

Barker, Elisabeth. *Macedonia.* London and New York: Royal Institute of International Affairs, 1950.

Benedict, Ruth. *Patterns of Culture.* Boston: Houghton Mifflin Co., 1934.

Burks, R. V. *The Dynamics of Communism in Eastern Europe.* New York, 1961.

Casson, Stanley. *Macedonia, Thrace and Illyria.* London: Oxford University Press, 1926.

Christowe Stoyan. *Heroes and Assassins.* London: Victor Gollantz Ltd., 1935.

Clarke, Grahame, *World Prehistory.* London: Cambridge University Press, 1962.

Cloché, Paul. *Un Fondateur d'Empire: Philippe II, Roi de Macédoine.* Paris, 1955.

Cousinéry, M. E. M. *Voyage Dans la Macédoine.* Paris, 1831.

The Cultural Monuments of the People's Republic of Macedonia. Skopje, 1961.

Cvijić, Jovan. *La Péninsule Balkanique.* Paris, 1918.

Dedijer, Vladimir. *Tito.* New York: Simon & Schuster, 1953.

—————. *Jugoslovensko-Albanski Odnosi 1939–1948.* Beograd, 1949.

Deroko, A. *Sveta Gora.* Beograd.

Diehl, Charles. *Byzance, Grandeur et Décadence.* Paris: E. Flammarion, 1920.

Documents of the Vienna Archives on Macedonia 1879–1903. Skopje, 1955.

Doflein, Dr. Franz. *Mazedonien.* Jena, 1921.

Edwards, Lovett F. *Macedonia.* London: David Harvey Publishers, 1971.

Ellis, Havelock. *The Dance of Life.* New York: Grosset & Dunlap, 1923.

Frazer, Sir James George. *The Golden Bough.* New York: The Macmillan Company, 1963.

Gllover, T. R. *The Ancient World.* London, 1935.

Graves, Robert. *The Greek Myths.* Baltimore, Md.: Penguin Books, 1961.

Hamilton, Edith. *Mythology.* Boston: Little, Brown & Company, 1942.

Herrmann, Paul. *Conquest by Man.* New York: Harper Brothers, 1954.

Heuzey, Léon, et Daumot, H. *Mission Archéologique de Macédoine.* Paris, 1876.

A History of the World, vol. I. Chicago: Rand McNally & Co., 1960.

Hofmann, Otto. *Die Makedonen.* Goettingen, 1906.

Ilindenski Zbornik. Skopje, 1953.

Istorija na Makedonskiot Narod. Nova Makedonija: Institut za Nacionalna Istorija, 1969.

Ivanoski, Orde. *Makedonskite Sloveni od VI do IX Vek.* Skopje: "Kultura," 1962.

James, E. O. *The Cult of the Mother Goddess.* London: Thames and Hudson, 1959.

Jovanović, Marija. *Vostanijate na Makedonskiot Narod vo XI Vek.* Skopje, 1963.

Katardžiev, Ivan. *Ajdutskoto Dviženje i Karpoševoto Vostanie vo XVII Vek.* Skopjie, 1958.

─────. *Antantata i Makedonskoto Prašanje vo Tekot na 1918.* Godina.

Kavadias, Georges B. *Pasteurs Nomades Méditerranéens; Les Karakatsans de Grèce.* Paris, 1965.

King, Robert R. *Minorities Under Communism.* Cambridge, Mass.: Harvard University Press, 1973.

Kolaja, Jiři. *Workers' Councils: the Yugoslav Experience.* New York: Praeger, 1966.

Koneski, Blaže. *O Raxvitku Makedonskog Književnog Jezika.* Beograd, 1958.

─────. *The Problem of the Macedonian Literary Language During the Nineteenth and Early Twentieth Century.* Belgrade: The Macedonian Literary Language, edition "Jugoslavija," 1959.

─────. *Towards the Macedonian Renaissance.* Skopje, 1961.

Kratak Pregled. Makedonske Istorije, Izdanje Istoriskog Društva NR Srbije. Beograd, 1955.

Liszt, Franz von. *Das Völkerrecht.* Berlin, 1925.

Lukacs, John A. *The Great Powers in Eastern Europe.* New York, 1953.

Macedonia. Published by "Jugoslavija," Belgrade, 1957.

Maclean, F. *Escape to Adventure.* Boston, 1951.

"Makedonia." Skopje: November, 1963.

Miljovski, Kiro. *Skica za Istorijata na Makedonskiot Narod za 1918–1941.* Godina.

Miracula, S. *Demetrii.*

Mosely, Philip E. *The Kremlin and World Politics.* New York, 1960.

Muehlestein, Hans. *Die Verhüllten Götter.* Wien-München-Basel, 1957.

Nešović, Slobodan. *Jugoslovenskoto-Bugarskite Odnosi vo Nedamnešnoto Minato.* Skopje, 1973.

Obolensky, Dimitri. *The Byzantine Commonwealth.* New York: Praeger, 1971.

Oldenbourg, Zoë. *Destiny of Fire.* New York, 1961.

─────. *Massacre at Montségur.* New York, 1962.

Ostrogorsky, George. *History of the Byzantine State.* New Brunswick, N. J.: Rutgers University Press, 1957.

Palmer, Stephen E. Jr., and King, Robert R. *Yugoslav Communism and the Macedonian Question.* Hamden, Conn.: the Shoestring Press, Inc., 1971.

Pares, Bernard. *A History of Russia*. New York: Alfred A. Knopf, 1947.
Perdrizet, Paul. *Cultes et Mythes du Pangée*. Paris-Nancy: 1910, Annales de l'Est; 24 Année, 1910.
Plutarch. *Lives of the Noble Greeks*. New York: Dell Publishing Company, 1959.
Popovski, Jovan. *Skopje and Its Surroundings*. Zagreb, 1963.
Pribichevich, Stoyan. *World Without End*. New York: Reynal & Hitchcock, 1939.
Rački, Dr. Franjo. *Bogomili i Patareni*. Beograd: Srpska Kraljevska Akademija, 1931.
1903–1904 Reports of Austrian Representatives in Macedonia.
1903 Reports of Serbian Consuls, Bishops and School Inspectors in Macedonia.
Rexine, John F., Norwich, John Julius, and Sitwell, Reresby. *Mount Athos*. New York: Harper and Row, 1967.
Rice, David Talbot. *The Art of Byzantium*. New York, 1959.
Rohde, Erwin. *Psyche*. Leipzig: Alfred Kroener Verlag.
Runciman, Steven. *Byzantine Civilization*. London: Edward Arnold Ltd., 1933.
Russell, Bertrand. *History of Western Philosophy*. London, 1948.
Schevill, Ferdinand. *The History of the Balkan Peninsula*. New York: Harcourt, Brace & Co., 1933.
Schultze-Jena, Dr. Leonhardt Sigismund. *Makedonien*. Jena, 1927.
Scott, Bickham Sweet. *Political and Economic Survey of Greece 1939–1953*.
Seton-Watson, Hugh. *Eastern Europe Between the Wars*. London, 1945.
Shoup, Paul. *Communism and the Yugoslav National Question*. New York, 1968.
Spengler, Oswald. *Der Untergang des Abendlandes*. München, 1923.
Stewart, Cecil. *Serbian Legacy*. London, 1959.
Šofman, A. S. *Očerki po Istorii Makedonii i Makedonskogo Naroda*. Kazan, 1960.
Taškovski, Dragan. *Bogomilstvoto i Njegovoto Istorisko Značenje*. Skopje, 1951.
————. *Karpošovoto Vostanie*. Skopje, 1951.
————. *Samuilovoto Carstvo*. Skopje, 1961.
Teofilakt, Žitije. *Klimenta Ohridskog*.
Tito, Josip Broz. *V Kongres KPJ: Izveštaji i Referati*. 1948.
Toynbee, A. J. *Hellenism*. London: Oxford University Press, 1959.
Trever, Albert A. *History of Ancient Civilization*, vol. I. New York: Harcourt, Brace & Company, 1936.
Vasković-Vangeli, Vera. *Samostojnite Feudalni Vladateli vo Makedonija*. Skopje, 1963.
Volkov, V. K. *Operacija Tevtonskij Meč*. Moskva, 1966.
Wells, H. G. *The Outline of History*. New York: the Macmillan Company, 1926.
West, Rebecca. *Black Lamb and Grey Falcon*. New York: Viking Press, 1941.

Articles, Encyclopedias and Periodicals

Andonovski-Poljanski, Dr. Hristo. "San Stefano Bulgaria," *From the Past of the Macedonian People*. Skopje, 1969.

Andonovski-Poljanski, H. G. "Situacijata vo Makedonija po Ilindenskoto Vostanie i Mirćstegskite Reformi," *Godišen Zbornik (Annuaire)*. Kniga 8 Filozofski Fakultet na Univerzitetot, Skopje, 1955.

Andriotes, N. P. "History of the Name 'Macedonia,'" *Balkan Studies*, vol. 1. Salonika, 1960.

Athens News, February 22, 1962.

Balkan Studies, vol. 8, No. 2. Salonika, 1967.

Belovski, Dimče. "The Ten Days of the Kruševo Republic," *Review*. Belgrade, 1963.

Benac, Alojs. "Medieval Tombs of Bosnia and Herzegovina," *Jugoslavija*. Belgrade, 1962.

Bićanić, Rudolf. "Economics of Socialism in a Developed Country," *Foreign Affairs*, July 1966.

Bihalji-Merin, O. "The Stone Carvings of the Bogomils, Bogomil Sculpture," *Jugoslavija*. Belgrade, 1962.

Bogoev, Dr. Ksente. "Početak Kraja Zaostalosti," *Politika*. Beograd, February 11, 1972.

Brockhaus, *Die Grosse*. 1952.

Burck, Gilbert. "Adam Smitović on the Sava," *Fortune*, May 1967.

Burke, James. "Alexander the Great," *Life*, May 3, 1963.

The Cambridge Ancient History, vol. I, II, IV, VI, VII, VIII.

Dimitrovski, Todor. "The Macedonian Literary Language Today," in *The Macedonian Literary Language*, edition "Jugoslavija." Belgrade, 1959.

Fermor, Patrick Leigh. "The Black Departers," the *Atlantic*, June 1962.

Firfov, Živko. Lecture at the Majestic Tavern, Windsor, Ontario, September 14, 1961.

————. "Makedonskite Narodni Ora."

"The Frescoes of the Church of St. Clement," *Jugoslavija*. Belgrade, 1961.

Gadd, May. "Origins of the Folk Dance," *The New York Times*, September 20, 1964.

Georgieva, Milica. "Bojadisuvanje i Šaranje na Veligdenski Jajca vo Skopje i Okolijata," Glasnik na Etnografski Muzej. Skopje, 1960.

Hadži-Manev, Vasil, and Firfov, Živko. *Journal of International Folk Music Society*, vol. VIII, 1961.

"Ilinden 1903—Breakthrough and Signpost in the National Revolutionary Struggle of the Macedonian People," *Sovremenost*. Skopje, June 1968.

Jovanović, Stevan. "Tobacco Exports," *Review*. Belgrade, July–August, 1972.

Jugoslavenska Enciklopedija. Zagreb, 1962.

Jugotutun. *Ekonomska Politika*. Oktobar 1, 1973.

Katardžiev, Dr. Ivan. "The Formation and Activities of VMRO up to the Ilinden Rising," *From the Past of the Macedonian People*. Skopje, 1969.

Kempner, Mary Jean. "The Little Churches of Ohrid," *Harper's*, April, 1964.

Kličkova, Vera. "Božićni Običaji vo Skopska Kotlina," Glasnik na Etnografski Muzej, Skopje, 1960.

————. "Veligdenski Običaji vo Poreč, Glasnik na Etnografski Muzej," Skopje, 1957.

Koneski, Blaže. "Kliment Ohridski," *Sovremenost*. Skopje, September 1966.

————. "Ohridska Književna Škola," *Slovo, Vajsov Zbornik*. Zagreb, 1957.

Konstantinov, Dr. Miloš. "Bitolski Evrei," *Prilozi*. Bitola: Naučno Društvo, 1960.

Korubin, Blagoje. "The Macedonian Literary Language in Its Definitive Form," in *The Macedonian Literary Language*, edition "Jugoslavija." Belgrade, 1959.

Larrabee, Eric. "Letter From Skopje," the *New Yorker*, October 7, 1964.

Marco. "Srpsko-Turski Rat 1912 Godine," *Nova Evropa*. Zagreb, Novembar 26, 1928.

Matkovski, Dr. Aleksandar. "Podatoci za Nekoji Ajduti od Zapadna Makedonija (1622–1650)," *Glasnik za Institutot za Nacionalna Istorija*, God. V, No. 1. Skopje, 1961.

————. "Tragedijata na Evreite od Makedonija," *Glasnik za Institutot za Nacionalna Istorija*, Godina II, Broj 1. Skopje, 1958.

Mitrev, Dimitar. "Makedonski Preporoditelji," *Politika*. Beograd, Avgust 9, 1959.

Nasledova, N. A. "Makedonskie Slavjane Konca IX–načala X.v. Po dannim Ioanna Kamedniati," *Vizantijski Vremennik*, Tom XI. Moskva, 1956.

The New York Times, September 24, 1972, "Nine Years Later Fear in Skopje."

Nigg, Walter. *Neue Zürcher Zeitung*, 28 September 1959.

Petruseva, Anica. "Skutinata Kako Sostaven Del od Maškata Nosija vo Makedonija," *Glasnik na Etnoloski Muzej*. Skopje, 1960.

Petsas, Photios M. "Pella," *Balkan Studies*, vol. I. Salonika, 1960.

Politika. Belgrade, August 12, 1966; July 16, 1972; August 28, 1972.

Popović, Čed. A. "Srpsko-Bugarski Rat 1913 Godine," *Nova Evropa*. Zagreb, Novembra 26, 1928.

Popovski, Jovan. "Makedonski Ilinden," *Politika*. Belgrade, August 2, 1973.

Pribićević, Dr. Stojan. "Sa Puta po Kosovu i Metohiji," *Novi List*. New York, Oktobar 21, December 2 i 4, 1952.

Pribichevich, Stoyan, "Albania: Key to the Adriatic," *Current History*, March 1939.

Putar, Rade. "Freske," *15 Dana*. Zagreb, Januar 1, 1962.

Queen, April 24, 1962.

Radojičić, Djordje Sp. "Hilandarska Riznica u Opasnosti," *Politika*. Belgrade, Mart 4, 1962.

Rand, Christopher. "Christmas in Bethlehem and Holy Week at Mount Athos," *The New York Times Book Review*, October 13, 1963.

Razgledi, Year VI, Nos. 5–6, Skopje.

Reed, David. "Yugoslavia: Time Bomb in Europe," *Reader's Digest*, April 1973.

Review. Belgrade: March 1961; August 1961; September 1963; October 1963; May 1971; July–August 1972.

Semiz, D. "Rusija i Borba Srbije za Vardarsku Dolinu," *Nova Evropa*. Zagreb, 26 Novembr a 1928.

Simović, Dragan. "Macedonian Black Gold," *Review*. Belgrade, July–August 1965.

Stillman, Edmund. "Farewell to the Balkans," *Harper's*, January 1963.

Stojanović, Dr. Aleksandar. "The Karpoš Rising," *From the Past of the Macedonian People*. Skopje, 1969.

Stojanovski, A. "Kon Prašanjeto za Hristijanite-Spahii vo Makedonija," *Glasnik na Institutot za Nacionalna Istorija*, No. 1–2. Skopje, 1960.

Sumarska Enciklopedija, I-II. Zagreb, 1963.

Tošev, Krum. "Die Mazedonische Schriftsprache," *Süd-Ost Forschung*, XV, 1956.

Toševski, Dr. Jordan. "Goce Delčev," *Review*. Belgrade, July–August 1972.

Werner, Ernst. "Theofilos-Bogumil," *Balkan Studies*, vol. 7, Number 1. Salonika.

Yugoslavia, An Economic Survey. New York: Bankers Trust Company, October 1973.

The Yugoslav Review, January 1956; September 1956.

INDEX